all the best,
Mark Rosen
WCCO T.V.

Enjoy! Best to
you — Jim Burton

Best Seat in the House

MARK ROSEN'S SPORTS MOMENTS
AND MINNESOTA MEMORIES

BEST SEAT

IN THE HOUSE

MARK ROSEN

with JIM BRUTON

FOREWORD BY DON SHELBY

MVP
BOOKS

In Memory of...

DARCY POHLAND: An unstoppable force in our newsroom. I so miss our daily chats by her desk, hearing her passionate pleas about the Vikings, Twins, or her beloved Gophers. She could report on the toughest of stories, but she always brought a smile to the faces of our viewers when she grabbed her pom-poms, put on her Gopher gear, and let 'em have it from the heart!

BOB RAINEY: I will always remember the excitement in his voice, calling it his dream job to come to the Twin Cities to report on his favorite team, the Minnesota Vikings. How he loved to play golf with the most unorthodox swing I've ever seen! And in the end, he fought a very private battle with cancer. I'll never forget the words he spoke to me in his final days: "This could happen to any of us—cherish your time!"

BILL CARLSON: Bill knew my father, Joe, long before I met him because of his association with the movies and my dad's job with Paramount Pictures. There was no one ever more comfortable in front of the camera or an audience than Bill Carlson, especially at the State Fair, where he loved to broadcast. He did it all at WCCO television. A true legend!

DAVE MOORE: Everyone will know from my early chapters how in awe I was of Dave Moore. Oh, how he would have loved outdoor baseball again at Target Field. I believe he stepped foot into the Metrodome just once, to offer an ode to Metropolitan Stadium and his disgust in having to watch baseball inside.

HAL SCOTT: My boss, my mentor, my friend. They broke the mold with him. Hal's storytelling and his love of fishing, golf, boxing, and a late-night whiskey made him a mythical character in the history of WCCO television.

To my mother, Doris, for her boundless passion for life, family, and friends. You are my inspiration.

First published in 2012 by MVP Books, an imprint of MBI Publishing Company and the Quayside Publishing Group, 400 First Avenue North, Suite 300, Minneapolis, MN 55401 USA

The information in this book is true and complete to the best of our knowledge. All recommendations are made without any guarantee on the part of the author or Publisher, who also disclaims any liability incurred in connection with the use of this data or specific details.

We recognize, further, that some words, model names, and designations mentioned herein are the property of the trademark holder. We use them for identification purposes only. This is not an official publication.

MVP Books titles are also available at discounts in bulk quantity for industrial or sales-promotional use. For details write to Special Sales Manager at Quayside Publishing Group, 400 First Avenue North, Suite 300, Minneapolis, MN 55401 USA.

To find out more about our books, visit us online at www.mvpbooks.com.

ISBN-13: 978-0-7603-4132-2

Library of Congress Cataloging-in-Publication Data

Rosen, Mark, 1951-
 Best seat in the house : Mark Rosen's sports moments and Minnesota memories / Mark Rosen ; with Jim Bruton ; foreword by Don Shelby
    p. cm.
 ISBN 978-0-7603-4132-2 (hardback)
 1. Rosen, Mark, 1951- 2. Sportscasters--United States--Biography. 3. Sports--Minnesota--History. I. Bruton, James H., 1945- II. Title.
 GV742.42.R66A3 2012
 796.092--dc23
 [B]
                            2011050524

Editor: Adam Brunner
Design manager: James Kegley
Book designer: Helena Shimizu
Cover designer: Simon Larkin
Front cover & author photos by: Sean Skinner

Printed in the U.S.A.

Contents

Foreword

By Don Shelby

There is a piece of film I've seen a hundred times, and each time I see it I understand Mark Rosen a little better—and I know why he had to write this book. It is a clip, shot by an unknown photographer, of highlights from the Twins' 1965 World Series. Most of the film shows the big bats and future Hall of Famers playing for all the marbles. The editor stuck in a five-second crowd shot as it reacted to a dramatic Twins highlight.

Remarkably, in the crowd and easily recognizable, is a boy. It is a young and gawky 13-year-old from St. Louis Park, Minnesota. The kid in horned-rimmed glasses barely able to contain himself in the excitement is Mark Rosen.

For Mark, no matter the section or seat number, he knew he was sitting in the best seat in the house because, simply, he was witnessing history and watching his heroes. Watching that clip, I like to think I am seeing the birth of one of the best sports reporters in the country.

Mark has been my friend and colleague for 32 years. My family would often complain that I spent more time with Mark than I spent with them. Looking back over those years, I find their assessment completely true. We shared, over those years, thousands of stories—some of which appear in this book. Some of the stories we shared had never been heard by another soul—such is the nature of our kind of friendship.

Don Shelby and I during a "Roof Top Special" broadcast of *Rosen's Sports Sunday*. As usual, Don talks and I listen.

One of my joys was listening to Mark, speaking in a man's deep baritone (but with the heart of a boy), telling me about who he had just met, or the venues of sport all over the world. My favorite story of his, which I never grew tired of, took place in Lake Placid, New York, when he watched a bunch of kids, many of them Minnesotans, beat the vaunted Russian national team in the game that became known as the "Miracle on Ice." He was there as a reporter. But, when he told the story, I could distinctly hear the voice of a boy.

People in the audience don't always recognize a simple truth about reporters. We learn to hide the most obvious indications that would put the lie to our above-it-all, objective façades. In our quiet and secret heart, we just can't believe we often found ourselves at the center of the action, and calling the heroes of our youth friends. Cut open a sports or news reporter, and you will find an overlarge heart and a deep sense of gratitude that fate (and hard work) had allowed us to live out our childhood dreams. When you read *Best*

Seat in the House, I hope you will hear the underlying notes like the throaty cello strings anchoring a symphonic piece. Broken out and played solo, the cello is saying, "I can't believe how lucky I am." Listen closely. It is in every chapter of this book, and in every chapter of Mark Rosen's career.

So, while this book is about famous people and historic moments in sports, it is really a story about a boy who loved the game and thrilled at the sight of watching the great players and coaches. The boy's career has now run nearly a half century, and I've seen something remarkable happen along the way. I've seen young players and coaches who may be bound, one day, to hero and hall of fame status, who are humbled to be interviewed by Mark Rosen.

The boy has become the hero. I watched it happen. I count that experience as one of the most fascinating in my life. In this book, Mark gets up out of his seat and gives it to you. Now you have the best seat in the house.

Introduction

By Jim Bruton

I doubt there will ever be a career in broadcast journalism like that of Mark Rosen. Forty-plus years at the same major television station is unheard of and likely will never happen again.

Mark didn't start out as a student placement or an intern. He didn't spend weeks in a program of on the job training or have a trial period on probationary status. He didn't work his way up from a smaller market and then hit the "big leagues" with a flattering résumé. Mark Rosen began his career at WCCO television by "hanging around."

With permission from a neighbor (who happened to be a reporter at the station) to come in on a Saturday morning to observe, Mark found a career all laid out before his very eyes. What was supposed to be a few hours of watching a newsroom in action turned into a career of more than 40 years. He watched and observed that first Saturday morning and never left.

Mark brings a passion and deeply engrained enthusiasm for his work and for people worthy of the highest esteem. He understands all aspects of his responsibilities and what is expected from his viewing and listening audiences. He knowingly appreciates that his true bosses are the sporting public, and yet he has developed profound loyalties and friendships among his clients and media colleagues.

Mark Rosen is not just a face appearing in your living room or a voice on your radio several times a day, but rather an individual who has used his self-made platform in broadcast journalism to make a difference in the lives and hearts of others. Whether it be taking the time from his busy schedule to chat with an admiring fan or spending many hours at or assisting with charity events and fundraisers, he has been a true example of understanding the positive effect his celebrity status can have on others less fortunate.

His love and deep devotion for his career is present in everything he does. He has experienced multiple moments characteristic of most fans' dreams. He has been alongside and interviewed some of the biggest names in sports and life.

Now for the first time, Mark Rosen brings the reader along with him over the past four decades and into the world of television and radio journalism. This is his autobiography, but it is not a book centering on sports. It focuses more directly on his personal experiences with some of the most interesting and fascinating people imaginable.

Travel with Mark into the basement studios at WCCO television during his early days of "hanging around," and go with him to the "Miracle on Ice," at Lake Placid in 1980, and on the airplane with the Minnesota Twins as they became World Series bound in 1987. Join Mark during his greatest of interviews, and stand with him at the front of the line with his all-time favorite athletes.

Let Mark take you into his heart and soul and learn about Bud Grant and Harmon Killebrew, and discover why he has dedicated entire chapters to these two famous icons. Find out what goes on behind the camera and the lights and the nuances of breaking the big story. Enjoy with Mark his radio highlights and his incredible run for governor. Get an inside view of it all, including his most difficult time period at WCCO television.

This is not just a book about a sports personality. This is a book about a remarkable broadcast journalist—his life, passions, memories, beliefs, and disappointments. This is the man behind the face on television and voice on radio.

For many years, Mark Rosen has wanted to share his four decades of great moments and fascinating experiences with others. He has now completed his dream. Come on along and enjoy the great ride with Mark. It has been more than he could have ever fathomed. And he took it all in from the greatest of locations; he had the best seat in the house!

A NOTE ON WRITING THIS BOOK WITH MARK ROSEN

Mark Rosen grew up in St. Louis Park, Minnesota, and for countless weeks we sat at Bruegger's Bagels in the very same community and formulated his book. I found every moment stimulating and inspirational, and I quickly developed an impatient need to get his words, experiences, and anecdotes on paper.

There was never a dull moment. Each time we met, I found Mark more passionate and more caring—a person with deep loyalty and respect for others. I have been truly honored to have had the opportunity to play a small part in his journey.

One of the very first things Mark said to me involved his appreciation for being a broadcast journalist. He told me, "Jim, for the past 40 years, I have had the best seat in the house and I want to share it with everyone." There could not have been a more appropriate title for Mark Rosen's book.

Mark's story has been told. It comes about with honor, humor, and a passion second to none. I have loved assisting him in the process. The recap of his journey is over and in print, with an invitation for everyone to jump on board and enjoy the ride.

And the best part of it all for me is that I am honored to call Mark my friend.

1

A Kid in the Newsroom

I was overwhelmed and just sat there and watched with the widest of eyes. It was truly an unbelievable sight seeing Kirby Puckett, Kent Hrbek, Dan Gladden, Frank Viola, and all the other players celebrating, laughing, jumping around, hollering, and partying in jubilation, like a bunch of little-leaguers. It was an incredible moment in Minnesota Twins history and I was there with them. We were on the team bus headed to the airport, and my memory of that special night will live on with me forever.

They were our Minnesota Twins, big-time professional athletes, and they were 10 years old again, on their way home from Detroit to play in the 1987 World Series. Although I will never forget the moment, this was just the beginning for the Twins that evening. What was to come later upon the team's arrival in the Twin Cities was more than anyone could have anticipated. What awaited the new American League champions was absolutely breathtaking. It would become one of my all-time favorite memories of the past four decades, a period in which I have been fortunate enough to live out my childhood dreams.

I was 10 when I put on my first little league baseball uniform. I remember the day as if it were yesterday. I reveled in the moment.

With Twins great Kent Hrbek after the 1987 World Series.

A cold chill ran up my back and throughout my body as I raced down the street on my bike to show my mom and dad my new attire. I can still feel the tires on the pavement, the sweat on my hands, and the excitement in my belly as I pedaled anxiously toward home.

It was one of those grand occurrences in life when you have to pinch yourself to make sure it's real. It was simply too good to be true. I made the team. I can't imagine anything replacing that moment, that feeling. I don't think hearing my name called out over the public address system at Yankee Stadium—"Batting fourth for New York, No. 7, Mark . . . Rosen"—would have created a bigger personal celebration. I was overpowered by the moment.

I once was a ballplayer, and now some two decades later the Minnesota Twins and their special night had become a reminder for me. There they were, grown men, great athletes with superior skills being boys again, just like me, when I got my first uniform.

I always thought when I was a young boy that if I could someday sit on the 50-yard line of a Vikings game or have a seat behind home plate watching the Twins, I would be living a fantasy. At center court

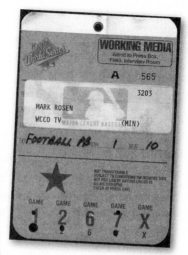

What a great series it was!

for the Gophers or the Timberwolves game would be a dream come true, or to sit 15 rows up at center ice for the former Minnesota North Stars or for today's Wild would be a once-in-a-lifetime experience. As a youngster I loved sports, and my imagination took me to the country's greatest ballparks, fields, rinks, and courts. But in the real world, just getting to a game was enough for me. I craved it, and once we were at the park or stadium it didn't matter where our seats were. I would later have the opportunity to regularly sit in a prime seat and attend any game I chose to be at, as my career allowed me to experience firsthand all my childhood passions.

My early interests seemed to always venture toward the sports arena. I followed religiously the teams, players, coaches, managers, and everything available from the newspapers, radio, and occasional television. We didn't have sports programming like we do today.

There wasn't any ESPN or daily radio and television programs focusing on sports. I got what I could from what we had, and I looked forward impatiently to special events like baseball's "Game of the Week." For the fans and viewers, it truly was what it was called. It was the only game on television during the week. It was a big deal. I would look forward to it and recall waiting for the days to pass until Saturday's game.

In 1961, the Minnesota Twins and Vikings arrived in the Twin Cities and became an instant attraction to go with my great passion and excitement for Minnesota Gophers football. The early 1960s were exceptional for Minnesota fans as we watched head coach Murray Warmath build consecutive Rose Bowl teams. His squads were highlighted by an abundance of exceptional players, such as Bobby Bell, Carl Eller, Sandy Stephens, Judge Dickson, Bill Munsey, and a host of others who wore the maroon and gold. It was a thrilling time during that era of Golden Gopher football.

The Minnesota Twins brought with them from Washington, D.C., such young future stars as Harmon Killebrew and Bob Allison, and they took the region by storm. I became an instant supporter and fan. I was the first kid on the block to get a Twins cap, and I proudly showed it off to everyone in the neighborhood. They became my baseball team immediately, and I spent a lot of my free time listening to their games on the radio. The Twins television broadcasts were few, but I recall watching the Hamm's Bear in those wonderful old commercials. The words and tune still flourish in my thoughts and ears: "Hamms the beer refreshing . . . Haaaammmms!"

Back then I hadn't given much thought to what I was going to do for a living. Most kids never do. But as I reminisce, I knew I was enamored with the broadcasting skills of legendary announcers Vin Scully of the Los Angeles Dodgers and Jack Buck, who did the St. Louis Cardinals games. I can recall falling asleep at night listening to the voices of Scully or Buck while creating in my mind what was occurring, as their voices resonated through my bedroom. But in reality, I was more into the actual game than the attributes of the broadcasters. They created the setting and the action for me. It was later on that I developed an interest in their skills and expertise.

I was around 10 years old when all of this was taking place, and during the daylight hours my imagination would exercise at full speed. For most of my summer daylight hours, when I wasn't playing sports with friends, I was in our front yard at our first house on 27th and Hampshire in St. Louis Park, throwing a baseball against the steps. If it bounced back over my head, it was a double. Something was really clicking inside me as I made up the live action, inning by inning. I was intrigued by every part of the game and made every effort to relive it. The atmosphere I created and the whole concept of sports, especially big-time sports, engulfed my youth.

I would play an entire game in my front yard. The Twins would be playing the New York Yankees or maybe the Boston Red Sox, and I was in the middle of all the make-believe action. I was Dean Chance and Harmon Killebrew—and Mantle, Carl Yastrzemski, and Zoilo Versalles. The setting had everything the ballpark had. I was in Yankee Stadium, Fenway Park, and Metropolitan Stadium in Bloomington. It all came to life for me at 27th and Hampshire. St. Louis Park was slightly different from the Bronx in New York or the heart of Boston, but at the time I was entirely fooled by the drama of the moment.

I went through the lineups and the innings, and I even kept track of the entire box score—runs, hits, and errors. No one watched. There weren't any hot dogs and Jack Buck never saw me throw the ball at the steps, but it didn't matter because I lived it. I was fully indulged, and in my mind the broadcasting voice of the St. Louis Cardinals called the play-by-play.

This deep love I had for sports was beginning to shape my career early on, and I didn't have a clue what was happening. However, I did pick up something valuable in the process. I was developing a vivid imagination, which later proved to be invaluable to my career. It was forming a solid foundation for what was to come in the years ahead.

As television became more acquainted with sports programming, I recall paying attention to such prominent personalities as Jim McKay and *Wide World of Sports*. I was still quite young, preteen as

I had that Harmon Killebrew stance. Dad is ready to throw a fastball to me.

I recall, yet I was becoming attracted enough to these television and radio icons to start thinking about becoming a broadcaster some day. I was fascinated by their commentary.

As I got older and with my interest in sports continuing to peak, I began to spend more time watching some of the local television personalities. Although I still wasn't into it to the point where I would say "I want to be that guy" or "I want to do television sports," I was becoming more and more captivated with every aspect of the sports scene and those reporting it.

At around the age of 15 or 16, I became familiar with the work of Hal Scott on WCCO television. He did the local sports and did it well. Of course, Hal was the brother of the famed Green Bay Packer and Twins voice, Ray Scott, maybe the best to ever broadcast a game. So I started to watch more intently and more frequently, and I became inspired by their work.

Hal's backup at WCCO was Jack Lavallier, and I remember I saw him once at a downtown movie theater. He came to life right there in front of me, and I was too scared to even go up and say hello. It seemed like such a special moment to see a television personality in real life. I guess in some ways I thought that the people behind the screen weren't real. I knew better, yet I never actually encountered anyone until I saw Jack Lavallier at the movies.

Another person locally on television who really struck a chord with me was the legendary news anchor at WCCO television, Dave Moore. Just thinking about Dave and what he later meant to me personally gives me a chill, as I recall his magnificent skills and character. He was one of those people you meet in life who carve a niche in your soul.

As a youngster, I often went to football games with my dad at Memorial Stadium on the University of Minnesota campus to see the Gophers play. I loved every minute of it—the setting, excitement, ambiance, and all the action. It was invigorating, and I couldn't wait to tell my friends, family, and everyone I knew about what I had experienced and observed on those beautiful fall Saturdays.

Hal Scott did that, too. He told people watching television about the games, and he did it for a living. "Are you kidding me?" I used to think to myself, "This is actually a job that some people have? They report the sports news of the day?" It was mind-boggling. You can actually do this for a living? You can see where all this was heading.

A neighbor of ours back then was Phil Jones. Phil was a news reporter with WCCO television and a very good one. Our family had moved to Stanlen Road in St. Louis Park, and we had been there for a few years when I first became infatuated with what Phil did for a living. I was fortunate to have grown up in two wonderful suburban areas, where my family has continued to maintain lifelong valued friendships with our neighbors.

Phil stayed at the station for seven years before moving on to an eventual illustrious career with CBS News. He held such prominent posts as White House and Capitol Hill correspondent, and he was recognized for his work with the CBS program *48 Hours*. But before all this, he was just Phil Jones my neighbor and an occasional employer—when I would babysit his kids.

I became enthralled by Phil and his work with WCCO television. I would see him on the news in the evening, become engrossed by his reporting, and then later see him cutting the grass across the street. It was surreal. He was a television celebrity and I knew him. But it wasn't enough. I needed more, and I began bugging Phil to let me come to the studio to watch what was going on. I didn't want a job; I just wanted to watch. I wanted to hang out at WCCO.

I was watching a lot of WCCO television then—the sports with Hal Scott, the *Murray Warmath Show* with Rollie Johnson, the *Bedtime Nooz* with Dave Moore, and everything else when I had the opportunity. I wanted to know how it all came together. How did they do the news, the weather, and the sports? I was becoming driven to find out and totally charmed by the magic of television. And I kept bothering Phil to set it up for me to come to the studio.

Phil was hard-nose, a grinder, and one of the best reporters ever. He was in the process of leaving WCCO toward the late 1960s, and I was really on him to help me out. I had to find out more about what went on where he worked. I was totally taken in by his profession.

Phil had piqued my interest level along with Hattie Steinberg, my journalism teacher at St. Louis Park High School. She was amazing, and she was responsible for me and many others developing an interest in the media. My speech teacher, Pete Peterson, was also a very special person. I remember Pete as an outstanding instructor and also for his role in some television bank commercials. With those kind of influential people in my life, I was really zeroing in on a passion for the work and a desire to learn as much as possible about the media.

St. Louis Park High School really did a terrific job in developing talent and working with aspiring students in a variety of ways. As an example, three very successful friends of mine and former students have also been influenced by their educational surroundings. Marc Trestman has been a winning football coach at all levels in the professional ranks; Thomas Friedman is a Pulitzer Prize–winning columnist and author; and Jeff Diamond has been an executive

I was ready for the "big time." Once I entered the WCCO newsroom, I never wanted to leave. Forty-two years later, I'm still there.

with the Minnesota Vikings, with the Tennessee Titans, and in the business world. I cannot forget Jeff Passolt, a solid anchor at KMSP television, and of course Academy Award–winning brothers Joel and Ethan Coen. All hailed from St. Louis Park High School.

My persistence eventually paid off, and Phil set it up for me to go to WCCO on a Saturday morning in the spring of 1969 to observe. Phil's presence on the screen and in the neighborhood made his work come to life for me, and I'm sure he never realized the impact he would have on my career when he set up my first visit to WCCO television.

There were no internship programs then; in fact, what I was asking to do was practically unheard of. Nevertheless, Phil arranged for me to go in and observe. He worked it out with Hal Scott.

I still recall the feeling of excitement I had the day Phil said to me, "You're all set. Hal said you can come down and hang out." It was an unbelievable feeling. Phil and Hal Scott had been talking about me.

Hal said I could come down to WCCO television and hang out! I was overjoyed by the news and couldn't wait to go.

This was overwhelming to me. Another one of my imaginary moments, perhaps? No, this was real. I was going to WCCO television. I had permission from Hal Scott. My desire and anticipation for the opportunity had arrived. I still recall the thrilling feeling of just the thought.

Phil later told me about the conversation he had with Hal. "I got this kid who keeps bugging me about wanting to come down to WCCO and watch what you are doing. Hal, would you please just let him come in and observe what is going on?" Phil was convincing.

It was arranged for me to go into the studio the following Saturday. I didn't know if this would be my only visit, and that bothered me some. Here I was, clamoring for the opportunity to come to WCCO television to observe, and now I was worried about maybe this would be my first and last trip there. Maybe they would say at the end of the day, "Thanks, kid, for the visit; you can't come back." I hadn't even arrived, and I was terrified I couldn't come back. I didn't know what to expect.

I remember I wore a blue sport coat from Fitwell Clothing on Hennepin Avenue. I think it was my only coat, but I wore it proudly. I was so nervous. Phil said they told him to have me come in on a Saturday when the newsroom would be less busy. I had my driver's license so I drove downtown, found a place to park, and headed to the newsroom on 9th and LaSalle. It was around noon when I arrived.

My thought was to stay in the background, watch what was going on, and make sure that I didn't get in anyone's way. With my nerves getting the best of me, I walked in the door and was further unnerved by the attractive young receptionist who greeted me. I'm sure she wondered what in the world was I doing there—probably even more so when I told her, while trying to sound confident and important, "I'm here to see Ralph Jon Fritz." By then I was blushing and even more nervous. I felt about 14 as I pondered the likelihood of her next job as a Hollywood motion picture actress.

Ralph worked with Hal and was apparently supposed to be there to greet me. He wasn't in yet and, to make matters worse, Hal had forgotten to tell anyone else I was coming. There was no one in the newsroom who knew a thing about me being there. My pride had taken a big hit after proudly announcing to the young receptionist that I was there to see Ralph Jon Fritz.

I was in severe distress just to be in the building, and my ordeal at the front desk didn't help calm me down. Maybe I wasn't going to get in at all. My dream was quickly vanishing before me when things finally got worked out. Jim Davis, one of the sports producers, heard about the confusion in the lobby and came up to get me. "Big Red," as everyone called him, was really nice to me and brought me downstairs to the newsroom. I had passed my test at the front desk, not by much though, and I was in.

Just going down the steps to the newsroom was quite the experience for me. It wasn't what I had expected. I was surprised by how close-quartered everything seemed. I almost bumped my head and had to crouch some just to get to the newsroom. I was tall even as a kid—I stood about 6 feet 6 back then, so it was awkward for me just to get down the steps.

I thought it would be brighter. To say it wasn't would be an understatement. It was dark, dreary, and crowded. It was not a bright, sparkling newsroom with hustling and bustling about as I had thought it would be, but rather a basement with narrow hallways, low ceilings, cramped and crowded small desks, and cigarette smoke everywhere. I didn't know for sure exactly what I was expecting, but I knew for sure this wasn't it.

I can say this for sure about my initial impressions of the WCCO newsroom. I didn't care. I was there and ready to observe, and I was pumped. My nervousness had been replaced by an overwhelming passion to learn and watch what was occurring.

I introduced myself to a few people, and Jim could absolutely not have been nicer to me. He got me situated to observe. He sat me down near where Hal Scott worked, and I was ready. I could not have been more excited if I had been sitting behind home plate during the seventh game of the World Series or on the 50-yard line at the Super Bowl.

I was watching and totally engrossed. I really didn't know what this person was doing or what that person was doing, but it didn't matter. I watched and I listened. After about an hour or so, Dave Moore walked through the newsroom, and I thought to myself, "Wow, that's Dave Moore." He was not just a television face any longer. I was now sure that he was real. He was right there in the newsroom with me. He actually existed. I was a star-struck kid, no question about that. I will never forget that moment when I first saw him.

Dave Moore was a media icon. He had been around since the early 1950s, and he was one of the most recognized personalities in the Twin Cities up until his death in 1998. He anchored the WCCO news broadcasts for over 30 years, and he added to his visibility and popularity by also hosting the famous WCCO *Bedtime Nooz*, which appeared on Saturday nights at midnight.

The *Bedtime Nooz* was a program news classic, filled with great theatrical performances in satirical delight for those who stayed awake to watch. With Moore's passion for comedy and the talent from other studio personalities, such as weatherman Bud Kraehling, the show was a huge success, broadcasting for more than a decade. Locally, during its successful run, the program reached the equivalency of *Saturday Night Live* for its loyal followers. People literally cut their evenings short in order to be home in time to catch the *Bedtime Nooz* before retiring.

And there he was, Dave Moore, in the newsroom with me. I was like a kid standing outside a ballpark waiting for an autograph. It could not have been more emotional for me if Mickey Mantle or Joe DiMaggio had strolled past.

Moore walked briskly by me, chewing on a pencil (as I later learned he often did). I wasn't going to say anything to him. I kept telling myself, "Just watch, observe, and stay out of everyone's way." Someone told me that he always came in on Saturdays about this time to begin working on the *Bedtime Nooz* for that evening.

After he passed by, I didn't see him again for some time. Later that afternoon, I had the opportunity to introduce myself. It was a thrill. I recall saying, "Mr. Moore, I'm Mark Rosen. Hal Scott said I could hang out and watch what was going on." He looked at me and said, "Hey, kid, would you mind helping us out with something?"

Instant shockwaves ran though my entire body. Dave Moore was speaking to me. And that was not all. He asked me to be a part of something with him. Dave Moore wants me to do something to help him out? I was just supposed to hang out.

"Sure," I said. "What do you want me to do?"

He took me into a back office area where they were going to do some filming. It was an area that I soon learned hosted some of the famous wrestlers of that time era. It was where they would do some 30-second promotion pieces for upcoming wrestling matches.

This was where Vern Gagne, "Mad Dog" Vachon, Nick Bockwinkel, and the infamous "Crusher" performed. It was all staged. I got to watch some later on. It was amazing!

The Crusher would come in as polite and nice as could be and say something like, "Okay, what do you need from me?" And someone would say, "Just 30 seconds about the match, Crusher." And Crusher would say, "I'M GOING TO KILL THAT VERN GAGNE. I'M GOING TO RIP HIS TURKEY NECK RIGHT OUT OF HIS BODY. THERE IS NOT GOING TO BE ENOUGH OF HIM LEFT FOR A FUNERAL. I'M GOING TO . . ." And when he was finished, he would say, calmly and quietly, "Was that okay?"

It didn't take long for me to realize that Dave Moore wanted me to be a part of the *Bedtime Nooz*. I was going to be in a skit, and my role was to simply take a blindfold off a particular wrestler. I can't remember who it was or even the point of it all. It didn't matter, but what came of it was actually unbelievable, because what I did that afternoon has remained in the archives to this day as one of the few saved episodes from the *Bedtime Nooz* with Dave Moore.

Here I am, a gangly 17-year-old, in my blue Fitwell sport coat, Beatles haircut, and oversized glasses taking a blindfold off a wrestler, on the *Bedtime Nooz*, during my very first day at WCCO. I was in heaven. I was as electrified as if I had just hit a home run in the bottom of the ninth to win the pennant for the Minnesota Twins. No different, not for me on that day.

I couldn't believe what had happened on my very first day at WCCO. The great Yankee catcher and broadcaster Joe Garagiola was famous for his remark about big-league baseball players: "Those guys in the bubblegum cards came alive." Now I could identify with what he had meant.

I remember like yesterday saying to myself while all of this was going on, "I have to come back here Monday. I am not leaving here and not coming back. This cannot be a one-time thing. I have to come back." I was really juiced!

In fact, as I was thinking this, it occurred to me that I hadn't even met Hal Scott. Here I was basking in the limelight, and at the same time worried about not returning, and I hadn't accomplished one of the reasons for my visit, to meet Hal.

A little later, Ralph Jon Fritz came in and was also really nice to me. I watched him write a sportscast and put it all together. *Watch, observe, and keep my mouth shut.* This was pretty good advice that I had given to myself, and it was working. I stayed out of everyone's way and I watched and learned and it was stimulating. I was fully energized.

I was there all day, and it was a day I will never forget. I was excited and exhilarated, and I knew that *this was for me!* I didn't know what exactly I wanted to do, but I knew I had to be there. I needed to be involved somehow in what was going on.

I came home and told my mom and dad all about the day. I told them that this was where I needed to be. I didn't know what it was about the place, but it was for me. It had literally swallowed me up. The setting, the atmosphere, the people, the work, and the overall environment had attached itself to every fiber in my mind and body. After just one day in the newsroom of WCCO television, I knew then, absolutely for sure, that this was what I wanted to do. The newsroom was a special place, and I knew it was where I belonged.

Al Austin (*left*) and Jerry Bowen (*center*), among others, in the legendary basement of the WCCO TV newsroom. I can still hear the racket of those typewriters.

So I went back. I can't remember if I was told it was okay to return or if I just showed up again. I knew there was no choice. Right after school on Monday, I headed back to the newsroom to find it was very different from what I had observed on Saturday. This was a Monday, the first day of the business week, and the operation was in full gear. I met them all—the crusty photographers, the producers, and many others. And I heard it all too—the language, the jokes, and everything that seemed to be missing from my first visit.

As before, the basement setting was again filled with smoke. It seemed like most everyone had a lit cigarette. The cramped surroundings were stimulated by the constant pounding of typewriter keys getting ready for a news broadcast. There were papers everywhere, and people moved in all directions with seemingly little order. The energy present in the room was magnifying, and I watched in amazement. This was for me. I absolutely loved it!

As I look back, I have often asked myself why I was attracted to all of this. I was in a basement. It was dark, crowded, dingy, and damp in feeling and appearance. The smell of smoke was staggering, and people were scurrying around doing what, I didn't know. The hallways were narrow, the ceilings were low, and the noise of the typewriters was never ending. It seemed like a setting bordering just short of total chaos. But the answer to the question of the attraction was simple. It was the end result.

All of these people embroiled in their duties were the working parts of a process. The adrenaline that flowed through all of them was unlike anything I had previously experienced. I knew it wasn't the cameras or the television setting that drew me to this bizarre world, but rather the people. It was their efforts behind the scenes in putting something together for the public to view and become educated. This is what attracted me to all of it. It was their tremendous passion, their connections to each other, their pride and expertise, all of which joined them on common ground as they worked toward a final product.

I got to watch the news in its infancy stages as well as the sports, where my passion had brought inspiration to my life as a youngster. I thought if I could help out in any way, it would be unbelievable. I would empty wastebaskets, clean up the room, sweep the floor, just to be a part of all this. The atmosphere, the setting, and the people had intoxicated me.

As my trips to the newsroom became more frequent, I began to fit in to some extent. People got used to me being around, and eventually they gave me some things to do. I would do anything they asked and put my heart and soul into every aspect of the work.

It looked like they were all overworked and understaffed, so I thought one day, maybe I could do something productive like tearing the ticker tape with the baseball scores. Wouldn't that be something? I must have created a good impression by observing, staying out of everyone's way, and helping out when I could because eventually they did let me tear the ticker tape and put the baseball scores together.

My job was to get all the National League and American League baseball scores along with the runs, hits, and errors for each game to be read or shown on television at the evening sports segments. I was helping out Hal Scott and Ralph Jon Fritz, and they were both wonderful to me. When they had the time, they began to teach me the business.

I soon realized that I was becoming a part of all this. My work was productive enough to occasionally be used on television. Soon, I got to do more and was working as a part of the sports coverage for the day. I was involved in something I truly enjoyed. I knew the teams, the players, the standings, the managers, and the coaches from my imaginary world. I was in dreamland, so my work, whatever it was, inspired me and motivated me. The bubblegum cards had come alive!

The days went slow at school because I couldn't wait to get to work. It took about eight months before they finally paid me anything. Hal went to work on that for me, and I will never forget the day when he told me, "I got you some money." It was great, but the most important thing for me was to be able to come back every day.

It was as if I was drugged by the business. I simply had to have more. I remember the tremendous frustration I felt when I wasn't there. I was missing something and could never make it up. During my early days at WCCO, while still in high school, I was working part-time at Town Drug in St. Louis Park. I did a variety of things, which included stocking shelves, delivering prescriptions, and just about anything they asked me to do. I can recall so many afternoons and evenings when I was working in the basement stock room listening to the Twins game on my transistor radio. I wanted to be there—not at the ballpark but at WCCO television working on the game highlights. I really missed it. It was in my blood, and I got to the station as often as possible.

While there I did what I was asked or told to do and was very careful to not overstep my bounds. I enjoyed opening the sports mail and occasionally got a chance to write script copy to be read on television, from the material taken from the ticker tapes. It was tough, a real struggle for me, but I worked hard at it and got guidance and assistance from many of the staff members who found the time.

I was there about three to four days a week and pleased to do anything to help out. Most of the staff were nice to me. However, in the beginning, some of the grizzled old veteran news folks and photographers ignored me, and I'm sure they must have thought, "Who is this kid who is around here all the time?" I knew I had to earn my stripes.

But I was there, and even though I didn't know anything, I made up my mind to do as much as I could to assist and still stay out of the way as much as possible. I seemed to be pretty good at that part.

One of my first important jobs would occur on Friday nights. As the high school football scores were called in, I put them together for the evening news sports broadcast. It was extremely challenging. It was done with a black-inked typewriter, and I could not make a mistake!

I would type up the scores and they would be entered on a roll. When Hal would be doing the broadcast, he would hit a button and the scores would roll through for the viewing audience to see. If I made a mistake in spelling or a score early on, I could start over, but once I had typed several, it was impossible to redo, so it stayed the way I typed it in. If I spelled Edina "Edena," it stayed on the screen. If I typed Bloomington "Blomingtons," it stayed. Now that was pressure! But I survived it and was thrilled by the opportunity.

The more I worked at writing copy, the better I got at it. Eventually, Hal started letting me write copy for him to read on the evening sports. I would finish the copy and give it to Hal to review. He would look at it and never say a word. He would just reach into his pocket, pull out a pencil, and go to work on my copy. He would cross out something and add something else. I remember the first copy I ever wrote; the page was full of corrections, scribbling, and lined-out words. I recall thinking, "Wow, that wasn't very good. I need to get better at this." So I continued on, drafting the copy while Hal made the changes and never said a word. He must have been somewhat happy with my work because he let me keep doing it for him.

When Hal died many years later, I spoke at his funeral and mentioned my copy writing and his endless editing. I recalled one of the best days of my life being the day that Hal Scott looked over my script for the evening news and his pencil never came out of his pocket. I knew in his eyes I had arrived. I had written copy that Hal Scott felt comfortable with. I had written copy that pleased Hal Scott. That was a big day for me.

The days got better and better as I learned more. I was in my kind of setting, an environment that I thrived in while learning every day and being a part of something that was important. I loved the enthusiasm, the energy, the passion, the expertise, and the end product. When the day was over and the work was done, I knew it would start over again the next day. I was developing a tremendous passion and intensity for the vocation that remains with me four decades later.

Once I had attained some experience, I got to actually cover sports and do interviews and become more of a part of the team. But as that kid in the newsroom, I just did what I was told and tried not to make a nuisance of myself.

As time went by and my experiences broadened, I realized how fortunate I was to be in a profession that I deeply loved. My interests, desires, enthusiasm, and passion for my work was relived every day. My imaginary world had come to life, and I was taking my seat on the 50-yard line.

As I've moved on from that dark, dingy, crowded, cramped, smoke-filled basement newsroom to my work today with WCCO television, I have known that I have been blessed with the best seat in the house.

2

Where Legends Are Built

Hal Scott was a real mentor to me. I'm not really sure if he intended to be in the true sense of the word, but he was. It wasn't as if he sat me down and told me how to do things. Hal wasn't like that. I gained incredible knowledge about the operations of the newsroom from just watching him. He was a great writer, a tireless worker, and special to me for many reasons.

To this day, because of Hal, I always take the time to help our interns and new staff as much as I can. He taught me kindness in the workplace, and I will always treasure his guidance.

Hal was definitely from the old school of journalism. In fact, I would say he was about as old-school as they get. Hal was a railroad guy and grew up in Johnstown, Pennsylvania, and like his brother Ray he made a career out of covering sports.

I'm sure Hal learned a great deal from Ray, but he was never a tag-a-long. He made it on his own with tremendous passion and a solid work ethic. He worked seven days a week. Ralph Jon Fritz, second in command in the sports department, would substitute for him on occasion, but basically Hal was in the studio and the newsroom all the time.

Hal worked hard and played hard, and during my early days in the newsroom he taught me more about life than could be imagined.

He was around the town a lot in many of the late-night establishments. There were some stories about Hal and some midnight brawls with off-duty cops and all kinds of things like that. He hung out with some pretty tough characters in many of those after-hours joints, but it never had any effect on his work. He never brought me along, but I heard all the stories. The reality was it never seemed to matter what Hal did the previous evening because he was always in the newsroom the next morning ready for work.

Things were different in the newsroom back then with Hal Scott and all the others. It was a close-knit group who worked together, and among them were strong personalities. But they made it work. They worked very well together and they often partied hard, but in the end they always did a truly professional job and the viewers got the news of the day.

Their close interactions with each other and constant drive to be the best are what had a dramatic effect on me as I watched and listened. It was stimulating and it was the reason I loved it all so much. They argued and fought with each other, and my eyes rolled around in my head like a pinball machine as I took it all in. They were a team, and I wanted to be a part of it.

From my first day in the newsroom and throughout all the time we worked together, there was never a doubt in my mind that Hal Scott had my back. For some reason, he took a real liking to me and watched out for me. I think he developed an early respect for me because he noticed how hard I worked. He knew I wanted to be there with him, and I think he appreciated it.

I know there was one particular time period when Hal really stood up for me. I didn't know what was going on at the time, but I found out later. It had become a situation where there was no doubt I was on my way to an early exit from the newsroom and probably from broadcast journalism. If it hadn't been for Hal Scott, I don't honestly know what would have happened to my career. He saved me, and at the time I didn't even know it.

Our general manager was Sherm Headley. I was told from a reliable source that Mr. Headley had a brief conversation with Hal about my future that went something like this: "Hal, look, you can't have this kid hanging around the newsroom all the time. Let him go."

Wow, that was shocking for me to hear, even some time later. My source further told me that Hal refused to follow Sherm's order and really stood up for me.

I was pretty sure it wasn't that the boss didn't like my work or anything like that. I really hadn't done much to that point. I didn't really think I was doing enough for anyone to not like what I was doing. I was getting paid some at the time, so it probably was a budget issue on top of the "hanging around" aspect. I guess I will never know all the reasons behind it, but I will never forget how Hal saved my bacon.

I still think about it occasionally and wonder how it would have all played out if Hal hadn't refused to follow orders. He could have easily come to me and said, "Mark, I have no choice here, the boss says I have to let you go." It scares me to even think about how my life would have changed. I get a cold chill even thinking about it.

In today's world of corporate journalism, I can't imagine something like that scenario occurring. I would have been gone, out the door, down the street, never to see the lights, cameras, and film again. It would have merely been a painful parting of the ways.

In addition, as a part of this occasional reoccurring nightmare, I was informed by my reliable confidant that not only was Hal told to let me go, but he actually received some sort of note to that effect as well. Apparently, he listened to his instructions, ignored them, and proceeded to put the written order in his desk, never to see the light of day again.

Hal knew I was a tireless worker, and he must have seen something good in me to stick his neck out like he did. I loved every minute of my job, and I suppose it must have showed because as time went along I was getting more to do. I guess Hal must have thought, "Hey, if I'm going to go to the wall for this kid, I better give him some real work to do."

So, I got more work. I knew what I wanted for my future, and I was actively involved in it every day. I cannot image being more engaged

I loved Hal Scott. He truly was my mentor and friend.

or working for anyone other than Hal Scott during my early years at WCCO television. I would like to believe we made a great team.

Although I admired many things about Hal, the one thing that really stood out for me about his character was his incredible people skills. Hal wasn't always careful about whether he was liked by everyone, but he did want to be respected—and he definitely was. People respected him as a person and as a professional. He had an opinion about things, and he was never afraid to express it. He never was concerned with whether people agreed with him or not.

Hal loved to cover the Vikings, and he had great respect and fondness for Vikings head coach Bud Grant. He also loved boxing, and I got to meet some real characters because of it. Jim Beattie, the Flanagan brothers, the Bobicks—they were all a big part of Hal's world, and there I was, taking it all in.

With his demeanor and long trench coat, Hal could have been assigned to WCCO right out of central casting. He was made for the job with his look and personality. But there is no question, it was his solid work ethic that impressed me—and more importantly, impressed management and his viewers. He was my mentor, and I really admired him.

I think another reason Hal took an early liking to me was that he sincerely appreciated what I did for him. My job was to make him look good, and I was willing to work endless hours to make that happen. As I learned more, he trusted me more. He knew I was going to give my all, and he took notice of the fact. We had a wonderful connection, and to his dying day I so appreciated who he was and what he did for me.

* * *

By 1970, I had graduated from St. Louis Park High School, was attending the University of Minnesota, and working full-time in the newsroom of WCCO television. It was quite the time in our country's history. With the Vietnam War in full force and the unrest on college campuses everywhere, there was no shortage of news headlines. Because I was on the university campus during the day, I saw firsthand what was happening. Then, when I got to work, I saw how the WCCO staff put it all together to inform the public. They were truly the best at what they did, and I was in awe of everything.

It wasn't just sports that I was involved with; it became so much more than that because of the times. I was working mostly in the sports department, but I had a front-row seat to watch and learn all that was taking place, and it was surreal.

Once I had figured out what was going on and earned some trust, I was given more and more things to do. I was producing and writing some of the sportscasts. My responsibility in that area was to put things in order of interest level and develop how it would be read on the air.

Maybe we would lead in with the Twins game and Hal would come on and say something that had happened in the game that day. There were times when I would observe Hal on the air and have to literally take a deep breath and think to myself, "Wow, I wrote that. I'm writing scripts for Hal Scott." I was afraid if someone at that very moment came in and pinched me, I might wake up and it would all be a dream.

As I got better at it, I was assigned to write the whole show on the weekends. Hal might come into the studio a few minutes before he was to go on the air and say, "The Twins beat the New York Yankees today 4–2 on a ninth-inning home run blast by Harmon Killebrew, breaking a 2–2 tie ballgame."

It wasn't much, not something left in the hands of a rocket scientist, not an earth-shattering breaking news announcement, but I had something to do with the broadcast and the public was listening to it. It was an amazing feeling for me, and I was very proud of my responsibilities. I guess in many respects it was a feeling of accomplishment and, more than anything, just a real sense of belonging and a beginning to paying my dues.

I was really learning all about the news/sports broadcasting business. I would take film from the game and fit in the words consistent with the film length, and we would put it on television. One night it might be the Killebrew home run, the next a Rod Carew double that we would highlight, and my job was to make sure it was ready for the broadcast.

I might decide we would end the segment with a Killebrew interview or some other related element to the game. It sounds simple, but it was much more complicated than one would imagine. I would have to be careful to balance the length of the film with the narrative and correlate it all to the timing of the segment. It had to all fit. The more I did it, the better I got at doing it. It was challenging, but the end product was the reward. This was long before we had videotape cameras. It was a cumbersome process.

We might finish a segment on the Twins on a particular night and move on to "The Vikings are getting ready to meet the Green Bay Packers tomorrow at Metropolitan Stadium and Grant has the team ready."

Think about it, for a kid who loved sports, I was now fully engaged in actually writing it—about the Twins and the Minnesota Vikings. All I could think was, *are you kidding me?* I'm pretty sure a magnificent dream best described my place of employment. Every single day I was showing up for work at Disneyland!

I had no social life at the time, just my work, and I loved every minute of it. Whatever I was doing, it wasn't enough. I wanted more. "Bring it on," I used to think. "What's next for me? Do you want me to scrub the floors when we are all done today? That's fine. I'll do that, too. Pick up the cigarette butts? I'm good with that. Just don't send me out there in the real world. This is where I want to stay. I want this to be home for me, right here at WCCO television."

I keep coming back to Hal Scott because he was a part of everything I was doing in the beginning. He was the one who kept me in touch with reality. He kept me in line, kept the ship sailing. He was so steady. He was there all the time. I don't think he ever took a sick day. He had a dramatic influence on me that has lasted.

My love for sports and my job in the newsroom created a passion for my work that lives in me today. I still feel it. It is a part of me, my personality, my character.

People are always amazed at my longevity with WCCO television, over four decades. It's an easy response. I tell them I never get bored, never seem to get tired, because the best part of my job is that I never know what is going to happen from one day to the next. There are never two days that are the same. It is what makes the work so exciting and keeps the passion burning inside me. I suppose it is also one of the reasons they kept me around for so long.

Everything about my job has changed through the years, which makes the baseline of the work challenging and exciting. We live in a world of technology today, but no matter what the change was, it really didn't matter because I was fortunate to always be around so many incredibly talented people. They were everywhere, and there were so many of them, and most helped me out when they could. I learned from the best. Ask anyone from back then and you will hear about the all-star team working at WCCO.

But in the end, Hal was my guy. I'm sure after all I have said about him, this would not come as any surprise. The fact is and the bottom line is, I wanted to please Hal Scott. I never wanted to disappoint him, and for me that's what it was all about back then and still is today. I always have felt that if you have an opportunity to work for a boss whom you have so much respect for that you never want to disappoint them, you have it made. I had it made.

I thank God for the opportunity I had and for the Hal Scotts of the world. If it hadn't been for Hal in the incredible WCCO newsroom sports department, I don't know what would have become of me. I think he felt he could always trust me. He likely never thought much about my future, but I felt that Hal thought I was worthy of hanging around for as long as possible. For whatever reason, he liked the fact that I had bought into the philosophy of putting in a hard day's work for a day's pay. He respected that in me. I know he did. He knew I wasn't some rich kid whose parents were friends with the boss, looking for a free ride and a handout. It's probably why we hit it off.

At Hal's funeral, I was fraught with so many wonderful memories of him, a treasure chest full. He taught me about loyalty, family, friends, and coworkers. He taught me trust, passion, and honor. He was one of the greatest storytellers of all time. He had that cigarette dangling out of his mouth, drove an old Pontiac Bonneville with one headlight in an odd direction, and was just the truest of characters. He was at the right place at the right time to do what he did best. And for me, well, I'm just eternally grateful I was there with him. The stars were aligned right for me when Hal Scott came into my life.

* * *

Ralph Jon Fritz was another of the best. He was the first person I met (other than "Red") who got me in the front door and brought me down the stairs to the newsroom that very first day. And R. J. was there for me like Hal, and we remain close today. He is one of my best friends, and we keep in contact regularly. The interesting thing about our relationship is that it is almost surprising that we have become such good longtime friends. We were sports sidekicks for 35 years.

In today's dog-eat-dog competitive world of television news, everyone seems to be always looking over their shoulder to see who their replacement is going to be. You wouldn't think having this high school kid hanging around the newsroom looking for things to do would be very attractive to someone who could have had that afore-mentioned thought in mind. But not R. J. He helped me out more than he will ever know, and we became very close. Not one time did he ever make me feel that I was intruding on his watch, taking up some of his space, or threatening his career. All he did was shower me with his kindness, professionalism, and friendship.

R. J. had a small-town charm about him, having grown up in Sleepy Eye, Minnesota, and he had such a great television delivery. He had such a down-to-earth kind of folksy way about him that people easily identified with him as they did with Dave, Bud, and Hal Scott. With all that was going on with me at the studio over the

With Ralph Jon doing the Minnesota State High School Hockey Tournament. It was one of the broadcast highlights of my career.

years, I truly believe anyone else would have hated my guts. There I was, this 17-year-old kid hanging around the studio and over the years working my way into great positioning with the sports news department. And Ralph Jon, well, he was always there for me to assist in whatever way he could.

I'll never forget the time I was assigned to cover the NHL All-Star Game at the Met Center in 1972. I was really excited about it and felt I had the plum assignment for the night. Ralph Jon was sent to cover the Gophers basketball game at Williams Arena against Ohio State. It turned out to be the game of the infamous on-court brawl. The game was halted by Gophers Athletic Director Paul Giel, who awarded the win to Ohio State.

R. J. did a great job of covering the story and actually spent the night at my apartment preparing for national coverage on the *CBS Evening News* with Walter Cronkite the following day. He did a wonderful job with the local and national coverage. I remember R. J. telling me recently as we talked over the unusual evening, "Over at the 'old Barn' on that night you would have thought it was the fourth of July. It was the only time I made the Walter Cronkite news!"

I recall one night we were covering a Twins game together and I lost my voice. During a commercial break, I told R. J. I couldn't talk and asked him if he would finish the broadcast. He told me to tell him what I was planning to say and we would have some fun with it. After the break, the studio tossed it to me for the closing segment. I said something like, "Well, that's it from the Dome tonight. It'll be Kevin Tapani pitching for the Twins against the Tigers tomorrow, looking to win his seventh game in a row. This is Mark Rosen reporting." I was moving my lips but nothing was coming out. It didn't matter. R. J. was the audio part of the closing. We had some great fun together. We have always had a very special bond between us.

As I look back upon everything, I realize today what was happening back then. I was thrown in with a group of the best news people who perhaps had ever been put together at one time. It was because of them that I am still doing what I love to do to this day. It has been over 40 years, and I can't for the life of me figure out where all that time went.

They were all there, some coming and some leaving at different times, but they were my colleagues and the best of the best. Don Shelby, Jerry Bowen, Don Kladstrup, Bob McNamara, Susan Spencer, Barry Peterson, Al Austin, Skip Loescher—all news folks, and what a team they made. It was the dream team of dream teams in the history of local television, period—exclamation point! No argument. No debate.

You can get caught up in all your sports debates about who is the best outfielder, the best shortstop, the best hitter, or the best pitcher, but I can assure you that no one in the country who knew anything at all about local television will argue against the fact that the WCCO news team was the best of all time. They made up the all-star team of all-star teams. It wasn't just Hal Scott or Dave Moore. It was everyone. The station was loaded and set into place a stone legacy forever. If the walls could talk, there would be a lot of stories, but in the end it was the standard they set—unmatched, unparalleled, and standing alone.

* * *

As I think about the old place on 9th and LaSalle, it brings a smile to my face. No television station today could survive in the setting or the atmosphere. If someone had been filming every day, it might have been a good James Cagney movie.

To say it was a unique place would be the understatement of all time. Just the physical layout was unbelievable. If a television station and newsroom were going to start out with this setting, the fire marshal would shut the doors on the first day of operation. In addition to it being closed for safety reasons, a keen observer of usable operating space would call it the most insane layout possible.

The newsroom was in the basement. The studio was on the fourth floor, and the control room was on the fifth floor. It made no sense at all. It was not practical by any sense of the imagination. Given the deadlines in this business and the fact that the staff members all needed to rely on each other, it was a nightmare setting to say the least.

On top of the logistical disaster was one elevator that moved at the pace of a turtle and often didn't move at all. There was a time, however, when I was in that elevator with a younger Sophia Loren, and I remember wishing it would slow down. Sometimes it would jam up and the news anchors and others would be stuck between floors. Many times I had to run the flights of stairs up or down, but you couldn't have the news anchors vaulting the stairways on the way to a newscast. For me it was okay—I was young and eager and I wasn't going on the air in a matter of minutes or seconds. The whole thing was ridiculous. The whole setting was a story in itself.

As I mentioned, the newsroom was in the basement—and that was another story. I think of it often when the show about hoarders comes on. I'm not sure if anything ever got thrown away. Just to get to the room was an experience with the low ceilings and cramped space. At the central part of the newsroom were a bunch of desks facing each other. To the right was a sports office where a lot of media guides and a typewriter were kept. Hal really never used an office. He sat right out in the open among all the noise and disturbances.

Everything was cramped and crowded. As you moved into the newsroom more, you would come across Dave Moore's desk area. Near him sat Skip Loescher. Nearby were some other reporters' desks. If you proceeded down a little farther, you'd find the restroom area and a place called "The Morgue."

It was a film morgue, but it might just as well have been a real morgue. For all I knew, there may have been some bodies stashed back there. It was where all the 16 mm film canisters were located. So if you needed old film for the news broadcast, good luck! You had to venture into "The Morgue" to try to locate it. Some were separated by date and some by story. There was no order to any of it and no such thing as videotape back then. I can't even fathom the number of hours I spent in that creepy, dark, damp area looking for film for a story. I shudder every time I think I must have stepped over a body or two.

Once you passed by the room full of film canisters, you would come upon an area where the film editors were located. They had stations that were set up for them to edit the film, and a couple of the editors actually had their own rooms to work in. Behind them but nearby was where the film processors worked. It was at this location that the infamous Lance Finberg set up shop. He was quite a character and was noted for his work on Dave Moore's *Bedtime Nooz* every Saturday night. This was the area where the photographers would bring their film to have it edited and processed.

The whole process seems unimaginable as you look back on it today. It was in some ways like when we used to take our film up to the drugstore and then pick it up the next day. However, this was different. There wasn't time to pick up the film the next day. It needed to be ready now. This is the news. The next day or in some cases even a few hours was not an option.

It was chaos. Film-processing chemicals were everywhere. Everyone was in a rush, and in the middle of the pandemonium there would be times when the film would get jammed up and everything that had been photographed for the news was gone.

Sometimes the film was dark because of the lighting at the setting where the film was shot, so chemicals were heavily used in the processing. This would bring about some of the dramatics of the moment in full force. There would be anger, sweating, and swearing, with lots and lots of doors closing and slamming. It was not a good time. And right in the middle of all that was the fact that a high percentage of those working with and in and around all the chemicals were smokers. Yelling, swearing, hollering, anger, confusion, chemicals, cigarettes, matches, lighters, and smokers. I wouldn't have been surprised if the whole place blew itself right out to the suburbs.

So there I was every day, right in the middle of it. Being too young and eager to realize what was occurring at the time, I would march right in with some film to get it processed and be in for quite a shock. I didn't know, didn't have a clue, but I sure found out quickly enough.

"Get out of here, kid, I have no time for your shit," I was told as I watched my film scatter all over the floor. I just stepped back and thought, "Whoa, what do I do now?"

Eventually I would learn when things got really testy to find something to do far away from the bedlam. You had these tough, crusty, incredibly talented photojournalists, such as Gordy Bartusch, Bob Sjoholm, and Les Solin, all trying to get their work accomplished, and it was something to behold. They had been to Vietnam covering stories and were the best at their jobs. I'm 17 or 18 years old and can't believe what I am seeing. It was combustion everywhere, and that included the staff.

From this area of flammable proportions we moved on to Ron Handberg's office. Ron was the news director and outstanding in every respect. Near Ron's office was the assistant news director, who had three giant televisions monitoring other stations. The newsroom was where all the major decisions of the day were made. Who was going to get what assignment. What stories we were going to cover for that particular day. What crews would be going out.

Another key part of the newsroom was a place called the dispatch shack. This was where the monitoring of police calls took place, where the codes used were figured out, and where cars were dispatched to newsworthy areas of the cities. Reporters and photographers were sent to the scene. "Car No. 4, there is a three-alarm fire at Franklin and Lyndale. Get over there immediately!"

Behind the dispatch shack was the Associated Press and the United Press International wire services. The sports ticker was located there, obviously long before the sophistication of ESPN.

Some days I would look around and think to myself, "I hope I can remember all of this to tell people about it," even though I knew no one would believe me. So, amid all the smoke, the coffee-stained carpeting, cigarette butts everywhere, paper and film strewn in virtually every location, it all came together. It worked. We all had a goal and always seemed to get there. We brought people the news.

I really enjoyed the weekends because I had the most responsibility. I would produce and write the weekend sports. I loved writing the stories. I didn't do a lot of the writing during the week, but I really practiced a lot. As I worked at it, I got better and better. I would gather the wire copy and take it into the sports office and practice writing a script for it. I would type them up and then retype them until I got it right.

I remember once writing a story about a major league ballplayer named Pete Ward who was traded. I wrote that story over and over trying to make it sound good. I don't know why I even recall the story to this day, but I do. I remember working endlessly on that little story with a countless number of draft copies ripped up and thrown into the basket. Finally, when I thought it might cut the mustard, I presented it to Hal for the broadcast. It must have been good because he used it. Wow, Pete Ward . . . I still remember.

It was all done on old-fashioned typewriters back then, with multiple copies given to Hal, the director, the assistant director, and the editor. I always thought if they didn't like my scripts, at least they would know that I was pretty good at changing the ribbon on those old machines.

When you look at what we have available today in modern technology, it is amazing that we could accomplish what we did. I am fortunate to remember how it was "back in the day." It was night and day from what it is now, but I cherish the memories.

From time to time, I might be assigned to interview a player. The interviews never made me famous, as only a glimpse of my hand holding a microphone might hit the airwaves. Early on, in 1970, I did an interview with Carter DeLaitte who won the state high school tennis championship. Carter was in my class at St. Louis Park High School.

Later that evening, the interview was on the air. I will never forget it, as all of my friends sat and watched the interview on the news broadcast. Unfortunately, only my hand made the screen. Most of the attention was on Carter, but inside I thought, "There's my hand, there it is. Without my hand, there would be no interview." I was on television, on WCCO TV with my high school classmate. Well, at least my hand was.

Every day that I was involved in something, I learned from it. Before I ever started working at the station, I regularly watched the news on television. I became awestruck with my neighbor, Phil Jones, and learned a lot from him by just watching. And then, of course, once I arrived permanently at WCCO, I had the benefit of the all-star cast around me every day.

I was fortunate that many of the cast helped me out tremendously. One of those individuals was a photographer named Doug Nemanic. He kind of took me under his wing. He taught me how to write a script that was descriptive.

I recall getting an assignment to cover the state high school cross country championship. I wrote the script with some pretty standard stuff in it. "Eighty teams from all over the state of Minnesota competed today in the state high school cross country championship at the University of Minnesota." Then I gave the name of some of the leaders and who eventually finished as the winner. It was pretty dry.

Doug read it over and told me, "There is not one thing in your script that tells anyone you were there." I will never forget that comment. He wanted me to write with descriptive passion, letting people know I had attended the event. As they listened to the story, they would feel they were there with me.

He told me, "You have to take the viewers with you to where you are. What did you observe? What were the weather conditions during the day. What did the sky look like? What was the temperature? Was there a wind in the face of the runners? What was the reaction of the spectators? You have the picture; now write to the picture so the listeners see it with you."

Doug Nemanic knew what he was talking about, and he really helped me out. I remember his words to this day. It was a real eye-opener for me. Instead of all the boilerplate nonsense, I learned how to develop a script that became descriptive.

"On a bone-chilling fall afternoon on the University of Minnesota Golf Course, the state high school girls cross country championship was held today with superbly conditioned athletes competing from 80 high schools. The brisk wind was in their faces most of the afternoon against a brilliant backdrop of glistening fall colors. One can only imagine that young Cassey Smith's fingers were numb and her face frostbitten, but she had the drive and determination to run those final yards as if she were competing for the United States Olympic team." This was the message I got from Doug. It was Grantland Rice all over: "Against the backdrop of a blue-grey October sky, the Four Horseman rode again." I got the message loud and clear.

I learned that developing a script was a process. It was not just putting words down on a piece of paper. It was taking the viewer or listener on the journey with you. Of all the things I do, writing is something I thoroughly enjoy more than just about any other aspect of my work. The description of the subject is what separates the great writers from the rest.

As I grew into my work, I loved it more and more. I had a passion for doing sports. It was my life as a youngster. I wanted no part of reporting on murders, fires, or politics. Leave that for someone else. Sports was my fixation, and I was surrounded by people who ignited the flame in me.

We were blessed in the newsroom with strong, vibrant personalities, and even though my work centered on sports reporting, I received a lot of help and guidance from many of the greats around me. I learned the basics, worked hard, and got to know these personalities—each in a different way. I had to earn their respect, win them over slowly, before I was going to get any help. Photographers such as Gordon Bartusch, a three-time Vietnam veteran journalist, would rip your throat out if you were off base with something. I approached him differently than the rest.

"Do your job. Don't mess up." I would tell myself this every day. It helped. I needed to show people I could do the work. I had to convince them they could count on me. I needed to do this so when it came time for them to work with me, they would say, "Hey, the kid is okay, he did a good job." At least I would hold my breath and hope they said it.

They watched me and saw that I wasn't a wise guy—that I was a hard worker—and that really helped me a lot. It helped because the staff began to believe in me and know they could count on me to do things and do them right. I was earning credibility.

On August 10, 1971, Harmon Killebrew hit his 500th home run for the Minnesota Twins. I had been on the payroll for a couple of years and was assigned to interview him when the monumental day occurred. We had been camped out at the ballpark waiting for the home run to occur. It took a few days, but when he hit it I was ready for the interview. It went well, and it was the first time I was given an opportunity to do an interview on the air.

Harmon, as always, was as nice as could be. But it wasn't a great night for Harmon even with his 500th home run because the Twins lost the game. That's the way Harmon was. He was so different from many of the modern-day players. Can you imagine that kind of an attitude today, putting the team first against such a giant feat? He was the ultimate team player. It was a big moment for me in my career. Because it was the first time they actually used my voice on a broadcast, I was able to join the union—the American Federation of Television and Radio Artists (AFTRA).

* * *

One of my early career interviews was a complete disaster. I had a chance to interview the great Willie Mays, and I blew it. Playing for the San Francisco Giants, Willie came here for an exhibition game. I did my due diligence and really prepared for the interview, but it didn't go well. In fact, that's probably an understatement.

I got too aggressive with my questions. While calling him Mr. Mays, I tried to get his thoughts on interleague play. It was a mistake. Willie didn't want any controversy, and he certainly was not going to comment on something like play between the National and American League teams. I never should have asked the question because he never even looked me in the eye. I might just as well have been invisible. He stoically replied, "Look, that's not for me to decide. Ask the commissioner about it. I just play the game." It was obvious he did not appreciate my question.

He shot me down. It was not one of my best performances. There he was, the "Say Hey Kid," paying little attention to my ridiculous question, just kind of looking out into space. But you know what—and I truly did think this after the interview—it didn't matter because I was at the ballpark standing near home plate interviewing Willie Mays, one of the greatest ballplayers of all time. Yeah, I could have done better, but I just interviewed Willie Mays! You have got to be kidding me! Wow!! I could not believe it.

I don't think Willie Mays liked my question. I was so nervous, and I really messed up the interview.

Things are so different today with satellite feeds and videotaping. Back then, we would be at the ballpark for maybe the first three innings and hopefully shoot something exciting that happened early in the game. We would take it back to the studio and get it ready for the 10 o'clock news. If something happened later in the game that was exciting or game-breaking, we didn't get it. It was the way it was done back then.

When I was at the games, the baseball writers would not allow me in the press box. They ruled it with an iron fist and were not about to let some wide-eyed kid trespass on their sacred ground. I would sit somewhere around the third base line. It was not too bad of a seat, and at least I was there at the ballpark. That was good enough for me. Larry Kohout worked with me a lot, shooting the film, and we later spent time together as a team at Lake Placid at the 1980 Olympics.

Larry taught me a great deal about taking pictures. If Rod Carew laced a triple in the gap and was racing around the bases, Larry showed me that you follow the ball with the camera. By doing this, you will end up in the right place and not miss anything. We didn't have multiple cameras. We had one, so you better not miss the action or you won't have it when you need it.

* * *

I was accepted pretty well by the Twins front office and the players. Now the Vikings, they were a little different. I loved to follow the team, but soon I learned there was a way to do things and a way not to do things. I learned my lesson the hard way.

I made the mistake of walking into the locker room after practice one afternoon and asking Fran Tarkenton and someone else (who I can't remember) for their autographs. I recall the interaction actually took place in the weight room, and Fran and Jim Marshall were there along with some other players. The autographs weren't even for me. A friend of mine had asked me if I could do that for him. Both players were very gracious and obliged. They weren't the problem. It was Bud Grant.

With Bud Grant on the set of *Rosen's Sports Sunday*.

Bud was standing nearby and saw me ask the players. He looked at me with those cold steel-blue eyes, and I just knew exactly what they said. "Don't ever do that again in this locker room. EVER!" "Yes sir," I thought loudly to myself. "I understand." And it never happened again. Bud hasn't coached here in over 25 years, but I know if I did it again, he would find out.

Bud never yelled at me or embarrassed me or anything like that. He didn't even call me by name. He just looked at me. In fact, he never called me by name until we did *The Bud Grant Show* together, quite some time after I had first met him.

In fact, I remember the first time he called out my name. I almost went into shock. It might just as well have been the pope calling me

"Mark." It couldn't have meant more. I almost dropped in my tracks thinking, "I cannot believe it. Bud Grant just called me by my first name." It was an important day for me.

For the most part, I was accepted by the Viking players and have developed some great relationships over the years. I recall the NFC Championship Game in Dallas in 1973, one of the greatest victories in franchise history. I remember on the plane ride home, running back Chuck Foreman came up to me and shook my hand like I was one of the guys. I'll never forget it. Chuck and I had somewhat of a bond together. In some ways, I guess we were both rookies that year.

When we got off the plane at the airport, thousands of fans were there to greet us. I walked along right with the players and really felt a part of everything. I even got patted on the back by the fans a few times. I'm sure they thought I was a ball boy or something. It didn't matter. I was accepted by the team and the fans and reveled in the moment.

* * *

As time passed, I was getting on the air more frequently. I had long hair and was sort of a goofy-looking kid back then, but I did my job. I was 23, 24 years old at the time and learning the business. I was a part of the team and couldn't wait to get to work every day.

In 1976, WCCO TV signed Gophers basketball coach Jim Dutcher to a contract to host a new program called *Inside Basketball*. Our news director, Ron Handberg, was considering people for hosting the show, and I quickly volunteered. "I'll do it," I told Ron, and to my surprise he agreed. I couldn't believe it. I was going to actually host a show. I was really excited about it. I was now in the heartbeat of television broadcasting, doing more than just interviews.

Jim Dutcher was the perfect person for my first hosting opportunity. Jim is a wonderful person and was fantastic to work with on the show. He made me feel so at ease. On occasion, because of travel difficulties, we would have to do the program on the telephone.

Dutcher often used his players for demonstrations, and they did a terrific job in assisting young players with the fundamentals of the game. Because of my work with the show, I got the opportunity to cover Magic Johnson's first Big Ten game when Michigan State hosted the Gophers.

Jim Dutcher made it all work for me, and I am forever grateful for his patience and assistance in the two seasons that we worked together. He has been a wonderful friend, and I am honored to have worked with him.

* * *

I was learning some things about scoops and verifying stories. I learned about sources and how to be sure a story you are going with is correct. I learned you do not stay long in the business if you get burned on stories very often.

I was learning from the best. And the best of the best was Dave Moore. Dave was of iconic proportions, but as I got to know him better, he was really just like the rest of us. To the public, he was different. He was the news.

People wanted the news from Dave, and he gave it to them in a down-home style as if their neighbor was talking to them over the back fence. He was really something—and some kind of a special reporter. I loved the man.

Dave did not have the broadcasting background of many of the other anchors of the past and present, but to this day he is revered in the newsroom. I wish I had a dollar for every time I heard, "I wonder what the old man would have said about this? How do you think the old man would have reacted to that?"

Dave cared about the product in the deepest of ways, something that cannot be said about all the other anchors. He wanted to report the news. I recall him saying many times, "Where is the news in this broadcast? There isn't any news here. Don't we have some reporters over at city hall? What are the beat reporters doing? Let's find some news to report." He had the passion for the business, and he never put it aside. There was no room for the Ted Baxters of the world.

Dave Moore was an icon in television news. I had such admiration for him as a person and as a professional.

Dave Moore cared. He cared deeply about what he reported to the viewers. Most newscasts have what they call a "kicker" at the end of a broadcast. This is kind of a "feel good" story to leave the audience in a good mood at the end. Maybe a story about a cute pet would surface, or something of that nature.

Most anchors, in order to have an unrehearsed reaction, don't even view the story ahead of time. Not Dave Moore. He would not only view the footage, but he mostly wrote the script as well. It was his time to shine, and he was incredible in getting the viewers to buy in. He would take the story, write it, shape it, and put forth his ability as an actor to perfect the delivery.

It was his personality that everyone loved. He could be as stoic and grim as the story needed and then take us to the *Bedtime Nooz* in different fashion on Saturday nights. Dave had a presence like no person I have ever known in local news. When the news was bad, viewers took comfort in the fact that Dave Moore was bringing it to them. He would report the most horrifying news and comfort you at the same time. He had our trust and the viewers' trust.

I often mention Dave in the same breath as the famous Walter Cronkite. I'll never forget Cronkite reporting the first man on the moon. He had that "Oh boy" broadcasting style that viewers really identified with at one of the most incredible times in American history. And of course, he was the same way when Kennedy was shot, but in such a different manner.

Dave never had the plastic look we often see today in the faces behind the camera. He was just this disheveled character in our backyard, on our patio, in our driveway, giving us the news.

Dave was on the WCCO softball team. He was the pitcher, our leader, wearing his Hush Puppies on the mound. He didn't care. That's who he was.

Dave never, and I mean never, just delivered the news. He gave it with his body, his eyes, and his feelings. He didn't read it. He felt it. He was a newsman's newsman with a tremendous sense of humor, someone who did his job in the most honorable way.

I really cared deeply for Dave because he did so many nice things for me and truly wanted me to succeed. He used to get really excited if I was doing something good. I really appreciated that. There was nothing phony about him. He used to literally go up to people and say things like, "Did you see what Mark is working on? It's really going to be good." Can you imagine how him doing this type of thing made me feel? It was unbelievable! To get Dave Moore's seal of approval on my work, now believe me, that was special.

Dave was a huge baseball fan and a member of what was then called "The Spectators Club." He got Ted Williams to speak to the club one day, and Ted met him at the studio before they walked over to the club. Dave asked me to join them. We walked down the street together. Dave Moore, Ted Williams, and me. It sounds make-believe as I mention it here, so I will say it again: Dave Moore, Ted Williams, and me. Unbelievable!

I was a huge Ted Williams fan. He was perhaps the greatest pure hitter who ever lived. He was known for having the best eye in baseball while he played. They said he could see the stitching on the ball as it propelled its way to home plate.

One of my favorite stories about Ted was when he was playing in a game against a rookie catcher. Ted took the first two pitches and the umpire called each a ball, much to the ire of the young catcher. After voicing his disapproval for a second time to the umpire, he was given a curt and short message by the man in blue. Removing his mask and stepping out from behind the plate, the umpire looked the rookie in the eye and said, "Young man, when the pitch is a strike, Mr. Williams will swing at it."

Dave was the general, the man in charge and the captain of our team. He was truly beloved by all who worked with him. He knew so much. I truly believe he had more news in him than anyone I have ever known, and he delivered it better than anyone as well.

* * *

Hal Scott and Dave Moore were good friends. And another friend in that group of beloved WCCO broadcasters was weatherman Bud Kraehling. Bud began his 50-year career as a favor to a pal by helping out at a radio station in Carthage, Illinois.

In 1970, Bud did a five-minute weather program on WCCO sponsored by Taystee Bread. He was a trusted reporter of the weather much like Dave and Hal in their specialty areas. He was one the audience could always identify with and became closely attached to them with his "Weather Window" report, as he wrote forecasts on the window for crowds gathered outside the television studio.

People loved Bud's laugh, his soft voice, and his wonderful smile. He could light up a room in his quiet demeanor. Bud was a weatherman, and guess what? People remembered what the weather forecast was going to be because Bud told it to them. He knew because he got it directly from the National Weather Service.

He had a great connection to his audience and was so easy to listen to on the air. He never gave you "the sky is falling" reports, as we often see and hear today; he just gave us the weather report.

He came across the airwaves as everyone's father, grandfather, neighbor, and friend. He had an easy manner about him with a quietness and sense of calm in his voice. And you know what, with all

What a great team—The best of the best! From left: Susan Spencer, Hal Scott, Bud Kraehling, and Dave Moore.

of the devices and sophistication of the weather reporting of today, I'm not sure we have it any better than what Bud told us many years ago. He gave us the weather in a folksy manner that identified him. And he did it day in and day out.

I was always impressed by the way Bud laughed and made fun of himself when he was wrong. We appreciated that about him. Sometimes he was wrong. Nothing wrong with that, and he said so. He was never above it all.

* * *

Our news director during all the fuss and chaotic times, putting things in place for the broadcasts, was Ron Handberg. He was a giant in the industry and very well respected. He had a steely disposition with tremendous ethics and great passion for the news. He had a true understanding for what was important to communicate to the public, and he had a thorough understanding of the community.

Ron was a phenomenal writer and would get directly involved in the actual writing of the newscast. It is different today. Ron would finish his work and often go home by 8:30 p.m. He knew things were in place, and if something came up there was someone on board to handle it. Ron was great to work with every day. He really understood what needed to be done.

I always thought the old manual typewriter he worked on was either going to blow up or start on fire because he really made those keys hum. He made tough decisions and found a way to balance out all the talent and egos in the newsroom. Remember, he was working with a very gifted, long-term, seasoned staff who knew how to do their jobs very well. Ron made them even better. He was well respected by all around him.

There was a time when, for some reason, the station had decided to take the popular *Captain Kangaroo* off the air. The decision was not received well by his audience, and a protest took place outside the station. I recall that word came down from the station's general manager's office to stay away from covering the protest.

Handberg hit the roof. This was news, and he was going to cover it. He went upstairs and told the bosses that we were going to cover the story and show the video we had of the protest, and they could have his job if they denied him. That was Ron Handberg and we respected him for the way he protected news journalism. No one was going to cloud his judgment of what was right.

Ron was the boss and our platform leader. He led the troops, and on that day when he went upstairs, he earned his battle stripes in spades. His respect in the newsroom was unwavering. I learned a great deal from Ron. We all did.

* * *

One of the very best writers in our group of talented news reporters was Bob McNamara. I really think Bob may have been the best. He was the wise guy of the group. He would always have something to say about everything. He would complain about this and complain about that. Something was always bugging Bob. He was the station rabble-rouser and quite the character. He was our James Dean.

Bob was an independent thinker and had so much incredible talent in writing for television news. He used to call me "Sid" after the *Minneapolis Star Tribune* reporter Sid Hartman. I hated it, and Bob knew it. I'm sure that's the very reason he did it.

In our dispatch room was a young women named Jane Nielsen. She was very attractive and very nice. I took her out on a date, as did some of the others around the newsroom. When Bob told us he was going to go out with her, we couldn't believe it. There was no way that Jane was going to have anything to do with Bob McNamara. They were just about as different as two people could be. Today, many decades later, Jane and Bob are still married and living in Arizona.

Bob became an outstanding news reporter with the network. He took no guff from anyone and got the story. He wrote it with precision and delivered it with accuracy and passion. He was the best, and I have had such tremendous respect for him through the years.

* * *

Another great personality and monumental talent was Susan Spencer, who became the first co-anchor with Dave Moore. She had to have guts to take on that role, but she did it and performed admirably. Over time, Susan blended in and did a fantastic job.

She was an outstanding reporter, but her real job was to win over Dave and the viewers. Eventually she achieved the goal, was accepted and respected, and did a great job. Susan was a great, down-to-earth reporter. She excelled at her work, and it came across to everyone involved. She didn't have to just pass the test of a good reporter. She had to pass Dave Moore's test. She did, and in the process she set the bar high.

There were so many others at WCCO in those early days, all unforgettable. People like Jerry Bowen, Susan Peterson, Barry Peterson, Don Kladstrup, Reid Johnson, Quent Nuefeld—all such talented journalists. I could never figure out what got them all together in the same place. These are the people you meet in your life who inspired you to stand a little straighter, stand a little taller, and speak a little clearer. Many went on to the network and excelled there as well. I am so proud to have met them all and worked with them, and I am so privileged to call them my friends.

One day, not so long ago, I was thinking about all those incredible times at WCCO in the early days. I was trying to figure it all out one day, making sure my memory was correct. I was sure some of my recollections couldn't possibly have been true. It was just so much insanity, too much craziness, and at the same time too very special for it to be real.

As I thought back on those early days, for my own sanity and well-being, I needed to find a verifying source, someone who could corroborate this bizarre world I had entered, someone who remembered it like I did. It was the only way I could be sure of my early history. So, I contacted my old friend Bob McNamara, who as I mentioned was one of the great newsmen of his time.

Bob is living a life of leisure in Phoenix, playing a lot of golf after his vagabond life as a TV correspondent. He was able to bring the past all back to life for me. He helped me realize that what I had observed and recalled was accurate. It wasn't a dream or a figment of my imagination. It happened, and it will be there for the ages. The following is Bob's early recollections of his time at WCCO television. Many thanks to you, Bob! You have brought the memories back and convinced me that I hadn't imagined the whole thing.

> I got to CCO in the summer of 1968, two weeks after Senator Robert F. Kennedy's assassination. I'd just turned 23, fresh from two years with the ABC affiliate KCRG-TV in Cedar Rapids, Iowa. There, for $105 per week, before taxes, I'd been a news and sports reporter, radio and TV anchor, cameraman, film processor, and film editor. When word

got around KCRG that I was leaving for WCCO, a station old-timer told me, "You'll be back in two months, Mac. You're okay, but you're not that good."

Going to the WCCO newsroom wasn't exactly like a trek into a West Virginia coal mine, but there were vague similarities. From a bright lobby, you descended a dimly lit stairway that entered a darker, narrow, short hallway with a ceiling so low that a six-footer had to duck under. On the right was a dusty, dingy sports office, with a desk heaped with film reels, wire copy, press releases, and old scripts. Usually, a guy with a permanent smirk named Jack Lavallier occupied the desk. When the newsroom was remodeled a few years later, the sports office was the first casualty.

The main newsroom featured an ugly wooden structure designed to be a six-person desk. Three reporters sat on each side of the contraption, typing their notes from stories, working the phones, or gossiping. The desk had a white Formica top, but its edges were yellowed and blackened by years of nicotine stains and cigarette burns.

Cigarette smoke was the odor du jour in the newsroom, which grew especially hazy in late afternoon as deadlines approached for the six o'clock news show. Discarded film cans were bent into ashtrays. Pipe embers commonly ignited wastebasket fires. Before 1970, I'd guess that at least 60 percent of the staff heavily smoked cigarettes or pipes. I couldn't write a story without a cup of black coffee and a Camel or Winston going. The air was so foul that even nonsmokers might have been diagnosed with at least a pack-a-day habit.

If the room had a watering hole, it was the assignment desk. Usually manned by the assistant news editor, it was the first stop for reporters and photographers to find out what assignments they'd be working on each day. On the wall behind the desk, three television sets were often turned to CCO's competing stations, but in those days there was only one competitor: KSTP. At news time, reporters and photographers pulled up chairs or stood around the desk to watch how our work compared with KSTP—stories they had that we missed or vice versa. By and large, we always believed

CCO's product was superior to the other stations in town. As far as we were concerned, KSTP was a steppingstone for people on their way down or out of the business. Few ever left WCCO to work at KSTP.

The newsroom "outback" was the film screening and editing area, where stories were assembled for air. The room echoed with a Mickey Mouse chorus as reporters, photographers, and editors quickly rolled through the sound footage reviewing and choosing shots. Around a corner, in a room of its own, was the giant stainless-steel film-processing machine. Fifteen feet long, five feet high, and three or four feet wide, it had a two-man staff to run it. One of the two guys was nicknamed "Tuna," because he actually looked like one. If you weren't on the photo staff, the only reason to go there was to get a cup of coffee.

My first impression of the CCO staff will never leave me. With a few exceptions, I thought it was a collection of aloof, arrogant snobs. Sure I'd come from a rinky-dink broadcasting backwater, but the fact was many of them had, too. If they hadn't worked in Iowa or Indiana, they were in from the Dakotas or down from Duluth. When it was clear I was being treated like a Jehovah's Witness missionary lost in the building, I set out to introduce myself to reporters and photographers one by one.

One of the few exceptions was Phil Jones. Jones was the star reporter and he knew it. He was the man among the boys and one girl on the reporting staff. He was welcoming and, as was his way, he stood there sizing me up as we exchanged details of our backgrounds. Jones had recently gone to Vietnam, where he and a station photographer had produced a documentary on Minnesota soldiers fighting the war—a move that would be copied by local stations coast to coast. WCCO's political reporter, Jones routinely broke stories night after night. The bumbling Minnesota governor, Harold LeVander, quaked when Jones asked him any question. To me, Jones was always encouraging. In fact, he recommended me as his replacement when he became a correspondent for CBS News. Several years later, it was he who dropped my name to a CBS executive and led to my own job with the network. For that I am forever indebted.

The "world's greatest news director," as I'd been told, was Joe Bartelme. Slim, professional-looking, and quiet, Bartelme had a reputation as a terrific writer and reporter. He was an Iowan who'd come to CCO from the same Cedar Rapids station I had. The previous year, Bartelme had done something few affiliate reporters had ever done; he reported a cold-weather story that aired on the *CBS Evening News* with Walter Cronkite. As news director, he excelled at organizing coverage for scheduled events, such as state political conventions and election coverage. He was a good judge of who and what worked best on news broadcasts. And he had a reputation for going above and beyond the call when CBS News needed station facilities to produce stories.

Still, in a station that billed itself as the "Communication Center for the Great Northwest," Bartelme could be the most uncommunicative of all. His apparent management strategy was to keep reporters in the dark about whether they were doing a good job or not. It came to be concluded by most of us that if he called you "shit head," you were golden. If he said nothing, you were on thin ice. After work, Bartelme would occasionally join a few of us for beers at a bar down the street. If he had too many, he was known to dance on the hoods of parked cars. Several years later, Bartelme left WCCO to become news director of KNBC in Los Angeles. His anchormen there included Tom Snyder and Tom Brokaw, who would someday be anchor stars with NBC News. When I met Brokaw on a story in Montana decades later, I asked him what Bartelme was like in L.A. Rolling his eyes, Brokaw said, "Great guy, but get him drunk and he gets a little crazy."

Led by Phil Jones, the reporting staff in the late '60s and early '70s was a collection of young, talented, hard-working men and one woman, still long on potential but sponging up as much experience as possible in a place where you could learn from the best.

WCCO's anchor team could not have been better for its time and place. In any other large television market, each probably wouldn't have been hired, but for the Twin Cities, the team was just the right fit. The 10 o'clock news, *The Scene Tonight*, as it was called, was appointment viewing for many Twin Citians. It was headlines, humanity, and a little humor on the side.

Anchorman Dave Moore was, as newspaper ads depicted him, "your friendly neighborhood newscaster." While news anchors in other like-sized markets drove Cadillacs or Lincolns, Moore's transportation was a beat-up maroon Chevy Corvair or a VW bus.

If there were newsroom prima donnas, they were the photographers, and there were a dozen. Veterans, such as Gordy Bartusch, Les Solin, and Bob Sjoholm, had filmed just about every kind of story in the Twin Cities at least three times and let you know it. They were some of the best in the business, and you would grow to realize it. New reporters were often looked upon as another rookie that photographers would have to train to do the job their way, and they were right. In no uncertain terms, a photographer let a reporter know that without their pictures, your work was nothing more than radio. Photographers liked covering stories with reporters who wrote well, since they knew that good writing gave even more meaning to their pictures. Reporters had favorite photographers and vice-versa. Good pictures and sound meant better material to write a good story.

Photographers often edited the stories they shot, so out in the field they were demanding about getting all the shots and angles they'd need to be able to package a film segment properly. If someone else was editing their story, they'd be doubly sure to get all the necessary shots so they didn't get chewed out by the editor.

Was WCCO a broadcasting field of dreams? For sure, in the late '60s and early '70s, it was a field of dreamers, like me. WCCO was the perfect environment of peer pressure and opportunity for someone willing to work hard and learn a craft to advance their careers from the best in the business. Peer pressure from the great writers like Al Austin and photographers who wanted their work to shine in your story made us all better at what we did. Unlike the networks, where executive producers brought political or social causes to their broadcasts, WCCO was agenda-free. For correspondents at the network level, it was every man for himself, while at CCO reporters were team players.

With Phil Jones' help, I became a CBS News correspondent like he did. Don Kladstrup, Jerry Bowen, and Susan Spencer became CBS

News correspondents with my help. Quent Neufeld and Jim Anderson would become CBS News producers, and Bill Stewart chose to join ABC News as a correspondent. In later years, a number of others would join CBS or NBC as correspondents or producers.

First time I saw Mark Rosen?

He was a tall, skinny, high schooler with glasses like snorkel goggles without the breathing tube hanging around the old sports office, but I didn't think much of it. After seeing him there a few more days, I asked Don Kladstrup, "Who's the kid?" Kladstrup said, "Oh, he's Phil Jones' neighbor. He wants to get into sports."

At the time, I was barely more than two years removed from being a Chicago newsroom copyboy, and I thought, "I hope this kid knows how lucky he is."

In the Chicago newsroom, a wise-ass reporter called me "Scoop" one day after I'd answered a phone call from a guy telling me that a well-known Chicago mobster had just been, as the caller put it, "dusted." He hung up. I passed the information on to the crime reporter, and it was the lead story that night. It was a "scoop" for the reporter, but for me "Scoop" became a nickname.

After a while, I had a feeling Mark Rosen would be a force, not just a hanger-on, so in honor of the Twin Cities' dominant newspaper sports reporter, Sid Hartman, I called Mark "Sid." I knew he didn't like it, but it was more a form of encouragement than a putdown. Little did any of us know that young "Sid" would have such a long, successful career at WCCO.

Many thanks for the above, Bob! It validates my recollections.

What great memories I have of those early days at WCCO television. And I'm still here after 40-plus years. No one does that. It will never happen again. No one will ever be allowed to hang around a newsroom and then make a four-decade career out of it.

In my early days, if someone had pulled Hal Scott aside and said, "Will the kid make it?" I would have hoped that Hal would have said something like, "I think so. He works hard and he knows his stuff." That would have been all I would ever need.

3

Do You Believe in Miracles?

It was 1980. The United States Olympic hockey team had just defeated Russia 4–3. I called Ralph Jon Fritz at the station and screamed into the phone, "DO YOU BELIEVE IN MIRACLES?" Al Michaels heard what I said and used it as his famous line at the end of the game. Well, not quite. But it makes a good story and has been a running joke for me for a long time.

And of course, it really didn't happen that way because Michaels had coined the line long before I made it across the street to my press office and the telephone. But the fact remains, and I still believe to this day, that perhaps we had just witnessed a miracle.

What a great memory: Lake Placid and the men's Olympic hockey team. I'm not sure anything in sports, amateur or professional, will ever equal what happened in that monumental contest against Russia. The ending became as surreal a moment in time as any sports event I have been associated with during my 40 years in broadcasting. I am thoroughly convinced that nothing like it will ever happen again.

I was pleasantly surprised that we were going to cover the Olympics. WCCO had made the commitment due mostly to the number of Minnesotans on the 1980 team. There was also mild interest in the hockey team, mostly because Herb Brooks was the coach but also

At Lake Placid
for the 1980
Olympic Games,
hours before
the opening
ceremonies.

because a number of former Minnesota Gopher hockey players were on the squad.

Ron Handberg was our news director, and he made the call. It was quite early in my career, and I was fairly inexperienced to be given such an important assignment, but I was well prepared—at least I thought I was. The fact is, no one was. No one was prepared for what was going to happen at Lake Placid that year. It was like going to cover an event and the result turned out to be something no one in a million years could have fathomed. No sports journalist will ever cover anything like it again, and I truly believe that no fan will ever see anything like it again.

WCCO sent a four-man crew to Lake Placid. The group included Larry Kohout, my sports photographer; Jack Brown, producer and director; photographer Jon Carlson; and me. My job was to provide coverage of the Minnesota athletes competing. I recall the station taking out a newspaper ad that read, "Follow our team covering your team."

The local press had given the hockey team some attention going into the Games. They had played some quality opponents on their pre-Olympic schedule, and many of the games were played at the old Met Center. Lou Nanne, the former Minnesota North Stars general manager, had arranged for his friend Herb Brooks' team to play a difficult minor league schedule.

* * *

In Minnesota and regionally, a number of the players were well known. Neal Broten, Rob McClanahan, Mike Ramsey, and others like Eric Strobel were popular athletes on the hockey front. We had watched many of these young men play in high school and college, so we were very familiar with their personalities and their play.

These were very talented young hockey players who made up a very formidable U.S. Olympic hockey team. But by comparison to the Russians, and even some of the other international competition, they were not even in the same league.

U.S hockey teams had not had a great deal of success in the Olympics since 1960, when the team was led to a gold medal by goalie and former Gopher Jack McCartan. During those two decades, Olympic hockey was dominated by the Russians. They had extremely well-seasoned teams with many of the players being together for countless years.

By comparison, the 1980 U.S. team was made up of a collection of college players with little time actually playing together as a team. Against the great Russian team in the Olympics, well, they really didn't stand much of a chance.

As we prepared to cover the Olympic Games at Lake Placid, I must admit I was somewhat interested in the men's hockey team and how they would fare in the competition, but I never thought they had much of a chance to be the lead story.

Our plan was to cover many other events in addition to hockey, and we were excited about our U.S. athletes, like Cindy Nelson from Lutsen. We felt like she would be a big story during the Games. As far as I was concerned, I was just happy to be there. It was a wonderful opportunity, and I was pumped and ready to go.

The four of us flew to Buffalo, New York, rented a car, and drove to Lake Placid a few days before the Games were to begin. The one thing I remember vividly as we arrived in the evening was the giant ski jump. It was amazing. I will never forget the feeling I had when I first saw it. "WOW," was the best way to describe it.

The funny thing is when I returned to Lake Placid 25 years later for the reunion of the hockey team, I got the same feeling when I saw the giant ski jump again. Nothing seemed to have changed. Everything looked the same. It was just a quaint little town, maybe like Hibbing, Minnesota, with that giant ski jump looking over the legendary community in the far reaches of New York. A quarter century had passed, but it seemed like only a day or week.

We got in late, picked up our press credentials, and went to our sleeping accommodations. We were staying north of town in a cabin-like setting. It was fine, but I remember that the transportation from our quarters to the Games was a nightmare. It was a complete transportation breakdown and caused massive problems in getting to and from the events. Jack Brown and I basically set our media coverage agenda, and we focused our attention on the local athletes competing, while at the same time we figured out ways to navigate our WCCO team to the events.

Believe me, it was not like today. I felt sorry for Larry Kohout. He would shoot the tape, get up at 6:30 a.m. the following morning, drive to the airport, and fly the tape back to the studio. As I look back, it was an amazing process compared to today. But hey, it was what it was, and in the end we got the job done.

We were set up in the media center, which was located at a school across the street from the ice arena. The bigger events were held in this newly built arena, with others held at the older building.

The night before the opening of the 1980 Olympics, the U.S. hockey team played its first-round game against Sweden at the new arena. The place looked half empty. There was not a lot of excitement generated before, during, or after the game.

The game ended in a 2–2 tie, and no one gave it a lot of thought at the time. But the thing that few people realized then, and for some even to this day, is that if the U.S. had not come back to tie that game against Sweden in the final seconds, they would not have had an opportunity to win the gold medal because the U.S. team would not have qualified for the medal round. So although it was a "ho-hum" game, the tie became huge as things progressed.

As more games by the competing teams were played in the Olympic competition, we would soon learn that the tie was against an extremely talented Swedish hockey team. Bill Baker's goal just seconds before the buzzer turned out to be one of dramatic proportions.

The next day was the opening ceremonies, and believe me when I say that no one was giving any thought to the future U.S. game against the Russians. Yes, we came up with a tie in the first outing and that was cool, but the Russians, well, that was several games away and, besides, everyone knew the U.S squad had little chance of staying in the game, let alone winning against the infallible Soviets.

As the days went by, the U.S. continued to win its games and the interest in the men's hockey team heightened. Their 7–3 win against Czechoslovakia was a stunner, and Brooks' team of college kids comfortably won its other games as well. As the U.S. continued to win, people started thinking, "Whoa, what is going on here?"

And all of a sudden coming up on the schedule was Russia. The great Soviet team had easily defeated its competition to that point and likely gave little thought to who its next opponent would be. I'm sure they paid little attention to the Americans. It had been just a couple weeks since they soundly defeated the United States 10–3 in an exhibition game at Madison Square Garden. To them, the upcoming game wasn't even a blip on their radar screen.

I remember for the first time since our arrival at Lake Placid starting to think ahead to the Friday night game against Russia. My first thought was, "Well, this will be fun to watch, but it will probably be a 10–2 game or something like that." I mean just a short time ago, the Russians had obliterated the U.S.

It was that earlier game against the Czechs that got my attention and that of the crowd at the game. It was the first time during that Olympics that the chant "USA! USA! USA!" reverberated throughout the arena. They played a fabulous game in defeating Czechoslovakia, and with their other games solidly in tow, it started to become quite apparent how talented these college kids really were.

I noticed that the more the U.S. won, the surlier Herbie got. He was tougher on the players than ever before and wanted them to perceive him as the enemy. He had the perfect strategy. He kept the team under tight wraps and controlled during all the media connections. He was focusing in on the Russians.

As it got closer and closer to the big game, the excitement was building. But let me stop here for a second and say this: There were no grandiose thoughts that the U.S. was going to beat Russia. There was no chance it would happen. I honestly believe that no one gave them even the slightest inkling of an opportunity to win. I certainly didn't.

I enjoyed the ride up to that point. The winning had been interesting to watch, but I recall thinking, "Well, this has been fun but it all ends Friday night."

I remember watching the Russian team practice. They were unbelievable. We had access to their practices, and it was pure and astounding joy to watch them perform on the ice. They were amazing skaters, stick-handlers, and shooters. They had all been together for so long that everything they did seemed so effortless. It was like a ballerina performance, as close to true perfection as possible.

The first time I ever saw this magnificent team skate, it was jaw-dropping. They were so robotic—their facial expressions, their movements, and their skills, as if in rehearsal for an opening on Broadway. For them, the Olympics must have seemed like another day at work. They were joyless, stoic. They had that "CCCP" on the front of their jerseys, and it was intimidating, yet awesome.

I watched them literally in reverence as they went through their almost choreographed drills, and I would then think about our team. We were a conglomeration of college kids, a bunch of goofballs having fun, having a good time, laughing their way along, until Herbie started cracking the whip on them. What a difference between the two teams. Did they have any possible chance to win? No.

As Friday night arrived, it was more than a hockey game. The setting was incredible. Not only was it going to be a big game in the Olympics but a big game for the countries. The Soviets were the evil villain in the world. They had just invaded Afghanistan and were viewed around the world unfavorably. They were more than an opponent on the ice. There had been talk of the Soviets boycotting the Olympic Games. There was a time when everyone thought they were going to pull out and not participate. So it was definitely more than a hockey game.

Coach Herb Brooks had his hands full with a bunch of space cadets about to face the mighty Russians. He knew he had to keep his players on track and get them ready. Herb believed that if they played their game—his weaving style of play—they could stay with the Russians. Could they win? Well, that was a matter to be determined on the ice.

We had been covering other events at the Olympics and were really busy, and all of a sudden it was Friday night and the game between the U.S. and Russia was on. I remember thinking whether the rest of the world was watching and if they were as intrigued and interested by the game as we were. There was no ESPN three decades ago, nor was there the national sports coverage of today.

The game against the Russians was not even in prime time and not even live. It was on tape delay. We were isolated from everything in Lake Placid, so I wondered how much everyone else knew. It was crazy. The network tried to get the game moved to prime time, but the Olympic Committee would have no part of changing the schedule. As it turned out, the greatest game ever played in the history of sports was on tape delay.

As the game time got closer, there was a buzz around the arena and tickets were tough to find. Electricity was in the air. I was in a jammed press box with a chill running up and down my back as the U.S. team took the ice to the chants of "USA! USA! USA!" It was riveting! I get the same feeling every time I think about it.

The sound bounded off the walls and was deafening. It was a passionate excitement that I had never witnessed before. I don't know how the players could feel the ice. They were flying high. Still, I would constantly have to bring myself back to reality. "Hold on here, don't get so excited, these are the Russians we are playing."

It had been just a short time before they had lost to the Soviets by a ton of goals, but for some reason, the previous exhibition game at Madison Square Garden was in the rearview mirror because our U.S. team was really on fire. They were incited by the crowd, and it showed in dramatic fashion.

The Russians, well, they didn't seem moved at all by the chanting and the noise. It was just another game for them, just another likely win. What did they have to worry about? This was a job where failure at work was not an option.

I have been asked many times to try to put some sort of an analogy to the game. The United States Olympic hockey team versus the Russians. Maybe this was like an average high school team playing a national champion Minnesota Gophers team. Maybe like a freshman in college trying to tackle Adrian Peterson of the Vikings in the open field—or me getting a date with Halle Berry. It was not going to happen. This was the greatest hockey team in the world, maybe the mightiest team ever put together—ever. They had easily defeated a group of NHL stars. They were invincible, to say the least. I'm sure they gave little if any thought to being defeated by the Americans—a casting of kids from the United States.

As the game started, all I remember is the Russian players soaring all over the place. The noise before the game and all the chanting hadn't fazed them for a second. They were everywhere. It just about took all the air out of the bubble. Russia scored first, and it scared us.

Nearing the end of the first period, Russia held a slim 2–1 lead when Mark Johnson scored a dramatic goal for the U.S., ending the period in a 2–2 tie. One period was over and it was even. It was the same as the beginning, even, but one period had elapsed with two to go. I thought, "Well, so far so good."

I think everyone at the game was in shock. We were even after the first period. But then common sense prevailed. Our thinking and wishing took a reality turn. The likelihood was it would be over soon and maybe finish 7–3 in the Russians' favor. It would have been a good effort but for naught. "Hey, we hung in there and have nothing to be ashamed of. Good effort."

But then something occurred that perhaps was the key to the game. The Russian coach pulled the greatest goalie in the world, Vladislav Tretiak. It was a fatal error in judgment and would come back to haunt them forever.

The Soviets scored once in the second period and held a slim lead of 3–2 going into the final period of play. We began to ask ourselves the question, "What was going on here? Two periods over and we're only down one goal?"

Still, I never thought in a million years we had a chance to win. There was a point when I changed my thinking, but it came much later. For most of the final period, because they were hanging in and keeping it close, I thought, "Well at least we aren't going to lose 10–3."

As the U.S. stayed in the game, the Russians never panicked. They must have thought they were being attacked by a bunch of little mosquitoes that kept pestering and pestering, and I'm sure they were figuring, "It's about time to show the Americans who's boss here."

The Russians were all over the place, and Jim Craig, the U.S. goalie, was making save after save. Again and again they attacked the goal in waves, to no avail. Craig was playing completely out of his mind, stopping everything they threw at him. The noise in the arena was devastating. Shot after shot, save after save, and here they come again!

Russia was attacking and firing the puck almost at will, but Craig was up for the task. They were in constant motion; poetry in motion. It was an unbelievable pleasure to watch that kind of hockey.

I was holding my breath, clenching my fists, and trying to keep my insides from busting out of my body. The arena was in chaos. I had never been a part of anything like this before, and I will never see anything like it again. Back and forth, back and forth the action went, and into the U.S. zone came the Russians time and time again, only to be turned away by Craig.

The U.S. never let down for one second; they never let up. My thought after the first period had been, "Okay, they have extended this game a little." After the second period, I began to change my thinking and had some mild hope.

It had become totally different for the players, especially after the second period, because at that point—I remember the guys saying later—they could hear the noise inside the locker room between periods: "USA! USA! USA!"

I was never able to get to the locker room, but I saw it at the 25-year reunion. It was very small. You could sense that the noise was such that you could hear it inside those walls. The chants reverberated throughout the place. And the U.S. team heard it full barrel.

Herbie said later that he told the guys, "Do you hear this? Are you listening to this?" "USA! USA! USA!" "You have 20 minutes left to show you understand what they are saying. You will never forget this!"

When the U.S. team came out for the third period, I really think they thought for the first time, "We have a chance to win this hockey game." Yes, they had a chance to win. I wasn't ready to believe it yet, but then I had not been in the locker room between periods. Still, are you kidding me? A chance to beat the Russians! I'm sorry. I don't think so.

The crowd was just berserk! I was in the press box and stood most of the time. I couldn't sit down. The third period was in full gear, and I was really excited. I had seen some pretty great sporting events with the Vikings and so forth, but nothing like this. Many of the fans were saying to me, "How about this? I can't believe this. What do you think?" It went on and on. All I could think was, "Will it last? Do we actually have a chance to win?"

I kept thinking to myself that maybe something will happen. They actually have a chance to win this thing. But deep down inside, I truly thought at this point the U.S would lose the game. Even if our kids stayed close, the Russians would be on top, the U.S. would have to pull their goalie, and they would eventually lose by two or three goals. I hated myself for thinking that way, but it was reality.

Even if that had turned out to be the ultimate ending, we would have walked away and said, "Wow, what an effort! What a great game! The college kids stood up to the big, bad Russians."

I think as the game progressed more and more into the third period, the Russians began to panic a little. They were off their game a little bit. They had never been tested like this before, and they didn't know how to react.

The U.S. was flying around them, playing aggressively, and playing their game. Herbie did everything to steady his team. "Play your game. Play your game," he kept telling them. It was their only chance to win. "Play your game." We couldn't hear it from upstairs with all the noise, but you could tell that's what he was saying, and it was confirmed later by the players. "Play your game. Play your game." And they did.

I recall looking down toward the ice as the period progressed thinking, "What is Bill Baker thinking right now? What is Mike Ramsey thinking right now? Here he is, 19 years old, and he is out there on the ice with these guys. And Neal Broten is out there and Eric Strobel; what are they thinking right now?" They were performing on the biggest stage in their lives and were trailing the Russians by only one goal in the third period. And then they tied the score. The game was even.

These were guys I had watched and done stories on since they were just youngsters. It kept flashing through my mind. "Wow! This must be absolutely unbelievable to these guys. Unbelievable! They are out there playing the best team in the world, and they are tied in the third period."

Here was Neal Broten from Roseau High School, where he had played pond hockey, and now he was in the 1980 Olympics tied with the Russians with minutes to go. Neal had certainly played in some big games in high school and college, but nothing like this. Not even close.

These kids had come from all over. Many were from the University of Minnesota and many from the Boston area. There was a rivalry between many of them, but now they were all together. Mike Eruzione was the captain, and his mom became kind of the den mother for all these guys.

There was a place called the "Hockey House" where they went from time to time outside the Olympic Village, and when we saw them there earlier, you could tell they were a team. Herbie had molded them into one.

As I said before, he had a plan. He brought them together with a resolve that "the only person they are going to hate on this team is me." And it worked. It's not going to be the Boston kids fighting the Minnesota kids anymore. It's not the name on the back of the jersey; it's the name on the front: USA. He molded them as one.

The Hockey House was a place where they all gathered, and I know I saw it there. They became "one," coming together as a team. This was not to say that they were all going to be best friends for the rest of their lives, but they were going to play together as a team.

* * *

And then came an incredible moment. With about 10 minutes to go in the hockey game against the Russians, Mike Eruzione scored and there was pure bedlam everywhere. The U.S. had taken the lead.

An interesting point about the great goal by Eruzione: Teammate John Harrington, who later became the coach at St. John's in Collegeville, talks and laughs about the game-winning goal. If you look closely at the replay of the game, you will see Harrington right in front of the net when Eruzione scores, ready to stuff the puck in on a rebound. Harrington has some fun with it and says, "Eruzione has made a career out of that game-winning goal to beat the Russians. Can you imagine how his life would have changed if his shot had been stopped and I banged in the rebound?"

Mike was a great captain but not a flashy, outstanding player like many of the others who went on to play in the National Hockey League. None of that mattered, because on this night in this place, he scored the biggest goal of his life.

After Eruzione scored the goal to put the United States in the lead, I thought I was going to go deaf. The place absolutely lit up. The noise just exploded. It was unbelievable!

But then, we looked up at the clock and thought, "Oh no, there is 10 minutes left in the game!" It was the longest 10 minutes of a hockey game that anyone could ever possibly imagine. And remember that back then, there were no TV timeouts or anything like that. The U.S. had to just keep going and try to keep the lead.

No one was sitting at that point. The whole arena was standing. It was getting louder and louder. Six minutes left, five minutes left, four minutes, three minutes, now two. It gives me the chills to think about it.

At this point, it became noticeable that the Russians had moved away from their game and were in panic mode. They were not used to this and had drifted from their natural play. The intensity was mind-boggling. No one in the arena that night could believe what they were watching.

As the clock continued to run down, I started to actually tell myself, "My God, this can actually happen!" All kinds of things were racing in and out of my mind. "Maybe we can get a tie. Maybe that's the worst that can happen. Can we hang on? Is it possible?" The place was ballistic. "USA! USA! USA!" The chants were deafening. Shot after shot and Craig was making save after save!"

Now we were down to the final seconds, and it looked like it might happen. I remember the fans counting down and my thoughts being, "I have to get on the air with this. I have to get this unbelievable upset reported back to the station."

So when the buzzer sounded, I bolted. I got out of that building. I had to do my job. I would have liked to have stayed for the celebration, but I couldn't. I had to get to a phone in the media headquarters across the street and get this back to the station.

I had to get the story to R. J. Fritz. It was about 6:15 p.m. in the Twin Cities, so the timing was perfect for the news and sports programming, which was already being broadcast. Remember, the game was on tape delay, so unless someone had been listening on the radio, they didn't know! *They didn't know!*

I ran across the street and got to the phone. I called our hot line number. It was busy—no, just kidding! I connected immediately and went on the air live.

I was screaming into the phone, "THE U.S. JUST BEAT THE RUSSIANS! I CAN'T BELIEVE WHAT I JUST SAW! THE U.S.

JUST BEAT THE RUSSIANS! THEY DID IT! THEY DID IT! MIKE ERUZIONE SCORED THE GAME-WINNING GOAL. JIM CRAIG WAS SENSATIONAL IN THE NETS! THE U.S. BEAT THE RUSSIANS! I CAN'T BELIEVE THEY JUST BEAT THE RUSSIANS!"

I was told later what Dave Moore said on the air that night: "I have never heard Mark Rosen that excited before."

I couldn't be objective in the report. We had just beaten the Russians. I was probably a little louder than normal in reporting it because there was so much noise already in the press room, but let me tell you, I was excited. It was such a grand moment in sports history. All I cared about at the time was getting this story on the air for the

Do you believe in Miracles?

minute or minute and a half that it would be featured. But it was more of a story than reporting the score.

There was a collectiveness in the electricity generated by the crowd. My ears were almost bleeding from the noise. But in reality I don't believe this was noise. Noise is noise. People get loud and are just being loud. This was passion. This was a combination of every emotion that a human being could experience. This was anxiety, nervousness, happiness, anticipation—every feeling in one's being came out. It was different.

If you go to a loud concert and your ears hurt, the feeling you experience is to want to say, "Stop it. It hurts." This wasn't that feeling. This was "I want more. Bring it on." They could have blown the roof off that place with what went on in the last 10 minutes of the game.

Turn your car radio on full blast. That's loud. This was so much more. People's emotions were pouring out of them. I think the crowd felt they could channel their energy to the players, and I think the players truly picked up on it.

* * *

When I went to St. Louis Park High School in the early 1970s, I was there during the Vietnam War. They were protesting the war everywhere. The protests were at my high school and at my college when I attended the University of Minnesota. There was a great deal of social unrest. At the university, I recall getting tear-gassed. I saw students burning the flag. I didn't agree with the war. I didn't like what was going on. I saw things that I wasn't happy about. I was taught to honor and respect the flag, and what I saw was in opposition to my beliefs. Our country at the time was in a state of unrest.

The point of this is that when I left the press room and got back to the arena, what I observed was mind-boggling. I'm outside the arena and people are breaking into song. They spontaneously sang "The Star-Spangled Banner." People were waving the flag everywhere, and there was a nationalistic feeling like I had never experienced before or after. There was complete harmony.

Another experience happened for me that night outside the arena that I will never forget for as long as I live. We were wearing our credential badges around are necks and there was this Russian man wearing a big fur coat, and he stuck his hand out to me and said, "Good game." He had that broken English and said in a solemn tone, "Good game." I was like, "wow!" It was one of the most staggering moments of my life. I can see him standing next to me, and I remember the look on his face like it was yesterday—I'll never forget it.

I could tell by his facial expression that he was in great pain, but he still had enough wherewithal to congratulate me as an American on the victory. If you were to close your eyes and try to picture a big Russian man wearing a fur coat, that was him. I don't know if he was an official or a fan. I didn't interview him, and it didn't matter. He was so incredibly gracious despite his anguish.

I remember wondering about what was happening with the Russians after the devastating loss. Then many years later, Herbie's daughter Kelly told me a story. She was about eight when her dad's team beat the Russians. After the game, she had to use the restroom and was taken down to a private area away from the general public.

I remember her telling me, "Mark, I went down there as a little girl, and all I remember was seeing the entire Russian team lined up against the wall at attention while someone chewed them out in dramatic fashion." She never knew who it was, but it was likely their coach, Viktor Tikhonov. "I didn't understand a word he was saying, but it was not complimentary." Maybe he was telling them that they were all being sent to Siberia! I can only imagine what they went through after the loss to the Americans.

I have never seen anything like the celebration. People were crying and hugging and cheering. My dad had told me what it was like to be in Paris on VE Day. This wasn't the end of a war, but it may have been the closest thing to it.

I recall telling my dad, "This is my VE Day." I don't want to compare this to the end of a war, but in sports, it was similar. Remember, the Russians represented what was evil in the world. So the win was more than just a victory. And it was all accomplished by a bunch of college kids who probably just didn't know any better.

I remember after the game, as happy as they were, they still had one more game to go to win the gold medal. They had to recover from this monumental victory and then defeat Finland. A loss in the last game would have quickly ended a dream and depleted a memory. It would have been staggering.

Herbie didn't make the same inspirational speech for this one like he did before the Soviet game. He quite simply told them, "If you f___ this up, you will take it to your graves!" That's exactly what he said before the game against Finland. He knew he had to get those guys back on track.

The championship game was played two days later on Sunday morning. I remember taking the bus from our lodging place over to the arena. I have never been more nervous in my life. I was sick thinking about the possibility of a loss. And of course, they got behind in that game just as they had in previous games, but they came back to win.

One of most cherished pieces of videotape we have was after the championship, when the team came back in the arena for the medal ceremony. I am literally on the team bench watching as the players each get called to receive their gold medals. I was 50 feet from them.

And then came the most tear-jerking moment of all, as Mike Eruzione invited the whole team up on the podium with him. All I can say is, it was an unbelievable moment. Afterward, they started skating around with the medals. I went out on the ice and grabbed a couple of them whom I knew well for interviews— Eric Strobel and Neal Broten—and they were crying. They were going, "I got a gold medal, I can't believe this. Look at this, I got a gold medal!"

Twenty-five years later at the reunion of the 1980 Olympic team, I was with Eric at the same place, and we kind of reenacted the whole interview. It was a chilling moment. Neither of us had been back since, and here we were again. It was an extraordinary time, one of the best times of my life. To have the chance to spend time with these guys 25 years later was imaginary.

Twenty-five years later at the reunion in Lake Placid.

It was a shame that Herbie was not alive to enjoy that special moment and all the grand memories. Because he had died in a car crash a few years before, it definitely took something away from the reunion. As much as many of the players disliked his methods of motivation, to them he was still their coach. Like Bud Grant, there was a distance about him that made him stand out, and yet everyone who ever played for them had an incredible respect for them.

As the reunion went on later in the evening, I asked some of the guys, "If Herb was here, could he have sat around with you and had a beer and reminisced?" The response from most was, "Maybe to a certain extent, but he was the coach and he would have always carried that persona." Here were grown men with families, 25 years removed from the 1980 Olympics, and Herbie still would have been the coach. They knew there was a method to all his madness, and deep down every single one of them knew there would not have been a gold medal without Herb Brooks.

As I have tried to put this in perspective with my 40-plus years of covering sports, I see it as a singular event. There is no way to compare it to the Twins winning the World Series or the Vikings' playoff games. Whatever the sport is, people don't really remember very much what happened from year to year. Players come and players go. But this truly was a miracle.

It was a miracle for several reasons. The U.S. stopped using college players shortly after that, which changed everything. The timing of the game against the Russians and what was going on in the world at the time was important, but most critical was the fact that nothing like this could ever happen again.

There will never be anything like this in sports again, and that's what really stands out and makes it significant. This was truly just a bunch of college kids who said, "Dream on."

Certainly in professional sports, no matter what the event— whether it be the World Series or the Super Bowl—for the most part the teams are evenly matched and it's a business. This was the Olympics. It was a dream for kids to try to achieve something special in representing their country, as opposed to a bunch of professional athletes. It was just not the same.

What happened at Lake Placid . . . well, no one could have even fathomed the possibility. The odds against were astronomical. It was an inspiration for others to follow. Not in a million years will anything ever come close to what happened at the little Olympic Village. I don't think about it too often, but whenever I do, it seems even more amazing to me.

I wish every person I know could have been there the night the Russians were defeated. I wanted to share it with everyone and still do today. I was so fortunate to have been there.

I mentioned earlier that there was an electricity before the game. Everyone knew that this was not just another game. If you had been in the arena that night, you would have realized that this was a different buzz than all the Final Fours, Super Bowls, and seventh games of the

World Series. This was not going to be replayed the next week or the next year or ever again.

This was our team, our guys, basically a little team put together in the backyard facing the best in the world. Who wouldn't have wanted to be there? The anticipation was so much for a victory. No one thought it could happen. But deep inside, there was the thought, "Could this be the night?"

I have often wondered if I've made too big a deal out of the whole thing. It's just a hockey game, isn't it? Or is it? I'm not the one to decide that. It will stand the test of time. I do know that what it represented to me and a lot of others was the feeling about our country and the fulfillment of a dream, a dream that will never happen again.

Many years later, I was sitting next to Herbie in the press box at the Xcel Energy Center in St. Paul. He was scouting at the time for the Pittsburgh Penguins. Herbie told me there was a movie being made about the 1980 United States Olympic team. It was being filmed in Vancouver, and they had asked him to be a consultant. I asked him if it was going to be a television movie, and Herbie said, "No, this is going to be a big-time Hollywood movie." It was then that he paused briefly and said to me, "I guess it was a pretty big deal." I looked at him in absolute amazement and replied, "Yeah, I guess it was, Herbie!" I am deeply saddened by the fact that a tragic automobile accident took Herbie away from us. He never saw *Miracle*.

* * *

The game in itself developed from an extraordinary set of circumstances that took place. It made for the opportunity to dream. Like Herbie said in his famous pre-game speech, "We can play them 10 times and they probably will win nine times, but not tonight. Not tonight."

The Olympics are popular to watch because the audiences are enthralled with the stories and the passion involved with young people. People want to believe. They want to root for the underdog, and they are inspired by the dreams. It's what makes it all so intriguing. That night at Lake Placid was all of it rolled into one game.

Maybe the closest thing to this on the professional level would be the Green Bay Packers. They are a community-based team owned by the community. For them, winning a Super Bowl must be close to the 1980 Olympics and the game against the Soviets. I can argue with the Green Bay fan with the best of them, but step back and take a look: They are the Green Bay Packers, for crying out loud, and look at them in comparison to the New York Giants or the Washington Redskins.

Big against little is what it is. Compare the Los Angeles Lakers winning the NBA Championship to the Green Bay Packers winning the Super Bowl. I think you know what I mean. The difference is overwhelming. Big market versus little market.

I want to put the climax to the "Miracle" with a little more about the reunion and the importance of reliving it a half century later. It had been a planned celebration. There was the naming of the arena—the Herb Brooks Arena—and the reunion of all the players.

I had recently read a book about the Games and the players' experiences and was thinking, "Here I am with them—my guys, friends, and athletes whom I had covered for many years." It was a great moment.

They were business people, bankers, financial advisers, and fathers, and yet they still represented the team. They were hockey players. As Herb said in his famous pre-game speech, "You were born to be hockey players."

I got their cell phone numbers and planned to catch up with them for interviews. I had a deadline for a large story we were doing on the reunion, but it got complicated because the next day was also the day that the Vikings traded Randy Moss to the Oakland Raiders. That was a big deal.

It was disappointing because I'm out in Lake Placid and this wasn't the big story anymore. So I wanted to make sure I did a really good job on the reunion because this time we were going to be able to go on the air live. No tape delay for this one.

We walked into the museum and set up our equipment in the arena, and before our eyes were all the players' uniforms set in glass. And I saw the guys looking at their jerseys and thinking, "I can't believe that

With Minnesota native Neal Broten at the reunion.

was my jersey and I was here." To them, it must have seemed like a day ago. I was standing next to Mike Ramsey, and we were watching the Russian game on tape. In the museum, the game was on a big screen. They had it playing for everyone to see.

I had a microphone on Mike and I asked him, "What are you thinking right now?" He said, "I'm sweating." And I looked down at the palms of his hands and they were full of sweat. It was such an emotional time.

We did the story, and I think the coolest moment was with Neal Broten. He had brought his father to the reunion and was able to take him to all the areas he had never seen. He got the tour of it all from his son. To see the tears in his eyes was so special.

And then we all went into the locker room, the same one the players used in 1980: Locker Room No. 5. And as they walked in, they saw all their jerseys hanging by the lockers. Chills were everywhere.

The movie *Miracle* portrays Brooks after the game going into a hallway, where he's by himself. The fact is that he went into a little restroom stall adjacent to the locker room. I know this to be true. He needed to collect himself, and he stayed there for a short time. It was not like the movie.

The moment that stood out for me was when we all went across the street to the pub, where they all got a chance to spend some time together. Steve Janaszak was the backup goaltender, and he was there. He met his wife at Lake Placid, and they have been married ever since.

I talked to Steve and Phil Verchota, Rob McClanahan, and all these guys. They were all there reliving the greatness of the 1980 Games. It was one of those nights that I wish had never ended. Herb's name came up, as I talked about earlier. They toasted him, and it was very emotional. I felt honored to be part of it. I was there that night, and I always felt they knew I had been with them back in 1980 as well.

* * *

As I wrap up one of the greatest sports stories ever told and certainly my greatest sports moment and memory, perhaps I have to use the most overused sports phrase in history: "Do you believe in miracles? Yes!" Well, I do believe because I saw it and I remember it.

For risk of sounding cornball, it was a miracle. It truly was. It was proof that you can reach the highest of highs. I always felt my career took off after that because it taught me to work hard and believe. It inspired me forever and has been the greatest learning experience of my life—to believe.

As special as the whole experience was, I have only one regret. Soon after the great win against Russia, I had the opportunity to talk with Herb Brooks. The first thing I asked was, "Herbie, what did you say to the guys before the game?"

He reached into his pocket and pulled out a piece of paper with a bunch of words on it. It was the famous pre-game speech shown in the movie, given and portrayed so well by actor Kurt Russell. There were the words right in front of me. "You were meant to be hockey players . . . not tonight . . . " The whole speech was before my eyes, scribbled down.

After Herbie showed it to me, he carefully folded it up and placed it back in his pocket. My regret, and I have carried it with me for years, is why didn't I just say, "Herbie, can I have that piece of paper?"

4

At the Front of the Line

I have been fortunate in my career to have had contact with thousands of sports figures and personalities. Some more than others have left an impact on me both personally and professionally. Bud Grant and Harmon Killebrew, for example, have left with me lifelong heartfelt memories, and I credit each for significantly influencing many aspects of my life.

As I reflect back on my 40-plus years of working in the broadcast media, there have been others who have stood above the rest. I always am troubled by trying to rank personalities and great athletes because I am sure I will leave someone out. Anytime I am asked to name the best baseball player, shortstop, quarterback, running back, goalie, team, coach, or whatever, I know later I will think about it and feel I left someone or some team off the list.

Yet having said this, I am comfortable in mentioning three people who have had a remarkable impact on my professional life. Each has influenced me in a special way and brought me profound memories. For me, they will always stand "at the front of the line."

When the name Dave Winfield is mentioned, the first thing entering my mind is his pure, raw athletic ability oozing from every pore in his body. He was the pure prototypical athlete of the 1970s.

I loved covering Dave Winfield. He was a great player and a great friend. *Focus on Sport/ Getty Images*

He stood about 6 feet 6 inches tall, had lean and long legs, powerful turbine arms, and a big smile on his face—and in college he had a little Afro going. I recall that he seemed to always be smiling, which was so contagious. He seemed to be such a driven person in every aspect of his life. Athletically, of course, he was as talented as they come.

David literally stood out in every crowd, not only because of his physical stature but because of his tremendous athletic ability. He was a spectacle, and everyone knew exactly where he was at all times. He could not be missed. His body structure and overwhelming passion to succeed exuded from him.

I met David for the first time when I was covering Gophers baseball at the University of Minnesota. He had been an outstanding athlete at St. Paul Central High School and was well known to sports followers for his high school exploits.

I recall a day talking to legendary Minnesota baseball coach Dick Siebert about Winfield and him telling me how he wished he could play Dave Winfield at all nine positions because he would be the best they had at each. Dave was skilled at every aspect of the game.

Back in the 1970s, college baseball was attracting a lot of attention, and the Minnesota Gophers were nationally recognized for their prominence. But it wasn't only baseball for Dave; he was also a dominant collegiate basketball player for coach Bill Musselman. And then to top it off, while never playing a down in college football, he proceeded to get drafted by professional teams in all three sports—baseball, basketball, and football by the Minnesota Vikings. I don't believe anything like that had ever happened before or after.

It was purely and simply complete validation of his incredible athletic ability. I'm sure the Vikings thought they could make a tight end out of him or most certainly find someplace on the field for him to play.

When it came to decision time for professional sports, I think Dave symbolized the line "What do you want, a bonus or a limp?" He went the baseball route instead of football.

Dave and I were close. We were born the same year, 1951. Dave was born on October 6, 1951, the day Bobby Thomson hit the famous home run for the New York Giants in the playoff series against the Brooklyn Dodgers, known as "The Shot Heard 'Round the World". I was born a month later, so in many ways our lives were parallel to each other, with Dave participating in sports and me covering them.

As I followed Dave's career, being the same age brought us together to some extent. I was doing a lot of stories and covering

Gopher baseball, and he was the big star on campus at the University of Minnesota.

Winfield was a dominant pitcher for the Gophers, and he was one of the very few who would pitch in a game and bat cleanup in the batting order. He was one of the rare athletes who, before anyone else, seemed to know where the finish line was. What I mean is that he was gifted so much athletically and still saw the means to the end.

He was going to pursue more than just a career in sports. He clearly understood there was an afterlife to sports and that he was going to be a part of that also. Dave Winfield was more than just a player. He had an entourage of strong mentors who helped him out, yet he had such a strong personality that he could have excelled at anything he undertook on his own.

It was perhaps the College World Series in 1973 that really stands out for me. It was as if he had chosen this period of time to release this tremendous athletic talent on the world for all to see, and it was absolutely magnificent to watch.

He had 15 strikeouts in the game against USC, a team that was locked and loaded. They had Anthony Davis, Roy Smalley, and a host of other great players when the Gophers faced them in the semifinals. I remember watching Winfield in amazement. It was as if he was going to single-handedly take the Gophers into the finals.

Although the Gophers suffered a late-game, monumental collapse that eliminated them from the series, it was a game I will never forget. I equate it to the Jack Morris final game in the 1991 World Series. Both of these great athletes, Winfield for the Gophers and Morris for the Twins, seemed to will their teams to victory, locking themselves in memory banks for the ages.

After the game, which the Gophers lost, Dave went right to professional baseball and never stepped onto a minor league field. He went from college baseball to the majors with no stops along the way—a very unusual occurrence.

If you look back, even some of our local great baseball players, such as Paul Molitor and Joe Mauer, each had their time in the minors before their ascent to the big leagues. But Dave Winfield went right from the Gophers to the San Diego Padres.

I kept in contact with Dave after he left the area, and I followed his career closely. I also kept in touch with his foundation as it developed here locally through his brother Steve Winfield. He was already giving back, which I thought was unique. His mother, Arlene, raised him and obviously had a huge impact on him. He knew that instead of being greedy, he was going to lend his support to the community immediately, and he started his minority scholarship program.

Dave picked me to be the master of ceremonies for some of his first programs, which highlighted his foundation and their work, and that meant a lot to me. It gave me one of my first indications that we were connected and had mutual respect for each other.

He decided early in his major league career that he was going to develop a program to become involved in his community. He was aware of kids coming from pretty rough-and-tumble neighborhoods, and he didn't want to see kids get lost in the cracks. Had it not been for sports, Dave Winfield might have been one of those kids, and he always had that thought in the back of his mind. He understood the value of education, and he wanted to be sure these kids had an opportunity. He was very giving and driven to make it happen.

Dave has tremendous passion for life and for what he believes in. He was like a visionary in some respects and very strong-willed and street smart. This was confirmed later in his career with his legendary locking of horns with Mr. George Steinbrenner, owner of the New York Yankees. He wouldn't back down from anything if he believed in a cause or if he knew he was right in his position.

Don't get me wrong, though. Dave could be and can still be very bull-headed and much opinionated when he needs to be, but his heart is always in the right place. This was something that I saw in him right away and likely was what attracted me to him. He is a good person.

As an individual, Dave Winfield was never going to forget his roots and what got him to where he was professionally in his career. Even though he had a great career in San Diego and went on to play in New York for the Yankees, St. Paul has always been his home and he has never forgotten it.

If I look back on all of the great athletes in the Twin Cities, I would probably rate Dave in the top two of all time. As far as high school and college goes, it's somewhat hard to evaluate because Joe Mauer of the Twins never played college sports, and Dave did. If Mauer had gone on to play football at Florida State, we might have another element to the equation, but as far as the greatest high school athletes of this area, they are Dave Winfield and Joe Mauer, no question, in my opinion.

When you look at the records of Winfield and Mauer in high school and beyond, they are on my list of the best nationally as well. How can you dispute what they each have done?

One of my favorite Winfield moments was when he was with the Twins and I had the opportunity during spring training to interview Dave along with Bert Blyleven. It was an amazing interview, one of my all-time favorites. I put a mic on each of them and stepped back. I really didn't have to say much at all. They just communicated with each other. I told them to go ahead and talk, and they sure did.

Here they were, two future Hall of Famers, acknowledging what the game had meant to them. They were each in the twilight of their careers, and the emotion and passion was flowing. I just sat back and listened.

They had such an incredibly rich history between them, and they just talked. It was almost like a couple of 21-year-old kids talking baseball. Their love of the game was so evident. It was one of my favorite moments of my career.

Dave Winfield had such great high school, college, and professional careers. To me, it all culminated when I was with him in Cooperstown, New York, when he was inducted into the Baseball Hall of Fame in August 2001.

It was my one chance to go there, and two of my favorite athletes ever were being inducted at the same time. The other was Kirby Puckett. They were two of the greatest players and people I have ever known. And how ironic it was that they went into the Hall of

Fame the same year. Witnessing it meant a lot to me both personally and professionally.

It was an exciting time when these two were inducted, and yet it was such a bittersweet week. Another of my favorite athletes, Korey Stringer of the Minnesota Vikings, collapsed at training camp early in the week and died. It left all of us with such a sunken feeling of heartbreak as we arrived at Cooperstown.

Both Winfield and Puckett were super athletes, yet they could not have been more different physically. Think about that. It shows that to excel, it takes all kinds and all shapes. It proves that the physical body dimensions and capabilities do not measure the size of someone's heart. Here was this mammoth Winfield being inducted next to this little short guy, Puckett. It was quite a sight. The skyscraper and the fire hydrant.

I never stopped smiling and laughing the whole weekend. They were each so incredibly different. Dave was a little more refined in how he was handling himself with his special moment, and Puck . . . well, he was just being Puck. He was on fire.

I treasure my relationship with Dave Winfield and have been proud of every moment I have known him. To me, he represents one of the best in ability and in character. And physically, he was a specimen.

* * *

Moving on from my friend Dave Winfield, I want to mention the guy who first stated calling me "Rosey." He is the short guy, the fireplug, the fire hydrant I just referenced, Kirby Puckett. He had a nickname for everybody. To interview Puckett was an absolute blast. "Hey, Rosey, what's going on, man? What's going on, what's going on?" It was like that every time you would interview him. He was a machine gun rattling stuff out of his mouth. Unbelievable!

He was as playful as could be, always laughing and having fun. He seemed to enjoy every moment. I would often hear him say something before an interview that would get me laughing, or he would say something that could never be used in any broadcast. It was Kirby and the way he was. It was playful, and he always had time for me. It didn't matter if he went 0-for-4 and struck out three times; he would have something to say.

I miss him so much to this day. He was the Pied Piper of Minnesota. He really was. He loved the game and every aspect of it. When I think of him, it is his laugh that I remember the most. Puck had the laugh. It was a bellowing sound of joy. It was expressive and nonstop; it could be heard seemingly miles away.

It could be a dismal, cloudy day, maybe a little rain in the air—it didn't matter. Puck in an instant could make you absolutely come alive. He had the attitude like the former great of the Chicago Cubs, Ernie Banks, who was famous for saying, "Let's play two." That was Kirby Pucket. "Let's play two."

When he came to the ballpark, it didn't matter if it was the first day of spring training or the seventh game of the World Series. He never stopped talking. He was one of a kind. He had a million stories, and there were another million about him.

I always felt that even though manager Tom Kelly was a polar opposite of Kirby that they always got along. There was no doubt that Tom recognized the tremendous talent that Kirby had. But they were so different. Tom was from New Jersey, gruff, hard to get to know, cheap cigars, wanted "ball guys" on his team. Kirby was a "ball guy."

If you weren't a "ball guy," Kelly had little time for you. His personality was not reachable. It made you uncomfortable. But Tom understood that it took all kinds of personalities to make up a team, and he went with that. I mean, with Kirby it was really rather simple for Tom. Just go to the ballpark every day and put No. 34 in your lineup and see how that works out for you. Well, it worked out pretty well for a lot of years.

It wasn't that every aspect of the game came easy for Puckett. He worked hard at it. He played the game to the fullest extent and never gave less than his most. He transformed himself from a singles hitter at the early part of his career to a power hitter, and he became a very dangerous threat at the plate.

I don't think most people realize how hard Kirby worked at the game. He was the first one out on the field and the last to leave. He would hit and throw and run wind sprints for what seemed like forever. Unfortunately, many people remember him toward the end when he had gained a tremendous amount of weight, which was not him.

Every single spring training was further testament to how hard Kirby worked. Some of the young players would watch him in amazement, thinking, "Wow, if Puck is doing these things, I better get going if I am going to keep up." He was such an inspiration to all around him.

He would show how the game was to be played. He would run wind sprints, shag fly balls, and do the little things that made him such a great ballplayer. He just had it all. "Jump on my back, boys," he used to say, and they did. He was a big-time player and a marvelous leader.

I think one of the reasons that fans could relate to Kirby and loved him so much was because he was like one of them. He carried a "lunch bucket." He didn't have the great body, the Hollywood screen appearance. He was just an everyday kind of guy who happened to be a terrific baseball player. He was 5 feet 8 and certainly didn't look at all like a major leaguer, but it didn't matter because the fans gravitated to him.

His popularity was nothing like I have ever seen. The lines were staggering for autographs. Everyone wanted to be near him, to talk to him, to get his signature or approval. He had that "It Factor." He had a glow about him and around him.

When it came time to win the game, it was like everyone knew he would do it. "Jump on my back, boys." He truly had it. He was the clutch player who fit into a select group of great athletes. When it was time to win the game, he would find a way to do it.

It was an absolute pleasure to be around Kirby. Everything he did, he did with such passion and joy. There are athletes who when the chips are down, they bite down on their lower lip, get into their zone, and deliver. Not Kirby. He would be chattering away, acting the same as ever, yet there was no doubt that he was all about business. He knew exactly what he was doing.

All you had to do was look at him in those pressure moments in the batter's box and then to the plate. I know opposing pitchers had to be thinking, "Are you kidding me, how am I going to get this guy out?" I could feel it at the ballpark. The fans could feel it. The vendors could feel it. The players and coaches could feel it. We all could.

We all knew Kirby was going to get the big hit. He was going to throw the guy out. He was going to make the big catch against the center field wall. Everything about him embodied his tremendous skills and his pure love of the game.

I treasured my relationship with Kirby and was fortunate he became a part of my career and my life. He had it all. He had that special charisma that made him who he was. I'll put it this way: If Kirby Puckett didn't like you, well, then there was something definitely wrong with you. If he didn't have a good word to say to you, then it would be time to check yourself some.

Kirby Puckett gave me the nickname, "Rosey," and I deeply miss this great friend.

Kirby thoroughly enjoyed everything he did. I recall him getting a hit off Greg Maddox, one of the greatest pitchers of all time. He called him Michelangelo. "Hey, I got a hit off you, Michelangelo. I got a hit off you."

And the opponents loved him. I don't think I ever saw a ballplayer who didn't like Kirby. Before the game around the batting cage, they all came around to talk to Kirby. It was amazing. I never saw a ballplayer who attracted more opponents to the batting cage. I don't care what team came to town in the Metrodome. They all wanted a piece of Puck. They would shake his hand, kid around with him, give him a big hug. It made them feel good.

When the game left him, it was tragic. The glaucoma he faced robbed him of more years, yet he publicly handled it so well. His words to this day are ones to live by. "Tomorrow is not promised to any of us," he said.

He handled the loss of his career with courage and respect for the game and an understanding that it was over. I recall him saying, "Look, I did it. I had my time, and now it's over and I accept it." He faced it better than most of us did at the time.

His time was cut short, and he was not done by a long shot. No one really knows what happened to him after that—I mean, in terms of what it did to him mentally. He said all the right things and people were inspired by his words, but it had to be devastating. His livelihood was taken away from him long before he was ready.

Granted, he ended up in the Baseball Hall of Fame and did all that went with it, but the fact was, he wasn't at the ballpark any longer. And when you are not at the ballpark, you are not with the guys. And especially with someone like Kirby, with his type of personality, where do you go to get all that? How do you replace that? I know it had an effect on him.

When I say this, I am not talking about the game itself, I'm talking about the hanging-out aspect of it with the guys, being on the road with the team and all that goes with it.

I'm sure Kirby was a rather complex person. Parts of him we never saw and will never know anything about. His personal life was none of our business, but because of his tremendous iconic status, it certainly took a major hit after his retirement, and that was too bad for Kirby and his family.

I happen to feel strongly that losing baseball from his life sent him mentally reeling, to a point where he had a hard time recovering from it.

As I said, he made it to Cooperstown, but the fact is that in addition to losing the game from his life, he lost the vision in his eye. And in reality, he lost a lot more than that. But the fans still loved him, no matter what. It was a tragic ending for the most beloved athlete I have ever known.

Kirby had a great deal of troubles later in his life. His marriage was failing, his legal troubles kept him negatively in the media, and his relationship with the Twins deteriorated.

My relationship with Puck for the most part was always good. I loved being around him, and even in his most difficult times I never forgot what he had meant to me as a friend. But even with our history, I recall a troubling time in our relationship.

Kirby and his ex-wife, Tonya, had a fundraising pool tournament for many years, which raised money for Children's HeartLink. This organization's doctors travel to underdeveloped countries to train other doctors to perform open-heart surgery on kids. It is an amazing organization that has prolonged the lives of many thousands of youngsters because of these taught procedures. It got to the point after many years that Kirby was not associated with it anymore, but Tonya was still on the board of directors.

With Kirby not doing the event any longer, Children's HeartLink came to me and asked if I would be willing to take over the event. I was honored to do it. I mean, after all, look whose name had been associated with it for so many years.

I am still on the board of directors, and as a parent who has adopted a daughter from Korea, I have a very soft part in my heart for organizations like this. I have seen the world come to me because of my very own daughter.

Kirby had been going through a pretty nasty divorce with Tonya, and when he heard I was taking over the event, he was not happy with me. It wasn't long after I had accepted the role that I bumped into Kirby at a Timberwolves game. And even though he was mad at me, I could never be the least bit perturbed at him.

He came up to me and with an angry tone said, "Rosey, what are you doing, man? What are you doing? Why are you doing that event?" I told him, "Well, they asked me to do it. You weren't going to do it anymore. They asked me. Did you want to still do it?" "No, no, no, no," I recall him saying, "but Tonya is still on the board and I would never do that to you, man. I would never do that to you!"

Kirby felt that I had crossed the line and disrespected him and was being disloyal to him. I said to him, "Kirby, I'm doing this for the kids, for the event, not for anyone else. I haven't even spoken to Tonya about it. She is on the board, but I never talked to her." He just shut me down and said, "I don't want to talk about this right now, Rosey, but I want you to know I am not happy about this. I'm not happy about this."

The confrontation bothered me. There was no question about that. It bothered me, not because I had accepted a role that I now thought was wrong for me to do, but that I had disappointed Kirby. I never wanted to do that to him.

I tried not to take the whole incident personally because I truly felt the whole thing was not about me but rather the relationship with his wife and her connection to HeartLink. It was a tough time for me, but I tried hard to keep in mind that it was not about me. I had to keep telling myself that.

I let it sit for a while, and then we got together a few times and it turned out fine. It was a great cause, and I was just doing what I thought was right, but I obviously hurt my friend in the process.

In many respects, as I look back on the incident with Kirby, I'm glad he confronted me with how he felt. My take on it was, if Kirby didn't think a lot of our relationship, he wouldn't have cared what I did. So in looking at it that way, in some way it made me feel good that he thought enough of me to tell me how he felt. If something is bothering you, get it off your chest. I feel that's a healthy thing to do in any relationship.

Our friendship ended by way of Kirby's death, and it was terrible. I was at spring training with the Twins and had been at the ballpark in Fort Myers early that particular morning. I got the word that Kirby had had a massive stroke in Arizona, where he had been living. I knew he was not taking care of himself. He had gained a tremendous amount of weight and was horribly out of shape.

I used to kid him all the time about being out of shape when he was playing. I told him he had better get back in shape and come with me to my workouts with the Fitness King. Kirby would grab a beer can and say, "Man, when I'm done playing, Rosey, I'm going to be lifting these beer cans, Rosey, that's what I'm going to be doing, man. When I'm done, I'm done. This is it, man. I'm going to be lifting these beer cans."

A lot of people were concerned about his weight. He had moved to Arizona and was with a new girlfriend and had also fallen out of favor with the Twins organization, although the connection was slowly on the mend. I had heard he was working at trying to get back into shape and trying to get back into good graces with his team.

At this time in his life, he was getting in the news for all the wrong reasons, and he seemed lost in methods to heal his reputation. He was still loved in the Twin Cities, yet he chose to run away from it and move to Arizona.

The horrible news came to us that he had suffered a massive stroke. Greg Coleman, the former Vikings punter and KFAN field analyst for the Viking games, was there with Kirby in Arizona and at the hospital. Greg, who's a good friend of mine, kept me informed with what was happening with Kirby. He was at the hospital all day and giving me regular updates.

As I talked and interviewed people about what was happening with Kirby, it was about as somber a day as I can recall. Even Pat Reusse, the crusty old sportswriter and radio personality, couldn't handle the news. I remember putting a microphone in Patrick's face and watched him walk off camera. He was having trouble facing the tragic situation, let alone talking about it. It was just too emotional.

This is a writer, not a teammate or close friend, but a writer. Kirby meant that much to him.

The media, well, we are supposed to be neutral. We are supposed to separate ourselves from our feelings and report the facts. With Kirby, you could not do that. You couldn't separate yourself because he infiltrated your life and your soul with his positivity and his outlook every day. He always had that smile on his face, and everything he did was so incredibly contagious.

We got the word on Sunday. I was doing my Sunday night sports show live, and I could barely get through it. I recall saying on the program that "Kirby Puckett is in grave condition after suffering a massive stroke at his home in Arizona." I knew he wasn't going to make it. Doing the show that night was very difficult, yet people wanted to know what was going on. I chose my words so very carefully.

The next day, Monday, I got periodic updates on his condition. Around the supper hour, I took a break to write a script about Kirby for the evening show. My cell phone rang. It was Greg Coleman. Before I answered it, I guess deep down inside I knew what the call was. I was right. Kirby Puckett had passed. He was gone.

I believe I wrote the best script of my life that night about Kirby. He was one in a million, and I treasure every moment I had with him.

* * *

I'm still at the front of the line, and there with Dave Winfield, Kirby Puckett, and me stands former Vikings great Jim Marshall. Jim is a classic, one of a kind, and an individual who has left an indelible impression on me.

Just thinking about Jim, I stop, take a deep breath, and think or say, "Holy cow!" He is really something. Jim and I had a great relationship. To this day, every time I see him, he says, "Little Markie Rosen, Little Markie Rosen!"

What a tremendous football player Jim Marshall was for the Minnesota Vikings. No. 70 seemed like he was there forever with other Purple People Eaters—Alan Page, Gary Larson, and Carl Eller.

He was so talented and had it all—speed, strength, durability, and stamina. I remember every time I shook his hand, mine would disappear in his mammoth hand. I have a big hand, but Jim's would swallow it up. The only time I came in contact with a larger hand was the day I met Bronko Nagurski. I would have loved to have seen the two of them shake hands.

It is hard not to love—and I use that word generously all the time—but it is hard not to love Jim Marshall. He attacked life like he attacked quarterbacks. He has gotten every ounce of every minute of life out of the amount of time we are allowed on this planet of ours, more than anyone I have ever known in my life. And probably often to his own regret.

Jim Marshall has one speed: foot on the pedal all the way to the floorboards. He had the pedal to the medal all the way down, whether it be in football or any other aspect of his life. Jim never knew how to coast or hit the slow button. His off-the-field endeavors could slow an army of adventurers. He got more out of his career than perhaps any other player who ever played the game of football. I mean, for crying out loud, he played defensive end in the National Football League at a meager 225 pounds.

I was just a kid when I first came across Jim Marshall. I could just as well have gone up and asked Jim for his autograph as cover him for WCCO television sports. I mean, these guys at that time were intimidating figures to me. I would walk into the locker room and there would be players around like Marshall, Fran Tarkenton, Carl Eller, and others who had made their mark as the greats of the game.

I remember covering the Vikings' NFC Championship Game in Dallas and hearing Jim telling Chuck Foreman after the game in the locker room, "We got one game to go, kid. We got one more to go," referencing the upcoming Super Bowl for football superiority. "Don't get too high now, we got one more to go," Marshall told Foreman and others.

It wasn't like it is today with the media all over the place. Back then, there might have been three or four of us in there among the players, and it was really something. And right there in the middle of it all was Jim Marshall, the leader, the one others took their cues from when the chips were down.

Marsh was the captain. What I have learned through the years by watching Jim is the tremendous loyalty he had to the team and they had for him.

Because of people like Jim Marshall and Bud Grant, I have learned a lot about what a word like *loyalty* means. I have seen the effect of it with my coworkers, with teams, and with relationships like the one Bud and Jim had for each other. You can come from the wrong side of the tracks, but if you have respect for people and for what they are about, it can be a magnificent connection. The team, your team, is what Jim was all about every day of the week.

Players did not make much money during Jim's era. It was all about pride, loyalty, and honor, and Jim Marshall gave it his all 24 hours a day. Bud knew it. The players in the league knew it, and Jim's teammates knew it. It was what made him so special.

He played for the love of his game. He came from Cleveland to the Vikings near the beginning of his career. The Browns had given up on him. They didn't think he could play. Do you think they were wrong? He got his chance here. He was an unknown at 225 pounds.

Jim had a bond with the team, with the Purple People Eaters, with Page, Eller, and Gary Larson, and the others who were here. They had their 50th team anniversary in 2010, and, of course, Jim was named one of the 50 Greatest Vikings. To see these greats of the game together is like looking at their version of Mount Rushmore.

The difference between Jim Marshall and Alan Page is like night and day, yet when they are together, just the way they look at each other is magnifying. The tremendous love and respect they have for each other is inspiring and beholding to watch.

How many people in your life can you say you have a bond with like that? It doesn't matter if it is athletics or family or in the workplace; it proves people do not have to be similar to have that special connection. I think it is hard sometimes for people to get out of their comfort zone to develop these kinds of special relationships, and the bottom line is they are really missing something special.

Jim Marshall is absolutely one of my favorite sports personalities. He started 270 straight NFL games, an NFL record that Brett Favre broke in 2009. *Vernon Biever/Getty Images*

I have seen it countless times in sports and in business, where people have incredible relationships and have become successful in life because they are willing to get out of their comfort zones. We see this with people who have the same people around them all the time, people with the same beliefs, people who have bonded with a great respect for the other.

Jim is like that. He gets it. He understands passion and loyalty, and those who love Jim see it in him.

We see this kind of thing a lot in athletics because they all come from different places, different economic backgrounds, and they find something in each other. When it all comes down to it, on that Sunday afternoon, they have one goal in mind, and it brings them close.

Jim sets the tone for everything I am talking about here. He is so respected by everyone, and it is the reason he has meant so much to me over the years I have known him.

As I mentioned, my career has given me the opportunity to cover thousands of athletes. Many stand out because of their abilities and unique personalities. Jim Marshall is one of those people who stands with Dave Winfield and Kirby Puckett. These guys were different. They were durable. They played to win at all costs and they played every day. But it was so much more than their consistency and durability as athletes.

Obviously, Kirby was a little different because his brilliant career was taken away from him before he could fulfill his ultimate potential. Who knows how many years he could have played?

But I look at those guys and I look at my career and what I have been doing for all these years, and I realize how much I have learned from them. I try to approach every day with the same passion and desire that these guys showed me for decades. I believe I have seen these three personalities different from the rest, and I know they have impacted my life in ways they could never imagine.

When I started out in this business, I was doing my job and covering games. And games are games—that's all they are. It is the people who make it all worthwhile and important. These people who are out there are unique, and unique for a reason. There is a reason we are all sitting in the stands and these people are playing the game. It is not about them being better people; it is something about them having that competitive edge.

It doesn't matter what the vocation is. It doesn't have to be in sports. It can be in anything you do. Puck used to always say, "Just be the best you can be every day."

I will never forget the statement made by the great Yankee, Joe DiMaggio, when asked why he played so hard every single game. His response, "Because there is always some kid who may be seeing me for the first time. I owe him my best."

Athletics is so different from other professions. Athletes are judged by box scores and newspaper clippings. We are not. It's not always easy to see how we are fairing in life and in the workplace. It is why they stand out. They bring something to the table. They aren't out there performing just because they show up. And Winfield, Puckett, and Marshall had it all. They brought more to the table than most, on the field and in life, and that part of them is what struck me.

I have watched these guys do their thing over the course of so many years. They had to prove themselves like others over and over and again and again and again. And they did. These guys brought passion to their work every day, and I learned that from them. Their passion pushed me. It inspired me.

I was very lucky and very fortunate to have crossed the path of these three individuals. They taught me about passion, desire, and loyalty. When I think back on all of my decades of covering sports, meeting athletes and interesting personalities, Dave Winfield, Kirby Puckett, and Jim Marshall are at the front of the line.

5

Behind the Camera—Before the Lights Go On

I am convinced there is a perception—and I'm fine with it—that people see me on television and say, "Oh, he shows up for work a few minutes before five o'clock, reads some stuff on the air, reads another couple more minutes on the six o'clock news, goes home for a few hours, and basically does the same thing on the 10 o'clock news.

I'm also pretty sure people say, "Wow, what a great job!" Don't get me wrong, it is a great job, but obviously there is so much more to it. The real rewards in broadcast journalism come from what goes on behind the scenes. It's not the gathering of the information that stands out but rather the people who you are doing it with every day.

We truly are a family. I might add, however, that it's an increasingly smaller family as compared to the way it was in the past. With all of the downsizing, budget cuts, and everything else that businesses face in today's economic times, we do the same with less in the newsroom, but in the end we always come up with a quality product.

Even though there is somewhat of a division between the news, weather, and sports, we still spend an extraordinary amount of time

With Carry Clancy, my producer, and Tom Ryther, my photographer, on the "Rocky" steps in Philadelphia.

together. It is sort of like a clubhouse in baseball. We all have to work in coordination with each other.

The rewards, as I mentioned, come with the colleagues. Take my producer, Carry Clancy; we are a team that puts it all together. She helps to organize the show. I count on her for almost everything, and she does an exceptional job.

We have conversations every day about such things as the lead story, what we are going to cover, how much time do we give to each piece—things like that. She is so important in organizing things and getting it all to work effectively and efficiently.

The two of us are kind of an island unto ourselves. There was a time when we had eight or even nine people working in the sports department. We had three full-time sports photographers, two or three producers, and full-time sports commentators like myself. Now we have Carry, Mike Max, Tom Ryther, and me. It is different, but we get it done and I'm proud of what we provide every day for the viewers. I feel very fortunate to have had the opportunity to work with many talented and wonderful colleagues during my four decades with WCCO.

We all have other responsibilities with other roles, too. Mike has his work with WCCO radio, and I spend hours broadcasting on KFAN radio in addition to my full-time job with the television station. We have been streamlined, no question about that, which is not unusual in this business today. What hasn't changed is the passion and excitement that I bring and those around me bring every day to the job.

In our department, Carry and I are essentially it, so to speak. We have to stay on top of what is happening if we are going to keep current and bring it to the viewers three times a day. We have to figure out what is important, how important it is, and how we are going to present the information on the air. Every day is so different from the previous or the next. It is what makes the work stimulating, inspiring, and exciting. It never gets old. I love sports, so you can imagine how this affects me. It's just great!

My favorite part of my job is writing, figuring out what I want to say and how I want to say it in a way to present it on the air so it makes sense and is interesting. With this, I go to the basics, what I have learned from some of the greats in the business, such as Bob McNamara, Al Austin, and others who taught me so much. I grew up with these people, and they taught me as I entered the business to express myself in a way that brings the viewers onto the scene with me.

As an anchor, it's not easy. There are movies and skits done on anchors. People laugh at that kind of stuff. It's trying to get away from becoming the Ted Baxter of the broadcast media. Baxter's role on *The Mary Tyler Moore Show* became the caricature of every newsperson. And to this day, whether it be on *Saturday Night Live* or wherever, it became, "*Good evening, everyone.*" Think about it: You get the low, slow, stern, cold, officious voice that brings you the news.

The fact is, the position—whether it be news, weather, or sports—becomes a role ripe for jokes and ridicule. Yet, we all know that people

Getting ready for a broadcast. Standing nearby is Rebecca Kolls, our meteorologist at the time.

are relying on what we do to get information, to keep them up to date on what is occurring locally and nationally. Today we have the ESPNs and the CNNs, but the fact is that people do rely on us local folks to give them what they need.

As I said at the beginning, people have an image of us showing up just before air time, running a comb through our hair, being sure there isn't some food stuck in our teeth, reading a prepared script, and going home. That might be the main thought people have about us. Well, I can assure you, it is not true. An incredible amount of time, effort, and preparatory work go into our broadcasts.

What about the makeup? Yep, I use it. So does everyone else.

Many years ago when I walked down those stairs into the basement of the old WCCO newsroom at the prime age of 17, I had no idea that someday I would spend as much time as I do at the makeup counter in department stores. In the old television days, we used to call it pancake makeup. We would put it on so thick, I often thought I would have to get some varnish or paint remover out of the garage just to take it off. Oh, I almost forgot another factor in the whole scheme of using makeup. If you happen to get some of that stuff on your shirt collar, the dry cleaner would just say, "Toss it."

I remember watching the old Lava soap commercials as a kid, with the lumberjack coming home after work and washing eight layers of grit off his hands. I actually gave some thought to picking up some Lava soap to see if it would help. I know what I used rarely did the job, nor did the nice company bathroom towels that took a horrendous beating.

In the late 1970s we had makeup artists, who eventually because of space limitations had to work in the ladies powder room at our old place on 9th and LaSalle in Minneapolis. It wasn't much fun sitting in a chair having our face work applied as ladies walked past us to use the restroom. But it was part of the business, and I knew eventually I would get used to it.

But things change. No matter what becomes the standard, hang with it for a time and you can be assured it will change. Like everything else, makeup has advanced through the years. I now shop for HDTV-ready makeup. The biggest issue with HDTV is that every one of your blemishes will shine through the screen, but this makeup is a lot cleaner and it helps when you go out in public between shows; you don't look like a forever tanned George Hamilton.

I can't believe I am talking about this, but you know what? I am actually waiting for the day when a woman asks me for advice about a foundation or blush. It would be a very nice diversion from "Do you think the Vikings will ever win the Super Bowl?" Just once, I think, it would be great to hear, "Mark, what is your advice on the best makeup?" Enough. Enough on the makeup.

I find putting together sports stories fascinating. It is challenging and interesting. And because I love sports and writing, I have tremendous passion for what I do. I am one of the lucky ones. I get up every day and look forward to going to work. It is a true pleasure.

When working on a story or news segment, we are looking for the visual aspects of what we're going to report. If we get an opportunity to interview a former Olympic skater, we will want to show some skating to support the feature. If we are talking with Joe Mauer, we will want to run some game action behind him. It is important because it adds to the story, makes it come together, and stimulates the viewers.

We have to think locally first even though we are inundated with ESPN national sports news coverage. The local viewer is much more interested in what the Twins are doing than the St. Louis Cardinals, and we have to play to the hometown interests. But it even goes much deeper.

I believe I have a responsibility to our viewers to offer up much more than a final score. I need to provide some insight and analysis for people to chew on. For example, I might say something like I said last spring when the Twins were struggling.

"The Minnesota Twins lost again yesterday, and as the losses pile up, there seems to be no end to this. It's only early May, and we see a bleak summer with a shortstop who can't hit or field the position, a bullpen fit for the minor leagues, and a group of regulars spending more time on the disabled list than on the playing field."

This kind of editorializing takes time and careful thought. I'm not afraid of expressing my opinion, but I want to be sure that what I say can be supported by facts. I also need the support of pictures during the exposé. The pictures back up the words, and the words convey thought, passion, and opinion.

I work closely with the photographer on a story. You cannot write a bunch of words if you don't have the pictures to demonstrate the subject you are talking about with your audience. People want to see something on television to go along with the script. They don't want to just see me talking away.

I am always looking for the story of interest. The Twin Cities region is a very active sports community. Even when our teams are not doing well, we have to find stories that infatuate our audience. The fact is, even though the teams may not be playing well, it doesn't mean there aren't stories there. The reality is that in most instances when teams are not playing well, there are more stories to be had.

What becomes important is how you present that kind of information to the listening audience. It can't be a bad-day rant. It can't be an opinion with no foundation. Our audiences are smart. They do their homework, and if you offer stories that aren't backed up by facts, you will lose them quickly.

With us in the reporting business, it is a constant. There never is a day off. Something is always happening. Many people in their businesses look ahead to the upcoming week or month and have planning meetings. We do the same.

In other professions, a business may have a budget meeting on Tuesday and a creative planning meeting the following Monday. We have those sorts of discussions as well, constantly.

What's on the agenda for tomorrow? What must we stay on top of this week? Who is about to make news? What's coming up next month? What about the trade deadline next week?

In my situation, I work what you might call the afternoon and evening shift, or perhaps some might refer to it as the night shift. On

With Carry Clancy preparing for a broadcast during the PGA Championship golf tournament at Hazeltine National. No two days are the same.

most days, I start work at 2:00 p.m. and work until about 11:00 p.m., but in reality I am on the clock all the time. I am getting phone calls and emails all day long, hundreds a day. And my radio gigs take me to even longer hours on and off during the day.

My schedule is a mess. I'm working, then I'm off for a few hours, then back to work, off, working. Every day for me is a little different. When a big story, a news-breaker, comes along, it might be that I will be on the clock all day. It will always depend on the day, the story, and the next agenda.

My cell phone is in use all day. I am in constant communication with such things as: Who will be covering this news conference? What will be our lead story be for the evening news broadcast? Do we lead with the Twins' win or the Vikings news?

I don't go to every single sports press conference. However, I am always on top of what we are doing and covering. During the pro football season, I go to just about everything. I am out a lot; twelve- and thirteen-hour days become the norm. My work does not involve only what I am doing; we have to be sure we coordinate with each other. Carry and I work closely with such things as being sure we have a photographer when we need one. Many other important pieces are needed for a successful broadcast. It all has to fit together.

Carry is a supreme organizer, and although we are independent from the news team, we have to keep them up to date with what we are doing. They want to know what we're going to be covering. Sometimes our sports news is important and significant enough that we will be on earlier than our time slot or even lead the news on some occasions. A big Twins or Vikings trade might be an example, unless the news has a bigger headline that particular day.

We do not have an offseason. We just keep going. Does the sports news stop at 4:30 p.m.? How about the weekends? Do we get a break on the holidays? It just keeps going. The reality is that after 4:30 p.m., on the weekends, and often on the holidays, the sports world thrives the most. So you can see what we have in front of us. For 365 days a year and the better part of every single day, sports news is flourishing. I'm not complaining about it. It is just the reality of the business, and I love every minute of it.

My job and what we bring to our viewers is in some way like going into a restaurant. Think about it for a minute. We do one show and it is like going out to eat. Someone goes into this place and has a really good meal and says, "Wow, that was great. I'm going to tell all my friends about this place." And so they come back the next night. And each time, the manager and the chef want to please them, so they return and keep telling their friends how satisfied they are.

If they come in and have a bad experience, they won't come back and will likely tell others what happened. It is sort of that way with me on WCCO television. Every time I go on the air and present myself, someone is watching and evaluating. A person in my profession wants to be consistent for people. I want my audience to know what they are going to get and never be disappointed. Every time the camera goes on, I have to perform. Like the chef, every time that meal leaves the kitchen, the customer is evaluating.

I bring up the Joe DiMaggio philosophy again: "There is always some kid who may be seeing me for the first time. I owe him my best." I am not comparing myself to the great Yankee, but it really is like that for me every night when I go on the air. If they are a first-time viewer, I want them back. If they are a regular, I want to keep them. I'm the chef delivering the meal.

When you are on, it's like *this is your time*. I could never understand how some people don't get this. They take days off even though they are on. I'm not saying they "mail it in" necessarily, but for some reason they don't have the drive to give it their best each and every time. Don't get me wrong, we can all have bad days, but somehow you have to get through them and still be able to perform at the top of your game. It is essential and critical to success. It cannot be any other way.

There might be someone out there who has not seen me perform, has not been to "my restaurant," or who comes back for that "second meal." I have to be at my best all the time. We must give a product that people enjoy watching and respect.

Many people have a phobia about speaking. They get a microphone in their hand and they freeze—or what sometimes is even worse, they can't find a way to put it down. Others find it easy to perform in front of others and understand the need for brevity and consistency. They know how to keep sentences short and how to work a room. Some are just plain naturals, while others have to work hard at it.

After doing the work for so many years, my experience has made it easier for me, but I still have to work extremely hard at being myself and relaxed when the lights and cameras go on.

At an early age, I never for a second thought I could do what I do now. I have learned how to be myself on television, but it is nerve-racking. It is difficult, and it takes a long time to become comfortable with the process. I don't want people to think I am a different person when the lights go on. I want to be Mark Rosen before, during, and after my "performance."

It is sort of like being on Broadway, in which you break through and develop this wonderful connection with your audience. There becomes a naturalism to you. You don't expect everyone to like you—it has nothing to do with that. It is just to let people know who you are.

I just talk to the audience. I am not broadcasting to them. I'm not that important. I just want them to listen to what I know and what I'm telling them, almost as if we were having coffee and a doughnut at a coffee shop.

The absolute hardest thing to do is to look at that lens, see a bunch of words on the teleprompter, and be able to penetrate those cold words. It is critical that I keep in the forefront of my mind that people are out there watching and listening, and my job is to connect with them in a personal way.

The majority of the time, there will be no reaction from the audience. No one is actually at the studio. They are at home, in a bar, or in a restaurant watching a television set. Maybe if I'm at the State Fair or at Twins spring training or at Vikings training camp, I might be able to feel from the people around me whether I am reaching them, but in the studio, never.

However, if something goes wrong on the set, we usually find out about it. You can be sure that some viewer saw it and will let us know. One year while we were doing the state high school hockey tournament, we caught Don Shelby off-guard. We planned to return to our studio from the St. Paul Civic Center for a news update in the afternoon between games. Don was unaware we were coming back so quickly and appeared on the air hurriedly with a crooked tie.

In addition to the tie off-balance, Don had just gulped a couple handfuls of popcorn right before he went live on the air. He reported the news while obviously holding back choking from the popcorn. He lasted only about 30 seconds when he was forced to duck away from the camera. His gagging could be heard, but he was not in sight of the viewers.

The phone lines lit up. Don's audience wanted to know why his tie was crooked. His survival from his bout with the popcorn was of little concern.

It's tough to not know how you are coming across. I sometimes wonder, "Are they laughing when they are supposed to be? Are they somber with a tough story? Are they groaning because I'm doing a bad job?" I am concerned with this aspect of my work. There is no feedback, so I have to get it for myself by constantly evaluating and asking for feedback from colleagues.

I approach it every night like—you know what?—this is my two minutes, or my three and a half minutes, or whatever it is, and you deal with it. You bring it. I give it my best shot. I really feel that way every single time I go on the air. I guess if the feeling ever leaves me, it is time to hang it up, call it quits, walk away. The high expectations I have for myself keep me on my toes before and during every broadcast.

I have been in this business for over 40 years, and I still have the energy and drive to get it done. Now, this is not to say I always do what I would call my best. There are times when I, like everyone else, have things on my mind. I have gone to work like everyone else with personal issues on my mind.

A person could have had an argument with their wife, matters with their kids, not be feeling well, financial stuff—whatever it might be—but you have to go on the air. It's not like I am going to work and filling out some paperwork and then go home and be moody or whatever. I have to go on the air, and you try your best to not let it show. But it's tough. There are nights (very few, however) that I can't wait to get out of the studio. It's part of living.

* * *

My job is to look and observe and then report my observations to the public. I want to bring the viewer with me to an event and have them see and hear what I am seeing. This is the key to what I try to do. I am still a romantic when it comes to the feelings I have when I walk onto a baseball field, and I want to convey it to the viewers.

In covering the big events, I still get the fan's goose-bump feeling. It's refreshing and real, and I want the fans to feel what I feel. The noise in the arena can make your hair stand up, but it is the little things often behind the scenes that become the key connection with your audience.

I do this every single day on the job. I pay attention enough to understand some of the behind-the-front-lines factors that may contribute to the headline news. As an example, I was driving along listening to the Twins game on the radio and Alexi Casilla made an error. The Twins went on to lose the game, and in reporting the loss it was much more than "The Twins lost yesterday to the Kansas City Royals."

I came out with the story that the Twins lost again with more mental and physical errors on the field. My focus then went to Casilla, and I said, "He has no right to be an everyday shortstop for the Minnesota Twins. I don't know what they were thinking when they installed him in the lineup as a regular. Enough of this already!"

So in that 10-second highlight and brief commentary, I told my audience much more than the score of the ballgame. Another Twins problem occurred when pitcher Carl Pavano beat up the wastebasket in the dugout with a baseball bat after being removed from a game. My commentary followed: "You know that those were the best swings

I have seen with a bat in several weeks." I hope I got a few laughs with the statement, which was tongue-in-cheek but perhaps somewhat true with the way the team was going at the time.

I have often been asked if I say something negative about a player or someone, how do I then go into the locker room and still do my job? In other words, do I worry about hurting someone's feelings or damaging my relationship with them? If they heard it or didn't hear it, it doesn't matter to me. Especially with professional athletes, this rings true. I don't care if someone gets mad at me. It is never my intent to take on someone personally, but I have no issue with taking on a player who has not performed up to expectations.

I try to say what I think. For local broadcasters who are tied in with the team, it is a little different. They're with these guys every day and they can't do their jobs if no one will talk to them. On the other hand, you can't gloss over issues and say, "Well, the boys are really trying . . . " I mean, this isn't high school. These are highly paid professionals, and if they aren't performing as they are being paid to perform, I see nothing wrong with reporting the facts to the fans. If they are stinking up the joint, it has to be mentioned.

Look, you have to be honest. I just said and I want to repeat that I would never disparage the character of an individual—that would be wrong and, I believe, unprofessional on my part. But to report bad play, effort, or failing to live up to athletic expectations, that's fair game. With Casilla, my comments had nothing to do with the young player personally; it had to do with what I believe was a mistake on the Twins' part to think he could be out in the field and in the lineup every day.

I believe this kind of reporting is what fans expect from me. I don't expect every person to watch every minute of every Twins game or every minute of every Vikings game or Wild game. So, keeping this in mind, I have to find a way to do highlights that accentuate what happened. I like to find a way to bring a personalization to the process. I'm looking for an edge to report on something in an interesting manner.

At our five o'clock news broadcast, we have changed things somewhat at WCCO. It is more designed now around a brief

Early on in my career—I look ready, don't I?

conversation that I have with news anchor Amelia Santaniello. It's something a little different and takes on some new perspectives on sports. Here's an example: In 2011, the Twins were playing very poorly, so we tried to take a more in-depth look at why. We wanted to give the audience some things to think about.

Previously, I mentioned some commentary I made on the failed experiment of using Alexi Casilla at the shortstop position. So we expanded on the thought:

"I know what the Twins are trying to do. They are trying to give this guy one more shot. But the Twins are coming off a divisional championship. Can they really afford to have this much of an unknown at shortstop without much of a backup plan? With Matt Tolbert as the backup plan, you are not going to get better at this position."

So we will talk about this some. We will put Twins general manager Bill Smith's hands to the fire as well as those of manager Ron Gardenhire to a certain extent. And I'll say, "Is anyone surprised this is happening? I'm not." It creates discussion, and I believe it's the way fans take the broadcasts to heart and become interested.

* * *

All of what I have been saying is what goes on behind the scenes in my work. It is the heart of what I do. I honestly think that the easiest part of my day, the part of my job I enjoy the most, is when I am on the air. It is like the day is over, the lights come on, and it's "go time." Let's go on the air and have some fun. It becomes the culmination of a hard day's work.

Sports is supposed to be a release for people. Everyone experiences many life issues. We all have a lot of stuff going on out there. So I know that if I, even with our losing teams, report more than just the facts, I'm doing my job. Take last spring. The weather was very depressing for everybody living in the area, so we went with this concept to relate to our viewers:

"Well, you think the weather has been depressing, then take a look at this. Take a look at the Twins and how they are playing. You think that's bad, well, take a look at this. See any comparison here?"

In some respects, you almost have to laugh through it, but you have to be pointed about it and you can't do it every single day. If the Minnesota Twins continue to lose, you cannot come on the air each and every day and go on and on about how bad they are playing. You will wear out your audience. You have to find balance. Find the good in the bad. Find one of the players who is doing well through the misery and report that story. "What is going on here? Why during all the struggles does Jason Kubel continue to hit and try to carry the team?" See what I mean?

The behind-the-scenes work I do is highlighted by my writing. It is what I really enjoy doing, and I think I get better at it every year. I have often heard people say, "Can you get better at something?" I think you can. I am never satisfied with things I do. I always want to improve. When I sit down at my computer and start to express my feelings, this is the part of the business I love.

I thrive on assisting young people coming into the business. I tell them it is not about impressing people with your vocabulary skills but finding a way to connect with the viewers, because it is all that matters. It is the hardest thing to do. You have to be able to express your feelings on a piece of paper, look into the camera, and then convey them conversationally.

I prepare and read over my scripts continually before I go on the air. However, there is so much more to it than that. You can't just read them to the audience. You have to make it seem like you are talking with the viewer. We are at lunch and talking across the table.

It doesn't always come out right. I may botch a name, miss a word from time to time, but I sometimes have to get through it by making fun of myself right on the set. For example, "I knew it wouldn't be long before I would butcher that name ... "

I have a built-in clock in my head because I am constantly aware of the deadlines that face us in television news broadcasting. I have nightmares about missing these deadlines, about showing up late with a crooked tie or my shirt not buttoned. Or maybe I come in late someday, look at my script, and it is all gobbledygook—and I can't read a word of it as I go on the air. I'm petrified.

I have all those thoughts in the middle of the night, but for the most part I love the pressure. I do my best under pressure. I have never missed a deadline, and I usually find a way to get through just about anything. I guess in many respects, because there are so many things that can go wrong when you are live on the air, it keeps it interesting, alive, and stimulated.

I have always felt that I can be at my best during the live broadcasts—at the State Fair, Vikings training camp, Twins spring training, and so forth. I enjoy covering the big events on location, where I can be live and tell the audience what has happened.

I have done hundreds of *Rosen's Sports Sunday* shows on location, and it is when I feel the best about my work. It has taken years to believe in myself to do this successfully. The experience of many years behind the camera has certainly helped in my comfortableness, but I truly do enjoy every aspect of the live broadcast. Everything seems so real when you can relate immediately to the audience. I love it!

I think doing years of radio has helped a great deal with the live broadcasts and my comfort factor. I have been able to trust my instincts to find the right word or phrase to get me through, to make sure what comes out of my mouth has actually started in my brain.

To this day I have nervous energy, and I believe it is beneficial. I think it makes one perform better. What I worry about is being overly tired because then I know I am prone to mistakes. When I am really tired, I get nervous, so I make every effort to be sure that I get enough rest, get my workouts in, and stay focused on my responsibilities.

There is a great scene in the movie *Broadcast News* with Albert Brooks, who is a producer getting an opportunity to anchor the weekend news. It is one of those scenes where you laugh and cry at the same time. He has this dress shirt and tie on, and he get the sweats like nobody's business. He literally sweats through his entire shirt. It is one of those great scenes. You become literally embarrassed for him watching the film in your own living room. It is that troubling.

Well, there was a time when I was doing the weekend sports, and just before I went on the air it felt like my heart was breaking through my chest. I don't know why, but it was one of those things that no matter what I did I could not calm myself down. It was frightening to me. It had nothing to do with the story or anything to do with the broadcast. I don't know what it was, but I sure do remember it vividly. It just happened, and I never could determine why.

This has happened to me a couple other times, including once not too long ago. I literally feel like I am going to turn to the news anchor before commercial break and say, "I can't do this," and walk off the set. It can be that bad for me. I have never followed through and walked off, but I have sure thought about it. I wish I could figure out what brings on the anxiety. I'll likely never figure it out. I guess it is just me, and it comes with the work.

Once in a while, I have to tell myself to slow down and relax. I do recall a time when I wasn't feeling well, and that probably contributed to the anxiousness I was feeling. You think, "Oh, I don't want to be sick on the air," and then you start thinking about it and it gets worse. That kind of experience.

There are those times when you don't feel well. We don't go to work every day and be just perfect. We all have moments, issues, health problems when we are just not at our best. But you have to find a way to get through it so that the viewers are unaware of what it may be. And sometimes, the fact is, it is tough to hide, but I work at it and do my best to hide it. But I know viewers; they are pretty smart, and you can't pull off too many things before they catch on. I have great respect for my audience.

* * *

For the most part, I haven't had any real disasters on the air. Regarding clothes, I have made some interesting decisions with shirt, tie, and coat matches where I have asked myself later, "What was I thinking putting that combination together?"

I'm fortunate to be with people who look after one another before the lights go on. If I have food dangling from my lip, I'm confident that someone will tell me, and I try to do the same for the others. I do have a mirror on the set, and I know people think I am being vain by looking in it. I'm not. I don't want to go on live television with a stain on my coat or tie or a piece of food stuck on my teeth. A shirt with a colorful ink stain on the pocket isn't an attractive article of clothing.

I know for sure that I will eventually mispronounce a name or say something I wish I could take back, but you move through it. I recall that I mentioned Vikings quarterback Brad Johnson many times on the air. And I knew it would occur sometime, and then it did. I called him Brads Johnson. I got through it by saying, "I knew I was going to do that someday," and everyone was laughing. It was just a fun moment.

The fact is, you have to be prepared mentally for anything that can happen when those lights and cameras go on. You don't want to show anger on the air, but there are times when you may feel quite upset.

Maybe a tape isn't there for the script and you are live. I would never want to respond by saying something like, "Hey, can you guys get your act together back there, and get the f____ tapes ready!" No, you wouldn't want to do that. Now, maybe later you might . . . well anyway, you get the picture.

You can't go down that road. No matter what happens, you have to get through it because an hour later, four hours later, or the next day, you are on again. Like I say, there is no offseason. You just keep going, and believe me, it sure does make it all interesting!

There is rarely the opportunity or the time where you can put everything on hold and say, "Let's take a few days or weeks to analyze our game plan here." No, you have no time for that. We go on every day. But you have to be ready for those moments when things fall apart, and it is those times that viewers likely remember more than a show that goes perfectly. This is when you have to trust your own personality.

You might have to bite the bullet and calmly say to the viewers, "It's just one of those nights here, folks, at the TV station. I know you've all had them." Fortunately, it doesn't happen all that often. But there are those nights. The tape is not there or it's the wrong tape or the sound doesn't work. You just kind of shrug your shoulders and know it will be better next time.

I know that viewers and listeners like to see things go wrong. It makes those of us who do the presentations seem more real. They don't want to always see everything perfect to the letter. So when we make mistakes, they do quite often enjoy it. It's why the programs called "Bloopers" are so successful in the ratings. People like to see that. They can identify better. It is more real and I'm sure much more interesting.

We have shown our "bloopers" from time to time. That's why I don't get too bent out of shape if I make a mistake, mispronounce a name, and so forth. But I don't want it to be a regular occurrence. I don't want to make a habit out of it. A name, a tough name, you get a pass once in a while. I wouldn't want to mispronounce Edina or Eden Prairie. You understand.

After a mistake with pronunciation, I recall saying on the air, "Where is Vanna with a vowel when I need her?" There are some people who are very unforgiving, however. I have been told, "How can you mispronounce a name like that?" Come on, give me a break!

We are competitive on the air. We are aware of what the other stations are doing, but I don't get real hung up on that aspect of what I do. Sure, we want the good ratings like everyone else does. But this market has been pretty fortunate because the sports anchors on the major local stations have been here for a long time and all do a good job.

Joe Schmit on KSTP, Jim Rich on KMSP, and Randy Shaver on KARE have been in this market for many years. Viewers have identified with us. We have been on television for a long time, and that's very unusual.

I think it's great. I am thrilled that we all have had extended careers in the Twin Cities. I think it shows that all of us have been doing the things for years that I have been talking about and survived—and survived very well.

Our bosses have recognized that we are doing our jobs. Joe was away for a while and is back, and the four of us have filled the sports news agenda for the fans quite well for a lot of years.

I have always felt it is nice to meet and get to know people from other stations. In the words of former quarterback Archie Manning, "We are all robbing the same train." We are all trying to provide for our families, do our thing, and please our viewers. Sure we would all like to always be number one in the ratings. But there is no trophy. You only get to keep your job and move on.

I am full of self-evaluation, just about every show. I even go so far as to tape shows quite often to watch and evaluate myself. I look carefully at my delivery. I literally write the word *SLOW* on my notes because I have a tendency to talk too fast. I tell young broadcasters all the time to be aware of their delivery speed. We are always so conscious of the little time we have, so there is the tendency to speed up and talk fast, and you can't do that. It makes no sense because you really can't read faster to make up time. It doesn't work that way at all.

I do read a lot of the script, but I work very hard at not making it look like I am reading. I want the audience to feel like I am talking to them, not reading to them. As I said before, I want my words to come across in a conversational manner. When my scripts, which I have written, come up on the screen, I do ad lib quite a bit because I don't want to get caught up in making it appear as if I am reading.

For the most part, because I have been doing this for so long, I would be comfortable without a script. But because of the nature of how we get our video on the air, we have to give "role cues" all the time. So, you have to have a script so the film guys know when you get to the last five to six words, and then it's time for the video. Those kinds of things. Everything has to be timed perfectly. Everything has to be properly aligned. I find it quite amazing at all the coordinating that has to be done for a broadcast to come together.

The hardest thing for a good interviewer is to be a good listener. You must be able to anticipate your next question and be ready when it is time for it. If you are looking at your notes and not listening, you might miss what the person is saying and miss the opportunity for a gem of a next question. If you missed the response, you have set the table for panic to set in. "Wait, what did that person just say?"

On *Rosen's Sports Sunday*, I use little-prepared scripts and go mostly from notes. Again, this comes from many years of experience. I am always trying to improve, to make it better. But I have to be careful and on top of what is going on because we have only so much time.

I am constantly aware of the clock. I can be on my show talking with Pete Bercich, Vikings radio analyst, about the quarterback situation and know I have to cut it off at three minutes, even though I could talk about it for 20 minutes. The clock is a part of everything we do, and as I have said many times, I absolutely thrive on the live aspect of it.

One of the biggest things that has changed through the years is the technology in broadcasting. There was no such television station as Fox Sports North, on which we could catch the whole game. There was no ESPN. There was no videotaping of the game. As I mentioned earlier in the book, we would go out to the old Met Stadium and tape a few innings and hope we caught something interesting for the news that evening.

I have taken the time to occasionally go back and look at some of our past clips, and I am totally flabbergasted. I sounded like some guy from a horror movie, completely unrecognizable. My voice sounded terrible. Even today, when I hear my voice played back, I can't believe it. It is pretty recognizable to others, though, because I am on the air so frequently.

I can be standing in a line and talking, and someone will turn to me and say, "Mark Rosen. I heard your voice." And I'll say something like, "Sorry, I know it's bad." And they will say, "No, no, no, I like your voice." But to me when I hear it, I am not so pleased.

The voice is so very important to the broadcast. You have to be able to coordinate with the video being played so that you get the right feeling, the right tone, the right emotion at the precise time, so that the audience can really identify with what you are trying to convey to them. It takes a lot of practice over a lot of years to make it work.

You have to be able to tell the story—make the viewers feel they are there with you. You are performing. Take a deep breath, get the right word, the right tone, and bring it on. My stuff on the air today is day and night from the past.

Clothes are also important to what we do. I probably have about 30 suits to choose from for work. As a guy, I have the opportunity to accessorize, mix and match, group, or whatever so that my audience can't focus on things like, "Didn't he wear that tie last night?"

Honestly, I have often thought, what if I wore the same things several nights in a row? How long would it be before the station or I heard about it? It would be kind of fun to give it a try. Who knows? Try it for four straight days. I'd wear a blue blazer, a white shirt, and the same tie every day. I wonder if anyone would notice. Maybe I'll give it a go sometime. It would be a fun experiment.

We used to have a set where we stood up all the time. Now we are sitting a lot, so on occasion—especially if I have been out in the field covering something—I might be doing the show with a nice shirt, tie, and sport coat on with shorts. It's okay; no one sees it. I just have to be careful not to stand up with the camera on me.

Our best connections are with our viewers. It is not just about our sources. We need to know what the fans want to see and hear about in order to do our job well. We have to think visual all the time. How can we show what we are telling our listeners? I get a lot of story ideas, a lot of tips from our audience. They are our eyes and ears, and we appreciate it.

Because of my profession, I have email, Facebook, and Twitter accounts. I might get as many as 150 or more tweets in an hour or so. I might get hundreds of emails in a day, and Facebook is always providing information.

Now with all this, it makes it tough to put it away and get some family time. Obviously, I cannot work all the time, even though it seems like it quite often. I'll give you a good example. I am at a movie with my wife one night when I am off work. We come out of the movie, and someone who was at the same movie as we were says to me, "Mark, how did the Twins do tonight?" They expect me to know. I mean, I just spent the last two hours with this person watching the same movie, and they want me to tell them who won the Twins game. I laugh about it, but they honestly think I know. I don't get mad, but I just kind of shake my head.

The fact that my business is constant, it keeps the juices flowing. It keeps me invigorated and brings excitement to the job. I am really proud of what I do. I enjoy the sports anchor job three times a day on WCCO and really like doing *Rosen's Sports Sunday*, which has been on now for almost three decades. This is unheard of in today's markets and makes me extremely proud.

I hope I have given a glimpse into what this business is all about behind the scenes, the lights, and the cameras. Whether it be in the preparation or in the actual delivery, I have had a love affair with my work for over 40 years. I cannot imagine doing anything else.

6

Breaking the Big Story

The presidential announcement that Osama Bin Laden was killed occurred on a Sunday night, May 1, 2011. I was in the newsroom getting ready to do my *Rosen's Sports Sunday* program that evening. We had received an alert from the network that the President of the United States was going to make a national security announcement at 9:30 p.m. Twin Cities time.

When we first heard the news that the President was going to speak, we had no information about the content of his address. The first thought I had was, "There is no question that whatever this information is, it is going to get leaked." With the resources available today like Twitter, email, Facebook, and so on, someone will know what is going on and report it to someone else. It is the reality of today's world with regard to the flow of information.

I initially thought that perhaps Khadafy had been killed or maybe there was some kind of threat to our shores or airports because the President of the United States does not come on the air on a Sunday night and make an unscheduled announcement unless it is big news. It just does not happen.

So, within 15 minutes, people are going absolutely nuts. I checked my goofy Twitter account on my phone and I'm reading somehow through

Donald Rumsfeld that Osama Bin Laden is dead. That's the word. As soon as I see it on my account, I re-tweet the information out, saying this isn't my source. I mean, I want it to be very clear that this isn't Mark Rosen saying this. What do I know? I want to tweet what is out there and see if I can pick up anything else, but at the same time I realize I am likely reporting to my contacts this information for the first time.

My attention is focused also on a national news network. This is where the immediacy of all news happens. This is going to be a worldwide announcement by the President, and there are rumors everywhere. It seems as if no one out in the broadcast media world will allow the President to come on the air and make his statement. There is this incredible need to get the information to the public before the President does. It actually seems like a race with no rules.

This is not about a baseball player being traded or a new coach being named to one of our Twin Cities teams. This is an announcement by the President regarding our national security.

I am watching a national news anchor, who is about as reputable a reporter as there is in the industry. He is sitting in their studio and they are prepping, so to speak, for the big announcement by the President. This is their pre-game. The network wants badly to get the information on the announcement out first before the other networks, yet they have to be sure of the accuracy of their sources.

I am convinced that the reporter knows the information. He knows what the announcement is going to be. But he has not got it confirmed, so he is not running with it. With something like this, you want to be sure that you are right. This is no time for a mistake. This is no time to go public with bad information. The timing is crucial, the stations are driven by the competition, and the pressure is intense.

So, all of us in the WCCO studio are watching the national news network because the CBS network has not as yet interrupted the regular scheduled programming. In fact, none of the traditional television networks have broken into their evening programs to this point.

CBS has a program running, and we are keeping track of what they are doing at the same time we were watching the national network. We aren't sure what CBS's plan is for local programs, so we don't know how it is going to affect us. It is a trying time program-wise and also tension-filled because of the mysteriousness of the upcoming announcement by the President.

This is fascinating. We are not really sure of the facts. I know what my Twitter account said, but is it right? Is Osama Bin Laden really dead and will this be the presidential announcement? We are pretty sure about this, but not 100 percent sure. And when you are not absolutely sure, you better not come forth with the information.

It seems like an eternity, but finally one of the stations—I'm not sure which one—announces what the President is going to say when he comes on the air. You know at this point that the national network anchor knows the story, and he must be biting through his tongue holding onto the news, but the fact is he has to have confirming evidence before he goes with it. He has to be sure that his sources, other correspondents, or whoever they might be has the information right. I really credit them for that because this part of the business is essential.

No one is going to remember later on who reported the information first. It is not critical who was first, but I will absolutely tell you that people would remember who reported the information if it was not correct. It can make the person, the network, and the station look tremendously foolish.

It turned out that a political reporter, I forget whom, released the news. There you go; I can't remember who said it first, and minutes later everyone had it. By the time the President came to the podium for the announcement, everyone knew what he was going to say.

I'm sure anyone who was extremely interested had figured out what he was going to say by all of the reporting. But I'm sure there were some who were not convinced until they actually heard the words come out of his mouth.

This is where there is an exemplary lesson to be learned on source checking: Making sure you are right before being first becomes the top priority. What made this so different was the immediacy of the story, as opposed to a story that has no specific timetable because it is going to develop over a period of days, weeks, or in some cases months. There is a different way of approaching the differences from a journalist's standpoint.

That particular night, every single network had to feel, pardon the expression, "under the gun" to get the information out there. But at the same time, the White House wasn't saying anything. All the normal sources out there did not initially release the information, and yet everyone knew that very soon the President was going to make the announcement.

In today's day and age, it is virtually impossible to keep news "under your hat," so to speak. It doesn't happen, especially national news such as this story. Someone who knows is going to tell someone, and they will tell someone and so on.

Everyone has a confidant. At some point, it is going to be reported, verified, and given to the public. On that particular night, the President's speech was delayed, which gave everyone even more time to gather the facts about Bin Laden's demise. It gave them more time to check their sources. The time crunch was extended, and the chaos was given more time to ignite.

I will guarantee you that every major network had at least one source that said that Bin Laden was dead and that the United States Armed Forces had his body. Now, do you think for one second when the first report came in, the person at the network or wherever receiving it said after all the years Bin Laden had been hunted something like, "Well, okay then, thanks, that sounds good. Goodbye"? I don't think so.

It would have gone more like this: "Are you sure? Who have you confirmed this with? Who have you talked to about this? Are you absolutely, positively accurate with your information?"

When you have critical information like this, you need multiple sources—more than one for sure—absolutely, positively confirming the report.

* * *

If you take what happened that particular night with the President on his monumental platform and then break it down to what we deal with in sports, you at least get a flavor of how the process works on our smaller stage.

I'll give you an example with Brett Favre, which became a signature story that I broke when he made his first trip here to sign with the Vikings before the 2009 football season. This was a huge story. We had been aware that this song and dance—"I'm coming to play for the Vikings, I'm not coming to play for the Vikings"—had been going on all summer. We knew the Vikings were interested in Brett Favre, and Favre was interested in coming here after paying his penance with the New York Jets, but nothing was confirmed. And it went on and on—a never-ending soap opera.

It was almost every day from about early May on: Favre might be a Viking. We were constantly hearing that he was working out with high school kids and that he was throwing the ball every day, and the drama went on endlessly. It was changing by the day. He was going to come back. He wasn't going to come back. We didn't know how his arm was after his injury in New York. His arm was good. His arm wasn't good. You couldn't find more theatrics in a Broadway play.

It went on with no real indication what the outcome was going to be. He wasn't telling anyone for sure if he planned to return, and if he did, we didn't know if his new team would be the Vikings. At this point, we all wanted to know what the decision was going to be. Was this former Green Bay Packer going to be a Minnesota Viking? Everyone's guess was just as good as another.

If it was going to happen that Brett Favre was going to be a Minnesota Viking, it would be huge news. If not, well then, we wasted an awful lot of time and energy. Most news media and fans, frankly, were plenty sick of it by the time the Vikings training camp opened and closed in late August.

I had no information at all that would lead me in any direction. It was a mess, and what made it more difficult to get a handle on was the fact that you were dealing with Brett Favre. He was known for this type of drama. He was a master at it. He had done this kind of thing for years with the Packers, then the Jets, and now the Vikings. "I'm going to play. I'm not going to play."

No one knew what he was going to do from one day to the next. He likely didn't know. He got up in the morning and changed his mind. Who knows? Although I was checking my sources regularly, it was tough to go after the story full bore because once you become comfortable in reporting something, it could change that fast.

As I mentioned, my sources vary. They are rarely players; usually they're people close to the story or within an organization. This story is a perfect case in point because there was absolutely nothing to go on. One day his shoulder was not right. The next day it was. The next day he was hanging his cleats up for good, and then there was a "maybe" attached to his decision. It was maddening.

With the Vikings breaking camp in Mankato, the timing and calendar were beginning to give an indication that he was not going to make a comeback wearing purple. In July, with the team heading to training camp, Favre was nowhere in sight. So, the thinking

With former Vikings coaches Brad Childress and Bud Grant at Sid Hartman's 90th birthday party.

at the time was that maybe the story was dead. I mean, the Vikings were heading to Mankato for training camp and Favre was not signed or in uniform. Now, training camp was over. It seemed like now we knew absolutely he had retired. Or did he?

Training camp opened with this nonsense having gone on the entire summer, where no one knew what was going to happen. Brad Childress' exact words on the opening day of camp were "Brett Favre has gone his way, we've gone ours. He is in our rearview mirror." That is an exact quote.

He went on to say, "We have Tarvaris Jackson and Sage Rosenfels, and they are our quarterbacks." After watching the first few days of training camp with those two directing the offense, the media was saying, "You have got to be kidding me."

Here we are, layman watching, and we saw what was going on. I know most of us journalists were thinking, "Here they are with this great football team and they do not have a quarterback." If we could see it from the sidelines, there was little doubt that the coaching staff could see it.

Camp went on for a few days, and it got real quiet with respect to any news about Favre. Even though Childress had made his "rearview mirror" statement, something had to happen. Most of us were thinking how badly they needed something to happen at quarter-back, yet Favre was not in camp. But then, of course, we all also knew Favre was notorious for hating training camp. So, the thought was, "Could it still happen? Yeah, it could." But as far as source checking, it was quiet. There was not any new information to dig up. Camp had come and gone, and no Farve.

I had covered the first few days of camp, and then planned to take a few days off. The Vikings were back at Winter Park, and everything was quiet on the Favre watch.

My daughter was planning to go to the University of Hawaii for her second year of college, and I was helping her get ready to leave. I had a speech scheduled at a high school south of the Twin Cities in Lake City, and I was going to hang out at home all day and then do the speech that evening.

It was about nine o'clock in the morning and my cell phone rang. I recognized the voice at the other end right away, and all he said was, "This is going to be a really big day for you." I replied, "What do you mean?" And he said, "This is going to be a really big day for you. Just get ready." My first thought was, "Wow!" He never mentioned Favre by name, but if I recall it right I believe he also said, "He's coming." So, I said, "Okay, okay, okay."

I hung up the phone and said right out loud, "Holy crap! Brett Favre is coming! Brett Favre is on his way here." Now I'm thinking, "I have to get this out there. How am I going to react to this? What am I going to do? This is not a local story. This is huge. This is national breaking news."

I also know that my source is absolutely reliable, totally credible. This person would never have called me with the information if it had not been 100 percent accurate, on the money. Yet, my head is spinning like a top. Within two minutes, I called my source back. I had to make sure in my own mind. I called him by his first name and said, "You understand I'm going with this right now. Are you 100 percent sure of this information." The answer I got was, "Yes, he is on his way." That was all I needed to know. Bam! I needed nothing else. My source was the only one I needed. He had this kind of credibility with me.

I have a great relationship with this person. Some years ago I kind of paved the way with him by saying, "If anything ever happens, please give me a call." So, my trust factor with him is as high as it gets.

Now, because of the all the drama with this situation and because it is Brett Favre, I was in competition with all the other local and national media for this story. I had to move with it immediately.

My daughter and my son were both home at the time, and I remember telling them before I left the house, "Brett Favre is coming to the Vikings! This is going to get real crazy." I ran upstairs and called Mike Caputa, who at that time was the assistant news director. I told Mike, "Let's get this on our website right now. Brett Favre is getting on a plane in Hattiesburg, Mississippi. He is on his way to the Twin Cities. He is going to sign with the Vikings. He will be on the field this afternoon."

Mike did not even question me. All I remember him saying is, "Okay, you got it." Bam! It was out there. Mike knows me well enough to know I would never give him this kind of blockbuster news unless I had the information correct.

Now, I was scared to death. I couldn't have been more worried or upset at that moment. This had nothing to do with my source. I knew his information was dead-on. But remember, this is Brett Favre we are dealing with here. He might change his mind again at the last minute.

Mike got it right out there, and it showed the world we live in today with regards to technology. I was watching ESPN and they said almost immediately, "WCCO television sports anchor Mark Rosen is reporting that Brett Favre is indeed on a plane from Hattiesburg to the Twin Cities to sign with the Minnesota Vikings."

Now I am really stressed to the max. I am going, "Oh . . . ! What if I'm wrong? What happens if he changes his mind?" The story is now everywhere, and there is not any confirmation from the Vikings.

I was in turmoil and still bringing on the story. I put it on Facebook, was talking with our news director, called KFAN radio, and went on live with Paul Allen, voice of the Vikings. I told Paul, "I have an impeccable source that Brett Favre is getting on a plane in Hattiesburg and is on his way to the Twin Cities to sign with the Vikings. As we speak, he is on the way."

Obviously, my first loyalty was to WCCO television, and so they were the ones that broke the story. And then within a few minutes, I got a call to go on ESPN live to tell the breaking news, and still there was no confirmation from the Minnesota Vikings. I had not had a chance to enjoy this yet. I was as busy and stressed as I had ever been. All I was thinking was about getting my story confirmed by the Vikings.

I was still upstairs in my home, and all this had taken place within about 20 minutes after I received the phone call from my source. After I hung the phone up from the ESPN interview, it took about another two minutes and the Vikings confirmed the story. Everything started with the phone call and the posting on the website, and the story just took off. I had not even left my home, and the story was nationwide.

As I recall, the Vikings came out with a press release confirming that Favre was coming to the Twin Cities. I believe Brad Childress and owner Zygi Wilf were quoted in the story. It seemed like an eternity from the time I broke the story until the Vikings confirmed it.

I was relieved but had no time to bask in anything. I think my sigh of relief could be heard all the way to Mankato. He was really coming, and he really was going to be the Vikings quarterback. In fact, because the Vikings confirmed my story, it really didn't matter now whether he changed his mind or not. He had done all the things I reported on. It was totally on him now.

To say the least, my day changed in a hurry. I had an adrenaline rush for the rest of the day. My phone was literally burning up. I got calls from all over the country. All these guys who I had done radio shows with were calling me, and I was going crazy, but a good crazy!

Now remember this was my day off and I was supposed to help my daughter get ready for school. I couldn't handle the calls coming, and I needed to get to Winter Park, the Viking offices in Eden Prairie. I asked for help from the WCCO public relations person so I could get ready to go to Winter Park.

I jumped in the shower and got dressed, put on a nice shirt and tie, and headed for Eden Prairie. I was also in touch with my news department and told them I had this commitment to speak at a high school that evening. I told them I really did not want to break the commitment. They were every understanding about it and let me attend.

I rushed to Winter Park to wait for Favre and to get prepared to do our local noon news broadcast. I have to say that I was feeling pretty good at the time. All the news stations were there, and, of course, they all knew I was the one who broke the story. Through all of this, I was asked only a couple of times who my source was. I think for the most part people, especially in the business, aren't foolish enough to ask such a question.

There was this palpable buzz like nothing I had ever seen before. This was an extraordinary moment. Favre was on his way in and now the Vikings had confirmed the story. It was incredible to say the least. The story became like a Hollywood script.

Brett Favre and coach Brad Childress on the way to Winter Park after Favre's celebrated arrival in the Twin Cities. When Favre walked out of the locker room in purple, it was a surreal moment. *Craig Lassig/AP Photo*

The media was everywhere, including the airport in St. Paul where the Vikings' private plane had landed. Head coach Brad Childress was at the airport in a white SUV picking up Favre, and the media followed them all the way to Winter Park. It was a replay of the *Seinfeld* episode and O. J. all over again.

Once the story reached the public, people were everywhere. I'm not kidding, it was psychotic. They lined the streets near Winter Park and followed the coach's car down West 7th Street to I-494. It was unbelievable. And then the car drove into the Vikings complex.

And now all of a sudden, there he was, Brett Favre, walking out of the dressing room and onto the practice field. He was wearing a red "don't hit me" quarterback jersey and putting on a purple Minnesota Vikings football helmet.

All I could think was, *you have got to be kidding me!* I mean, this was the most obscure, obtuse thing I had ever seen in my life. Here was the most hated player on the rival Green Bay Packers putting on a Vikings uniform.

When he walked out of that locker room for the first time, it was jaw-dropping. It was a sight. Here he was, a little grin on his face wearing the purple, one of the guys.

This was, without a doubt, major sports news. There was no time to do anything after I heard the news but go with the story. Fortunately, I had a reliable source and he was right. I will forever be thankful for that phone call.

With most stories, like when I reported that Joe Mauer was going to sign with the Twins, you have some time to gather your thoughts and do more checking of the validity. With this, there was no time. Favre was on a plane on the way to the Twin Cities. If I waited, everyone else would have the story, beat me to it, and it would be pointless. I had to roll with every instinct I had, and even then it was nerve-racking.

There had been so much leading up to the story, but then we heard Childress say at the beginning of training camp, "He's in our rearview mirror. I called him and he is not coming." Well, what are you supposed to think at that point—now he is coming? I mean, what a nightmare!

Training camp was over. The Vikings had left Mankato and were practicing back at Winter Park, and it was getting close to the beginning of the season's first few preseason games. It was early August, and I'm sure Favre was thinking, "Training camp—what do I need to show up there for?" The Vikings had a West Coast offense, and Favre could teach the West Coast offense. So, maybe, and very likely in his mind, he always knew he was going to be a Viking.

Once the decision was finally made, it broke quickly. It was simply trusting one source, which is generally not the rule of thumb when reporting a major story. We're taught to get two sources. But a credibility ranking of sources also becomes a reality, and timing—as in this case—can be critical.

* * *

Here is another example. If Lou Nanne called me and told me who was going to be the new coach of the Minnesota Wild, I would take it to the bank. That would be all I would need to know. That's good enough for me. Sure, I would do my job properly and try to get a hold of the Wild administration to confirm it, but I would go with the story as soon as I possibly could. Even if they responded with a "no comment," that would be okay. I would go with the story because my source had the utmost credibility. Lou Nanne would not call me with the scoop if he wasn't 100 percent sure.

With the Wild, I would understand where they'd be coming from with a "no comment." They might still be finalizing the deal. I mean, do you think they would say to me, "Okay, you got us—here's the deal"? No way. They would not let me rain on their parade; they would let the news out when they were ready. This is just an example of how something like this could work with credible sources.

Now, just quickly, my example is only for illustrative purposes. Lou Nanne would never do anything like my example. He would never upstage the Wild or any team or person, for that matter. He gets it, and although he would be a reliable single source, rest assured, I would not get such a call from Louie.

* * *

The Joe Mauer situation, with his long-term contract, was much different than the Favre fiasco. I was doing my radio show with Dan Cole—"The Common Man"—on KFAN, and we were talking about a totally unrelated situation with a shortstop, maybe Orlando Hudson (not sure). Anyway, we were discussing the fact that someone was going to be signing a contract, and I wanted some more information on it. So I called my source in Florida to ask about it.

While in conversation about the player-signing matter, Joe Mauer comes up in the conversation and my source tells me that the framework of a deal is in place for Joe Mauer to sign a long-term contract with the Minnesota Twins. I'm told it is going to be long-term in the range of somewhere between seven to nine years. And I'm told it is going to get done sooner than later.

Now, this news is huge. My source is what I call a secondary source. He has absolute credibility with me, but he is relying on his source for the information. Yet, I know he would not be telling me this if his source was not 100 percent sure.

So, I have the information. What do I do with it? In this case, I mentioned it on KFAN, and on the news as well, as a "developing story." I reported it just as it was reported to me. It was a difficult situation. I wanted to be on top of it. I was totally confident in my source, but this story was not about to come to any immediate conclusion. The final contract deal between Joe Mauer and the Twins was still a ways away.

I told our news director that I had the information, it was totally reliable, and I was going with it. When I went on the air, I had a story totally different from the Favre news. In that scenario, I was able to say, "Favre is coming. He is on a plane from Hattiesburg to the Twin Cities."

The Mauer signing story was very different. I said on the air, "A framework of a deal is in place with the Twins for Joe Mauer to sign a long-term contract. He is not going anywhere. I have tried to contact his agent, Ron Shapiro, and he is not acknowledging anything at this time, but believe me the sources I have talked to have told me this is going to happen."

I never said that he was going to sign soon or even in the near future. I just said the framework of a deal was in place to keep Joe with the Twins. But I got a ton of criticism for this. You see, here is the problem: The next day, Mauer happens to be in L.A. promoting something and he opens himself up to the media for interviews. Some of our local media are doing satellite interviews and ask him about the information I had come out with on the air the night before. "Joe, there is a report in town that you are about to sign a long-term contract with the Twins. Would you like to comment on it for us?"

Now, what's Joe going to say? "Well I don't know anything about it. I don't know where those things start." Now, it is very easy to discredit my report because of the Mauer comments and say that my story is an erroneous report.

I am getting my share of shots at this point—unfairly, I might add, because I never said he was going to sign now, tomorrow, or the next day. I repeat, I said, "A framework of a deal is in place. Here is the bottom line. He is not going anywhere, folks. The Twins are not going to let him leave." This is a far cry from saying the Twins have signed Joe Mauer.

Joe doesn't sign right away. And the time and the story go on and on, seemingly forever. But I am sticking by what I reported. People are poking fun at me and I'm really on the spot, but my source continues to tell me, "It is going to happen." I ask him repeatedly, "Is it still on? Is the deal going to work out? Is it still in place? Has it fallen apart?" And I get nothing but, "No, no, no, it has not fallen apart. Be patient, it is going to happen. Mark, believe me, stick to your guns. It will happen."

Joe Mauer in Fort Myers after signing his multiyear contract. *Steven Senne/AP Photo*

It went on week after week, and it was frustrating, but I knew that my source would know the facts on this matter and would not lead me in the wrong direction. So I stuck with it even though my information was coming secondarily.

As time went on, about two months, one thing led to another. I'm sitting in Milwaukee covering the Gophers playing in the NCAA basketball tournament and I get the call. Sure enough, the Twins are having a big news conference the following day at Fort Myers to announce the signing of Joe Mauer to an eight-year contract.

I recall how few actually remembered my exact words. I was even nitpicked about the eight-year deal. I may have said seven or perhaps nine years. The fact of the matter is that I reported that he was not going anywhere, and I was right. Mauer did sign with the Twins, and I had said he would.

* * *

Sources come from a lot of places. You will often read in the paper, "Unnamed sources have said . . . " You have to be very careful about unnamed sources. From a news standpoint or sports standpoint, these people may be former employees who are bitter at the organization and have a different agenda.

I don't ever mind getting information, but you have to keep in mind that person's point of view on the matter. The unnamed source could be anyone from the former bitter employee to someone in the training room. When the information comes to you from within an organization, it is usually the result of someone who cannot keep a secret very long. And even though their job could be on the line, they have to tell someone, so they do.

"Hey, I got this really juicy piece of information and I have to tell somebody. This is too good to be true!" I think once the information is given out, I think they feel a sense of satisfaction. "Hey, I'm the guy who told Rosen. I gave him the scoop."

Look, gossip is gossip. It's out there all the time. It almost becomes "white noise" to the public. We live in a world of such advanced technology that it is difficult to keep a lid on anything. There are so many unnamed sources out there. How many times have you heard the comment, "White House sources have said . . ."? What does that even mean? "Sources close to the White House have said." What does that mean?

It could be the guard at the front gate or a cook in the kitchen. How about someone who parks cars? He's close to the White House, isn't he? "Sources close to the White House have said . . ." Come on now. Who? Give me a break. But that's the way it is today with everyone in contact with everyone else. Email, phones, cell phones, Facebook, Twitter—it's unbelievable but reality. What does this mean? It means you have to be very careful.

It's important within the media to be first with a story, but we should never succumb to taking source information that's not credible. From the public standpoint, I doubt they care.

We all want to feel like we got the big story, but for every Brett Favre and Joe Mauer story, there are dozens of others out there that don't interest the public. This is why I took great pride in breaking the Favre and Mauer stories. Those kinds of exclusives don't come easy, and surely they don't come along every day.

In the end, like I said, no one really cares who broke the story, got it first, or whatever. What's important is how you presented the story. How did you get the information to the public, and were you right and were you accurate? These are the important issues.

My goal every single day is not to say, "I'm going to break this story." My goal is to get information from people I trust and put my perspective around it. I try not to take sides but try to report the facts accurately. I want to give a perspective and let the public be the judge.

I have been around here in the Twin Cities doing this work for four decades and some change. With each sport, I probably have a handful of solid sources that I can count on and other sources as well. Sometimes I don't even know who they are until they come forward, and they may come from a variety of places.

The foundation of everything I have done in my career has been built on honesty, integrity, and credibility. These are vastly important to me, yet I deal every day with people who don't honor those words the same.

Take the Brad Childress situation, when he sent three players to Mississippi to essentially beg Favre to come back to the Vikings in 2010. Three players were gone from the locker room, and when asked about their absence, the Vikings told a bald-faced lie to our faces. Does this kind of thing bother me? Absolutely it does.

We know the motive. They wanted it quiet. They did an end run on us, "a Statue of Liberty" play. I understand that it was certainly because of the intense media pressure, but lying is never right. "These guys aren't around. What do you mean they are not around?" Answering the questions would be much tougher than lying, so they lied and it was wrong. Sometimes I understand the motives. It is, in fact, their business, but it doesn't sit well.

A good source to me is someone who has developed a pipeline of information based on years of experience with or around an organization. But more so than what this person has developed internally is what I have developed with this person on the trust level, a trust that we have built up through the years. I have to have a tremendous respect for the person and confidence in him or her.

I have said many times that it is very important to be very careful and also to be aware of being used. Some teams will want to use you to get their point across, and for the most part I don't want to get into those situations.

In the process, you also have to be watchful of being burned by a source. I recall many years ago relying on a source that high school basketball star Janet Karvonen was coming to Minnesota. I reported it proudly. She never went to Minnesota. I was younger and wanted the story to be true. My source was wrong. I don't forget those kinds of things. I learned my lesson the hard way.

Here is the perfect case in point. Mike Tice was one who really talked to the media. Brad Childress came in and totally buttoned things up. Before Tice was Dennis Green, who always seemed paranoid about everything the media did. Green acted like everything was a major confrontation. They were so different.

Mike Tice was very easy to cover. He talked and wanted a good relationship. He also told me a lot of things that were "off the record." Anytime any source tells you something in that context, it must be honored. It goes the other way, too. Burn a source and you will never get any more information. It's that simple. This doesn't mean that the information can't be used in another context; it can as long as the source is kept away from it. This happens all the time, and sources know this and understand it.

With most of my sources, I have developed a professional relationship. I call them and they call me. It is definitely a two-way street. This is not to say that some of my sources have not been friends of mine because they have been. But I would say that for the most part they have been people with whom I have established professional relationships and mutual respect.

Some of these sources may be close to other people who have the key information but are individuals who won't talk. This is where the secondary source comes in, as mentioned earlier in the Joe Mauer signing scenario. Sources are not always used for the "breaking story," but they are utilized for background information. So when you have the story that eventually comes out, maybe being released from the team or whatever, you will then have some very important background information to accompany the story. This may be critical to support the story and, most importantly, make it interesting.

The information coming from the source may be a leak or it may be the organization instructing the person to get the story out there. Most times, the information, especially the small stuff, just gets out. I doubt any team is saying, "Tell Rosen this or tell Rosen that." This would be highly unlikely. It would be more a situation where the source is going to give you some good background information to the story.

The new Gopher football coach, Jerry Kill, is a good example. When he first came to town, we had lunch a couple of times so we could get to know each other. I have a professional relationship with him. There is some trust involved. I don't want to be his close friend. I don't want to be that close to him or any of these guys, but Jerry is a really good guy.

But as we get to know each other, Jerry may tell me things that I would never report on, and he trusts me with it. He may provide me with some solid background information on an issue or a player, which helps me to understand something better. It helps me to understand a perspective on something, which makes me a better reporter. Yet at the same time, he knows the information will assure accuracy in the story, and that works for him and the team.

In gathering information, I sometimes have been pressured to reveal my source. During my first few years with the station, I had to earn my trust with them. Now after all these years, I have an established credibility with the station and they surely know I understand the complexities and importance of getting a story right.

Even with the Favre story, I was never asked by the station to reveal my source. I didn't want to because someone could let it slip or somehow it could get out and then no question my source would be gone. But more importantly, I would have broken a trust with that person and potentially hurt their credibility.

I never have a problem, though, going through a checklist. I have bosses, and they need to ask me hard questions. I thrive on that. I want to be checked up on and questioned. It's part of the business, but it also keeps me sharp and on my toes.

"Mark, are you sure? Are you absolutely sure about your source?" This is the right thing for a boss to ask. It doesn't happen every day, but when it does, I appreciate it. I want to be checked up on. I want to know I am doing the right thing.

No organization would ever ask for me to tell them my source. They wouldn't dare do that. They know I wouldn't tell them anyway. I think in some respects they get kind of a kick out of the whole thing, depending on what bit it is. They know what we have to do and how it all works. It is kind of a game to some extent. They know the world we are living in and how it has changed with all of the technology and so forth.

I like to directly quote people with certain stories. Maybe it is Lester Bagley of the Vikings on the stadium issue or someone else.

But you have to be very careful on the slippery slope to get it right. I think it is good to come on the air with "I talked to this person or that person." I think the viewer appreciates knowing that I didn't pick up the information from someone else but rather I got it directly from the horse's mouth. "I was there. I looked him in the eye, and this is what he told me." Viewers like that. "I talked to so-and-so and he told me this . . . "

Fans want to feel like they are part of the team. Remember, this is sports we are talking about here. We are not talking about hunting down Osama Bin Laden. We are talking player movement or some other sports-related matter. Fans want to feel a connection to their team and players.

The Love Boat scandal with the Vikings is a perfect example of that. I was at a restaurant with Vikings head coach Mike Tice that very week in Edina. He came up to me and told me about this team meeting the Vikings had and said the players are this and that—all good updates on the Vikings. And two days before our conversation, the infamous Love Boat had occurred out on Lake Minnetonka, and he didn't even know about it. Two days later, the story broke and all hell broke loose. Talk about getting blindsided on it; even the head coach didn't know. It was the beginning of the end for Mike. He never deserved the blame he took for the antics of a stupid few.

* * *

I want to mention one of the most fun and perhaps one of the best stories I have had the honor to break. It involves my good friend and former great Vikings wide receiver Ahmad Rashad. He was working with the media in New York, and he called me the day before Thanksgiving.

He said, "Hey, Mark, you have to watch the Thanksgiving Day game tomorrow on NBC. I'm going to make a big proposal on the air tomorrow." I said, "You are going to what? You are going to make a marriage proposal?" He said, "Yeah, a marriage proposal." So he says,

With Ahmad Rashad at a formal event some years back. Ahmad was the first to work with me doing weekly broadcasts on Sunday evenings, a program that subsequently became *Rosen's Sports Sunday*. Through the years, we have maintained a wonderful friendship.

"You ever watch the Bill Cosby show?" I said, "Of course I watch *The Cosby Show*. Everyone watches *The Cosby Show*." Ahmad then said, "Phylicia Ayers, I'm going to ask her to marry me tomorrow on national television." I said, "What? Really? Can I go with this on my broadcast tonight?" He goes, "Yeah, go ahead."

So Wednesday night, the day before Thanksgiving on the 10 o'clock news program, I said, "You have got to watch NBC tomorrow because Ahmad Rashad is going to propose live on television to Phylicia Ayers, and she doesn't know about it."

Of course, I was at our local station in Minneapolis, and the next day Ahmad Rashad goes on national television in New York in the middle of this broadcast and says, "Phylicia, would you like to be my wife?" And it turned out to be this big ballyhoo thing, and I had the story the night before.

Now, here is the perfect case in point because this was back at a time when there was no such thing as email, Facebook, Twitter, or any of those kinds of information pieces. No one knew about it! If that had happened today, that story would have been out there and she would have known ahead of time, and the surprise would have been spoiled.

It shows you the world we live in today. Here we have a friend as my source actually telling me this great breaking news announcement. I thought I was going to have some fun with this. Ahmad didn't care because he knew there was little chance of this information reaching New York before he made the proposal. It was a great piece of information, no doubt about it, and I broke the story locally.

Oh, one more thing. I didn't need a second confirming source on that one.

7

Greatest Interviews and Associations

Over the past four decades, I have had the good fortune and opportunity to be involved in hundreds of television interviews. Each has been special to me, and for the most part each has been very different from the rest. Some of the interviews have been relatively short, and some have been lengthy. Some have been taped and many have been live, especially when they have been in-studio interviews on my show, *Rosen's Sports Sunday*.

I have had my share of interesting discussions with some of the most celebrated names in sports, and as a journalist I have been honored by each allowing me the chance to talk to them with the public listening.

I have to acknowledge that I have been inspired by most of my interviewees, some more than others. I have laughed and I have been embarrassed. There have been tension-filled moments, and I have held back tears of sadness. But I can honestly say that I am thankful to have had a career with endless opportunity to meet some of the most famous and interesting people imaginable.

I'd like to start by mentioning one of my very favorite characters of all time. His name was Calvin Griffith, the former owner of the Minnesota Twins. Calvin was a true purist of the game.

When I first met Calvin, I was starting my career in broadcast journalism and he was one of the last of the dinosaurs running a family-owned baseball team. His family originally owned the Washington Senators and then the Minnesota Twins.

They weren't some giant conglomerate with several multimillionaire ownership groups as we see today. It was Calvin, his sister, and brothers, and they had to make money with the team because there was nothing or no one else to back them up. I have always felt it was an honor to have had the opportunity to be in the presence of this man.

Interviewing an owner of a team in today's world of sports is much different than it was to interview Calvin. If you look at Zygi Wilf of the Vikings or Craig Leipold of the Minnesota Wild, they are not as accessible. You have to jump through some hoops to get to them.

I'm not saying these guys won't talk with you, but it is not like you can just walk into their office and start up a conversation. It doesn't work like that. Calvin Griffith was much more available, and he liked to talk.

He was unique for so many reasons. I can remember walking near his office, and if he saw me he would likely holler, "Hey, come on in, boy, come on in." When this occurred, I knew I was in for quite a treat.

He always had a messy desk, and a giant sailfish that he had caught hung on the wall behind him. So, I'd walk in and he would start chirping, "Did you see our attendance yesterday? We only had 20,000 out here and it was Bat Day!"

Those Bat Days at the old Metropolitan Stadium would drive you crazy because the kids were always hammering the bats on the railings and the noise was deafening. But anyway, back to Calvin. If I was interviewing him, he would come on the air and likely say some of the most outrageous or inappropriate things, but you know what? It was right from the heart.

As I mentioned, he might be all upset because of the attendance on Bat Day, and I might say, "But Calvin, your team is 30 games out of first place. What do you expect?" He didn't care; he thought the place ought to be filled if he was giving away bats. It was always about the money because, remember, his total income came from the ballclub. There was no other money or business he could fall back on if the baseball team lost money. His adopted father, Clark Griffith, made it in Washington that way and so did he, and he was not going to fail in Minnesota.

As I look back at my time with Calvin, I always think about how incredibly refreshing he was. He was old-school, and he so worried about the dollar that people looked at him and associated him with being "Mr. Cheap." Yet again, this was his only income. He had to be.

There are a million stories from the ballplayers about Calvin's protection of the buck. Harmon Killebrew made around $19,000 when he was a superstar. Rod Carew had a tremendous season and was offered a $5,000 raise—those kinds of things. He was legendary in this regard.

But no matter what was going on, I appreciated having the access to Calvin. He stood out. He was different; *refreshing* is a word I associate with him.

He was this curmudgeon-type character who had such an amazing history with his family running the ballclub that dated way back to their days in Washington, D.C. They were always successful in finding ways to survive. They were a family, loved baseball, and just happened to own a major league team.

Calvin would from time to time inadvertently stick his big foot in his mouth, but he really didn't mean anything hurtful by the things he said. That's just the way he was. He was not one of those rich owners who could often get by with things. Whenever he spoke, it was likely newsworthy.

He never fell into money or fell into the ownership of a baseball team. He worked his way up in the organization when his adopted father ran the ballclub, and there was no doubt that he knew the game. He was as true a baseball man as they come. He understood what it took to win and how to operate all aspects of the club.

Calvin would have his brothers walking around the ballpark making sure things were selling—the hot dogs, the beer, the peanuts. He counted the scorecards being sold. He didn't want to put the names of the players on the back of their uniforms because he was afraid the fans wouldn't buy scorecards. He came up with the idea to puts lots of ice in the drinks to save on the beverages sold.

Take a look at the throwback uniforms the Twins wore last year in honor of Harmon Killebrew. You don't see the names on the back, do you? Calvin knew what it took to make money, and he had to find unique ways to survive.

I loved the fact that no matter what was happening on or off the field, I could get to him. I didn't have to wait a few days or a week. "Come on in, come on in," he would say. I can hear him today, the sound of his voice, the look in his eye. He was special, and I was excited every time I got the chance to have a conversation with him.

There was no filter on Calvin Griffith. He was around all the time. You didn't have to go through all kinds of staffers to get to him. You could stop by his office, catch him on the field, or walk right up to him at spring training. It's too bad, though, that he didn't have a filter on his thought process because when there was a microphone nearby he might say just about anything.

When I think about Calvin Griffith, it always brings a smile to my face. Even the players who spent years with him—Killebrew, Blyleven, and so many others—often laugh when they talk about him. They really understood his penchant for the almighty dollar.

It definitely was not so funny when they were negotiating their salary with him because back then it wasn't like it is today. There was no team of lawyers, agents, and so forth, and there was not any free agency at the time. It was the player and Calvin, and the owner held all the cards.

He was about as tight with player salaries as he could be, and he built quite the reputation in that regard. I can't imagine in a million years Calvin today with the giant salaries, all guaranteed. I break out laughing thinking about Calvin Griffith and Joe Mauer. Twenty-three million dollars a year for eight years? WOW! He wasn't paying his entire team anything even close to that kind of money. Come on. I absolutely know that kind of money would have killed Calvin on the spot, or he would have sold the ballclub—whichever came the quickest. He eventually did sell the team.

I loved being around Calvin. He probably could best be described as a cartoonish-type character, a Fred Flintstone. He had a brusque, unique manner to him that stood out. He didn't need a bunch of public relations people around him. On the other hand, maybe he needed a few. His persona made him different from the rest, and special. He was sure special to me, I know that for sure.

It was impossible not to like the man. He was real. He was the man, the guy in charge. This is it. "This is who I am. Like me or don't like me." He wouldn't apologize for things he said. "Hey, this is me. This is the way I feel about this. We should have had more people out here today. I don't care if we are 30 games out of first. I gave away bats and they should have come to the ballpark!"

One thing for sure I can absolutely say about Calvin Griffith: He spoke from the heart and loved the game. I truly loved being around him, and I treasure my memories of him. Sometimes when I am out on the field before the ballgame, I look around and hope to see him. I know his spirit is out there counting the programs or measuring the amount of ice in the drinks.

* * *

Of all the interviews I have conducted during the past 40 years, there is one that stands out as being my all-time favorite, without even a close second. It's the time I got the opportunity to interview the great Sandy Koufax of the Los Angeles Dodgers. He was my boyhood hero.

I believe Sandy Koufax was the best pitcher of all time. He was so dominant. Here I am, this Jewish kid growing up looking at Koufax, and it was almost too much to fathom. I knew everything about him from his days in Brooklyn, what he had to overcome in his life, and his rise to superstardom.

Of course, he was here in 1965 with the Dodgers when they played the Twins in the World Series and beat them in Game 7, but I got to meet him and interview him when he returned as the honorary captain for the 1985 All-Star Game at the Metrodome. And not only was he the honorary captain for the game, but he pitched batting practice for the National League. I was in awe watching him.

He wore his old No. 32 on his uniform, and he still threw with the most fluid motion I have ever seen in a pitcher. I was absolutely dumbstruck watching him. It was the only time I had the chance to meet him.

I was very lucky to get the interview. Sandy is still a very private person. He to this day grants very few interviews. I'm not quite sure how it all transpired. I think I asked the public relations guy to help me out with the interview; I just can't recall. I might have had a mutual friend who set it up—something like that.

Interviewing Sandy Koufax was one of the most memorable moments in my career.

But it was arranged for me to interview him, and we did it live on the 6:20 p.m. sports on WCCO. It was amazing. I could have been on Mars for all that mattered at the time. It was as surreal a moment as I have had in my career. I couldn't even feel my feet.

I heard someone say once that Sandy Koufax had the left arm of God. I believe he did. Koufax was that good, that dominant in the game. But the fact that he agreed to do the interview and do it live, now that was pretty special.

I was so nervous. I think I said we were at the Met Center or some ridiculous thing like that instead of the Metrodome during the interview. And I remember just laughing about it. But you know what? I didn't care. I was too excited to know where I was. It didn't even matter. *I was talking to Sandy Koufax!*

I didn't try to hide any of my feelings, and he was such a gentleman about everything. The interview went great. It was probably about a two-minute interview. I asked him about the 1965 World Series and what it felt like to return to the area, that kind of thing.

He could not have been nicer or more gracious. He was a super interview and a super person. I have a picture of us together, one of my most prized possessions. I have this million-dollar smile on my face.

He looked like he could still pitch. Injury had done him in, but you have to wonder with all the medical technology in place today if his career could have been lengthened. He had a bad elbow, arthritis building up in his arm, and it all eventually did him in. In the 1965 World Series, I remember him pitching on two days' rest and he shut out the Twins. He was magnificent.

We in the media are not supposed to ask for autographs. This is kind of a big deal. We can have our credentials pulled. But this was Sandy Koufax. I figured this was different, so I had him sign a couple baseballs for me when we were off the air. I have never done that before, but I got them and he wrote, "Best wishes, Sandy Koufax." WOW is all I can say. To me, he was the greatest pitcher of all time. And as for that special day, it was my biggest thrill of all time.

* * *

As I talk about my greatest interviews, I would be sadly remiss if I didn't mention the time I sat down in a trailer and interviewed Evel Knievel. I can't believe I am actually saying this. I actually sat down and did an interview with one of the most interesting of all characters, Evel Knievel.

He was the greatest daredevil of all. He was in town on a Saturday to promote a jump he was going to do at the old St. Paul Civic Center. I would guess it was around the early to mid-1970s because I know I was still pretty green in the business and still just a kid. He was setting up at the old North Star Drag Strip so our photographer, Al Crocker, and I went out to the track to do the interview.

He had agreed to meet with us on a Saturday afternoon. Evel owned a private plane, and at about the same time as our interview was scheduled, his pilot was flying in to land nearby. As the plane approached, we began filming the landing. The pilot was not aware of power lines near his landing space.

It was soon after our filming began that we could see there was not enough room for the pilot to navigate around the power lines and land. The plane ended up hitting the strip. It went a short distance and crashed into a trailer. Evel was in the trailer. It was amazing. Fortunately, the plane didn't explode, the trailer was still standing, and we all lived.

We couldn't believe what we had witnessed. I was snapping pictures with a little Nikon camera and Al was filming away, and all of a sudden out of the trailer came Evel. He was absolutely nuts. He was hysterical, screaming, "Call the insurance company and tell them to get this million-dollar piece of crap out of here!" He had gone completely ballistic, and all I was thinking was how was I going to be able to interview him after what had just occurred.

Eventually, Evel calmed down and we went inside and I interviewed him. During the initial part of the interview, he suddenly announced, "I need a shot of Wild Turkey, and you're going to have one with me, kid." I was like 20, maybe a little older; it didn't matter to him. But I was working and not supposed to be drinking. I might have a couple beers once in a while, but Wild Turkey and on the job? I don't think so. But I had one with him, and I thought the stuff was going to rot out my insides for sure. Every time I tell someone about my drink with Evel Knievel, I still get that awful taste in my mouth.

I thought I was going to pass out from the drink. But I downed it. What choice did I have? I mean, this was Evel Knievel. I was not about to give up my interview opportunity over something like a shot of Wild Turkey. After we downed the shot, he says, "Say, kid, you were taking pictures of the plane crash, weren't you?" I said, "Yeah, yeah. Why?" Evel said, "Hey, I need copies of that film for my insurance." "No problem," I told him. "For sure, they're all yours."

What a dummy I was. I probably could have sold him those pictures for thousands of dollars. I gave him all of the film.

He was one of the most unique people I had ever met. He walked with a cane and had this unbelievable devil-may-care attitude like no person I had ever met before or after in my life. At that point, he had not yet attempted his famous Snake River Canyon jump, but he had already performed the infamous stunt at Caesars Palace in Las Vegas, where he jumped and broke every bone in his body. I think he jumped cars and buses and whatever else they could line up for him.

Evel was a great interview, a great storyteller. He always wore an Elvis-type jumpsuit, had his hair all slicked back, and was quite the personality.

We led the news that night with the story because of the plane crash. And here I am still wet behind the ears talking to Evel Knievel, one of the greatest of all showmen on WCCO television. It was a wonderful memory, especially the drinking part, which I have taken with me for a lifetime. "I had a shot of Wild Turkey with Evel Knievel!"

For me it was almost like meeting Elvis. He was that kind of personality and was such a great character. He had a lot of P. T. Barnum in him, performing some incredible and spectacular feats. With all of his antics and misfortunes in his stunts, he probably should have been dead a hundred times over. Amazingly, he survived until his ravaged body—full of alcohol and drugs—succumbed to his flamboyant lifestyle. In the end, he was a mess.

* * *

Another of my interviews I vividly recall was with the legendary Ohio State football coach, the one and only Woody Hayes. The one thing I remember most from the interview, which I did with some other reporters, is that not one time during the interview did he look up at us.

The Ohio State football team was in town to play the Gophers and had scheduled a walk-through at Memorial Stadium the Friday before the game. Afterward, the coach made himself available to the media.

I'm sure in Coach Hayes' eyes, the media was ranked slightly behind the tax man as far as who he wanted to spend time talking with before a big football game. "Tax man, hey come in and have a cup of coffee. Media, get the hell off my lawn!"

That was about what he thought of us. I can barely recall what he said in the interview, but what I will always remember is how he never made eye contact with any of us. He was wearing that red jacket that he always wore along with a white shirt and tie, and he kept his head down and his hands in his pockets during the entire interview. He never looked up once.

I remember thinking, "Come on, you're bleeping Woody Hayes. Talk to us." It was one of those moments that you always remember, and I recall thinking, "Why does he have to be this way?" I mean, I'm sure he knew he would beat the Gophers easily—it turned out that it wasn't even a contest—so he really didn't have a lot to fret about. "So come on, be nice." Well, he wasn't. He just performed like the bully, the big shot, and the too-good-to-be-bothered type. Too bad, because he was a great football coach. He must have had a lot to say, and I'm sure he could have been a great interview. He wasn't, and I lost a lot of respect for him.

* * *

In talking about Woody Hayes, it leads me in to another classic interview with a similar personality, Bobby Knight. The fact is, you don't interview Bobby Knight. He allows you to be in his presence. Bobby tells you when to start and when the interview is over.

The first time I had an encounter with him, I was following an interview Knight was doing with Tony Parker, one of our local competing-station sportscasters at Channel 9 television. It was the early to mid-1970s, and Bill Musselman was the coach of the Gophers basketball team. Knight and Musselman hated each other.

The interviews were conducted one-on-one instead of as a group interview. I'm not sure why, but it was the way Bobby wanted it done. So, we stood in a row waiting for our time, and I was next after Tony Parker. All of a sudden, Knight and Parker started arguing. It had to do with Musselman. They got louder and louder, and Tony, who had been in the business for quite some time, wasn't backing down. As the interaction got more and more ugly, all I could think of was, "Oh no, and I'm next."

Now I didn't have a lot of experience at that time in my career. But I did have the Evel Knievel interview under my belt, which followed his private plane crashing into his trailer with him inside, so I thought I must be able to handle just about anything. So, with Bobby Knight in a rage, I began the interview.

I approached Knight and said, "Bob, I just have a couple of questions for you. Let me ask you about Musselman." Knight starts screaming, "You, too, you want to talk about Musselman. What's the matter with you guys!"

I look at him and say, "What do you mean, me too? I just wanted to ask you something about the Gopher coach, Bill Musselman." He says back to me, "I can't stand Bill Musselman. Do you like everyone you work with? Well I don't, and I can't stand Musselman!" So, I tell him, "No, of course I don't like everyone, but that's not what we are doing here." It didn't matter. It was a terrible interview.

This was a younger Bobby Knight, and I remember that time so well because of his behavior. He was so surly and ugly about it. The interview soon ended, and I recall it so well because of the inappropriate way he handled it, so unnecessary. Here is this outstanding coach, like Woody Hayes, and he has to act this way. Very unfortunate.

Many years later, Sid Hartman set up an interview for me with Bobby. I remember asking him a question, and he answered it for about 45 seconds and did the same with another question, and then he walked away. I wasn't done with the interview, but he didn't care. It was obvious that his logic was quite simple: "Look, I gave you my time. Now I will tell you when the interview is over." You kind of just sit there and think, "Wow, that's it, the interview is done because Bobby says it is done. How unprofessional!"

Some years later, at Sid's 90th birthday celebration, I was the emcee and gave Bobby Knight a little shot from the podium. I don't know exactly what I said, something like, "It's all about him when he is being interviewed. Apparently his time is more valuable than ours." I didn't care what he thought. I mean, what is he going to do to me? Actually, he was a good sport about it and laughed when I poked at him some.

Here he is today, after all these years of giving the media a bad time, working for ESPN doing college basketball. A little irony in that, don't you think?

* * *

One of my favorite people to interview through the years, and frankly just to be around, is Lou Nanne. Louie is an absolute joy. We were involved many years back with the Minnesota State High School Hockey Tournament. It was the ultimate team effort at WCCO TV. In my opinion, there has never been a more unified station-wide project than that tournament during those memorable years. I believe one would be hard-pressed to find another station in the country that has ever put together a better product on the air from start to finish. I am so proud of the work we did on the tournament.

My longtime friend R. J. Fritz reminded me that we started broadcasting the tournament in 1983 and how we both had "yearned for the day we could become a part of the television coverage." R. J. recalled how our station general manager, Ron Handberg, had agreed to pay $555,555.55 for the three-year rights to do the tournament. All the 5s were in the contract to rub it into the former rights' holders at Channel 5!

For the action, Lou Nanne was the "color commentator" and we also utilized the expertise of Doug Woog and Herb Brooks in the booth. Here is the difference between Herb and Louie. During the game breaks, Herb would diagram plays on a napkin while Louie would make dinner reservations for later that evening at Mancini's restaurant.

And if the game happened to go into overtime, Louie would say off the air for my ears only, "Someone better score quick or we are going to miss the reservations at Mancini's!" He is the best! I loved working with Louie. No one knows the game better, and no one is more enthused and appreciative of the schools, players, and coaches than Lou Nanne. He has been doing the state high school tournament for just under five decades!

Not long ago, Lou was asked to recall those days in the booth. Here is what he said: "WCCO TV spared no expense, brought in top-notch talent, and worked tirelessly at producing sensational state high school hockey telecasts. The unmatched excitement of the eight-team tournament was accentuated by the professionalism of the station and its workers."

We all had a great time and produced outstanding tournament coverage.

* * *

After being in this business as long as I have, I can say one thing for sure: I have met some real characters. Latrell Sprewell, a former player with the Timberwolves, was one of them. He put himself on the map with his infamous statement about having to "feed his family." He was complaining about his salary offer of millions of dollars and tried to solidify his position by bringing his family into the discussion. What I remember the most about the aftermath was going back to him the next day and asking him if he wanted to clarify anything about his statement, and he said, "No, that's exactly what I meant to say."

Randy Moss was another. He was the most electrifying athlete I've covered in a rookie season. He turned the 1998 Vikings season into a frenzied, franchise-turning event. He made some of the greatest catches I have ever seen. He was a game-changer if there ever was one.

The one moment that stands out to me about Randy that year was after a victory in Chicago. He was sitting alone in front of his locker, and I asked him about a great block he threw that enabled Cris Carter to spring for a touchdown. He sincerely answered, "If I want to be one of the greatest to ever play this game, those are the sorts of plays I have to make." Here he was, talking about what's best for the team, not just for Randy Moss. His complexity always confounded all of us. Behind the scenes, Randy did amazing things for underprivileged or ill kids. He didn't want or need the media there to document them. If you recall, anytime he scored a touchdown in the far end zone at the Metrodome, he would always hand the football to a kid in a wheelchair who would be watching the game on the sidelines.

Cris Carter once told me that there was a disconnect between the right side and the left side of Randy's brain. It's too bad. I've never seen a receiver with more God-given talent, and he should have been a Viking for life, but he couldn't help himself during the tough times. His "I play when I want to play" quote has followed him his whole career and haunts him to this day.

His tremendous ability single-handedly made the Packers change the way they drafted players after he burned them on that memorable rainy Monday night game in Green Bay in 1998.

His speech in New England after he had returned to the Vikings was a classic, and his love letter to the Patriots and obvious regret in forcing them to trade him was perhaps the last straw. And of course, his insults to the caterer at Winter Park were also in the mix. On the field and off, he stood alone. No one seemed to ever know for sure what he would do next.

* * *

I have had a few controversial interviews in my career. One was with Mike Lynn, general manager of the Vikings at the time. This "moment" occurred during a preseason game played in Memphis, Mike Lynn's home. We did a half-hour pre-game show, and on that show we featured Lynn's antebellum home in Memphis. It was straight out of the Civil War, and therein laid the problem.

Sitting home watching the broadcast were a number of prominent African American Viking veterans who didn't make the trip to Memphis. Among them was Steve Jordan, their excellent tight end. When it came up about the area of the estate where the slaves had been housed, it created quite a stir. Of course, the Lynn family had nothing to do with slavery or that period of time. They just happened to have owned that piece of real estate.

We have heard the term *slavery* come up from time to time in the NFL. Lynn did nothing to help himself the one time he bragged about how cheaply he was able to sign Joey Browner, their number-one draft choice, which probably didn't help the perception of the story before it aired.

* * *

Interviews are always interesting, especially when they are not scheduled. I suppose a better way of approaching this is to say it was an unofficial interaction. It all started in about the fifth inning of the final game of the 1991 World Series, perhaps the greatest series and game ever played in the Fall Classic.

I had just opened Rosen's Bar & Grill in the Warehouse District in downtown Minneapolis about two weeks before the World Series. I was at the game and received a call from one of our restaurant managers saying that Charlie Sheen was in the establishment. That's right, Charlie Sheen, in my bar.

When the game ended, the Twins had won the World Series and pure bedlam flowed everywhere. I enjoyed celebrating with everyone

With Charlie Sheen at Rosen's Bar & Grill in 1991.

else and eventually made it over to the bar. Charlie was still there and in quite a good mood. He told me he had wagered thousands of dollars on the home team in each game of the series, and if you recall the home team had won each of the seven World Series games.

I ended up staying with Charlie until the wee hours, mostly to avoid the madness in the streets. It was obvious that Charlie was enjoying spending his winnings!

* * *

For a short time many years back, I was involved in preseason Vikings football on Channel 4. One of those years, I shared the booth with Brad Nessler, one of the really great guys and a very talented play-by-play broadcaster. We were joined by Scott Studwell, one of the all-time Vikings greats. Scott had just retired from his playing career, and we had a great time with the games and working with each other. Scott was always a pleasure to be around—a true professional and a solid interview. Besides being a real class act, Scott set an NFL career record for the most tackles for the same team. His career on the field and in the front office has spanned three decades.

Another year, we were joined on our broadcasts by Joe Kapp, the former Vikings quarterback, who served as the "color commentator." Joe led the Vikings to the 1970 Super Bowl and has always been recognized for his coined phrase "40 for 60" as he talked about his Vikings teammates. His passion for the game made him interesting because we were never sure what he might say.

Late in the first half of one of the games we were doing, Luis Zendejas came onto the field to attempt a 40-yard field goal. Kapp, who is Mexican American, said "this Chile Chomper" shouldn't have any trouble making the field goal.

My headset almost exploded. Back in the Twin Cities, the phone line lit up. Kapp was being ripped to shreds, and an apology was being

With Brad Nessler (*center*) and former Viking Scott Studwell (*right*) as we prepare to do a preseason Vikings football game.

demanded by the listening audience. Word got to me quickly, and I told Joe he had to apologize. I remember Joe looking at me and saying, "Mark, that's what we call each other." I said, "Well, Joe, that may be true, but 95 percent of our audience doesn't know that!"

So, as only Joe could do with his disarming charm, he offered up his version of an apology, and it was effective. Joe's a classic with a heart as big as it gets.

* * *

From a "crush" standpoint, my favorite interview and person would have to be Dorothy Hamill. She came to town about three years ago for the Herb Brooks Foundation, and I had a chance to talk with her and sit at the same table with her for the dinner.

When she first came on the scene in the Olympics back in the 1970s, there wasn't a guy in the world who didn't have a major crush on Dorothy. With her talent, that pixie haircut, and personality, she was really something. She still is to this day, just a wonderful person.

Comparing her to the Bob Knights and Woody Hayeses of the world, there is a marked difference. She is so engaging and gracious, and she has a fabulous personality. By the end of the evening she was calling me "Rosey," and it was a great evening.

Dorothy seemed like a blushing 15-year-old, and the interview with her was really outstanding. She has such great passion for everything and can relate so well to people and an audience. It has to go down as one of my favorite interviews. It was reaffirming to know there are people like her. I watched her as a young kid who was so successful as a skater and certainly as a very famous personality. It sure is nice when something comes full circle and you later get to meet someone like Dorothy.

Back some years ago when I was playing a lot of tennis, I had the opportunity to play with Chris Evert, Martina Navratilova, and Herschel Walker. Chris Evert was as charming and beautiful and nice as you could possibly be, and Martina was the polar opposite. She had a little dog back stage that she spent time with and was just grumpy.

Herschel I knew from his time with the Vikings, and he was great. But Chris Evert, again, was wonderful. She made me so relaxed. Think about it: I'm out on a tennis court in front of 15,000 people playing this exhibition match with Chris Evert.

During my career, there is no question that Chris Evert and Dorothy Hamill have been two of the most interesting and iconic figures in sports, and I was so honored to have had the chance to spend time with them. I don't mean to say that Martina was mean or anything like that, but she just had an edge to her that was quite noticeable.

The interview with Chris was fantastic. She was laughing and having a good time, and it was like I had been a friend of hers her whole life. She was really special, and the time I had with her was so memorable. She was so nice and such a class act—a real professional.

* * *

One of my early career interviews was with Bobby Hull. I remember going out to the Met Center to talk with Bobby as he neared the end of his career. He was the "Golden Jet," maybe the most exciting hockey player who ever lived. He had that giant slap shot that came off his stick like a bullet. When he circled behind the net and picked up the puck on a Blackhawks power play, there was nothing else like it in all of sports.

One of the things that really impressed me during my interview with Bobby Hull was the way he treated the media. He was so different from guys like Woody Hayes and Bobby Knight. Bobby Hull was so nice. He had so much class.

I was maybe 18 or 19 years old, and the first thing he said to me before we started the interview was, "What's your name?" I told him "Mark," and I introduced myself to him. And then when he answered the questions, he did something real special. Whatever I asked him, let's say I asked a question about the North Stars team that year, Bobby would answer with, "Well, Mark . . . ." He prefaced every answer by including my name in his response, and I cannot begin to tell you how that made me feel. It put me so at ease. It was like we knew each other for a long time and we were just having a routine conversation.

Here is the superstar of the National Hockey League calling me by my first name. It took Bud Grant 30 years to call me by name, and I told you what that meant to me. But Bud, well, that's the way he was with everyone. It wasn't just me.

I will never forget the fact that Bobby Hull before the interview made me feel validated. Bobby was such a tremendous hockey player. Well, I mean he was the "Golden Jet," and he had that big broad smile and was every hockey fan's hero, and yet he took the time to ask my name and repeat it throughout the interview. He made me feel special, shook my hand, and made it seem like, "Hey, Bobby Hull is talking to Mark Rosen"—not just doing some everyday interview with the media.

Today when I talk to college kids, prospective journalists, and others, I discuss the importance of using people's names, looking them in the eye, and finding a way to make them feel special. Bobby Hull did that for me, and I try to do that for others.

* * *

One of the real characters whom I met and had a chance to interview was former Detroit Tigers pitcher Mark Fidrych. They called him "The Bird." And let me tell you, he was a character of all characters. It was one of the looniest interviews I have done. I can't believe we did the interview live from the Tigers dugout at the old Met Stadium.

In 1976, he had a phenomenal rookie season. It was like he took over the whole league. Mark "The Bird" Fidrych, he was really something. We did the interview live, as I mentioned, the day before he was scheduled to pitch, and it was one of the most goofy interviews I ever had.

I kept asking him about his career, his season, and so forth, and he would just say he went out there to have fun and, in the process, he talked to the baseball. Yes, that's right, he talked to the baseball. I could barely get through the interview without laughing because he was such a goofball. But it was what made the interview work and be successful. I will never forget "The Bird" and his legendary "talks" with the baseball!

* * *

One of the most interesting and memorable interviews I have ever done was with Mickey Mantle. I got to spend a short time with him, and I was deeply saddened by it. It was during a tough period in his life. Mickey was in town for a promotion for Donaldson's department stores. This was a chapter in Mickey's life that was likely centering around, "He needs the money. He's still drinking, and it has become the ironically sobering part of his life."

We sat down for lunch. There were five of us at a table, and he told this sad story about a reoccurring dream that he was having. He is standing outside Yankee Stadium and all of his teammates are inside. Yogi Berra, Whitey Ford, Billy Martin, and all of his favorite guys, and he can't get inside to get to the game. And he is telling the story like he is telling it for the first time. It was really sad, mostly because of the extreme sadness in his voice as he told the story. There was so much regret in his voice. Here he had this meteoric career— he was the toast of New York—and he paid the price for it in so many ways.

His nights on the town, his drinking, his carousing, his fame . . . it was too much for him, and he paid dearly the latter part of his life. I felt like as he spoke he was really saying, "I wish it had been different." The sadness in his voice, in his words, and on his face spoke volumes about his life and where he was on that day compared to where he had once been.

He was just this green country boy from Oklahoma when it all started, and what a road he traveled. I was taken by the story because when someone talks like that with the emotion and passion in his voice like Mickey did, it tells you something about where they are at. But it had been his choice. He had made the decision to live that kind of lifestyle, and now he was living the results.

Just having the chance to interview Mickey Mantle, sit down at a table with him, and hear his story was really special for me. He was a magical hero who comes along only a few times in a lifetime. Mickey was all of that.

One of the first autographs I ever got was a gift from my aunt, an autographed baseball from Mickey Mantle. It was a prized possession that I kept in my drawer. It had No. 7 below his name.

* * *

Another very emotional and extremely sad interview for me was with the former Minnesota North Star Bill Goldsworthy, famous for "The Goldy Shuffle." He put the North Stars on the map. He was a Killebrew-type hero for all of us to watch. He was, no question about it, our "Golden Jet." He had the hair flowing before they wore helmets, and he could really bring the fans to their feet.

I remember when "Goldy" came to our high school journalism class. A classmate of mine invited him to come. She had gotten to know him some, and here was the great Bill Goldsworthy coming to my class. It was a real thrill. He was such a dynamic hero to us kids.

During my career, I had the opportunity to interview him many times. He, like Mickey, lived a careless lifestyle and ended up destroying himself. Bill ended up getting AIDS, and the end was very tragic.

I recall an interview with him that was so sad as the end neared for him. Here he was, a broken man who had fallen so deep into the despair of life. He was very accountable for his lifestyle, but it literally brought tears to my eyes to remember where he had come from to where he was at the end.

I had a lot of admiration for Bill and what he had done for the North Stars. And here I was talking to him one on one. He wanted to get some things off his chest to help people to "not do what I just did," and I respected him a great deal for his message.

* * *

I was always fascinated by the opportunities that my career presented for me. I mean, I got to be around some of the greatest sports stars and celebrities of the game and of life. Early in my career, I was much more enamored with sitting next to the superheroes than I probably am today. But many times still, I might have to stop for a second and say to myself, "I can't believe I am here with this person or these people."

Think about it for a minute. I'm the kid in the backyard pretending I am Mickey Mantle, pretending I am Harmon Killebrew, and now I had become a friend to Harmon and at lunch with Mickey Mantle. "Come on, Mark, wake up!" I often felt that way and still feel like that. Most of me is still that kid who hasn't as yet grown up around the greats of the game.

One of the proudest moments of my career was when I was able to get my mom to meet George Mikan, the former iconic center of the old Minneapolis Lakers. Mom was a huge Lakers fan and really loved

Look at the smile on my mom's face as she puts her arm around former Minneapolis Lakers great George Mikan.

Mikan. There was a Minneapolis Lakers reunion here a few years ago, and I took my mom. The joy I received watching her interact and meet George Mikan was a thrill I will never forget.

Dad used to take her to all the Lakers games, and she would yell at the referees, "Tell them to get their hands off Mikan!" And to see my mom next to Slater Martin, Bud Grant, Mikan, and the others, well, it is a memory lodged in my mind forever. All the guys were there—Vern Mikkelsen and so many other greats of the past—and to see Mom with them was fantastic. To get a picture with Mom and George Mikan, well, that was the best ever.

Mom was like a teenager. Although I never saw Mikan play, I thoroughly enjoyed interviewing him. He was such a graceful, gracious, gentle man and so nice to my mom. Dad had passed away by then, so I missed the fact that he wasn't there, but Mom's absolute joy made up for it.

* * *

Another of my favorite interviews and perhaps one of the all-time best interviews on my *Rosen's Sports Sunday* show was when I had Tony Dungy on with me. This was after he had left the Vikings, and he was in to talk about the postseason, as he often did. Tony, who played quarterback at Minnesota under coach Cal Stoll, had a very special relationship with Cal. They were very close when Tony played for Cal and remained great friends after Tony left the university.

We surprised Tony on the show with a birthday cake, and Cal brought it out for him. We had Cal on camera walking in, and it was a tremendous night. Seeing the connection those two had with each other made the show memorable. Not only were both successful in their careers, but they were also wonderful, caring gentlemen.

You can talk about how sports can form your identity. Well, sports certainly did that for Tony, as did the relationship he had with his former head coach, Cal Stoll. I truly enjoyed that show because the surprise and connection the two had wasn't just a private moment, but rather witnessed by our television audience live from the WCCO studio. It was a rare night for television sports.

Former Vikings quarterback Brad Johnson is a person whom I really got close to in my work. Brad was an outstanding quarterback and a really good person. He had that kind of "Opie of Mayberry" look and character, but he was a solid professional football player and a really nice guy. Brad was a low-round draft choice from Florida State, where he wasn't even the starting quarterback.

He had a great work ethic, and to see him fight the way he did to make it in the NFL and later become a Super Bowl–winning quarterback with Tampa Bay was really pleasing for me. He had an easygoing demeanor, was a great family man, and was a strong role model for kids.

I got to know Brad very well. Before the Vikings' historic 15–1 season in 1998, I spent several days with Brad down in Tallahassee, where he went to school, and did a story on him. Brad started that unbelievable season with a touchdown pass to Randy Moss. He then got injured in the second game, which opened the door for Randall Cunningham and his Pro Bowl year.

The next year he was traded to Washington, and eventually he ended up with the championship season in Tampa Bay. He was a guy who was not blessed with great talent, but he truly persevered in his dream and had a very successful NFL career.

Brad and I became pretty close friends, and he used to do my show quite often. One of my favorite lines from him was when I asked him a question about one of his game scrambles. I said to him, "Brad, what were you thinking on that play?" His reply was, "Run, Forest, run," referencing the blockbuster movie *Forrest Gump*, starring Tom Hanks.

One of my favorite Vikings was a bigger-than-life character, Dave Huffman, who died in a horrible car crash. He was a Notre Dame alum who really just "got it." He understood life and knew that football was just kind of passing through for him. I really miss Dave.

* * *

I interviewed Paul Newman. I knew the ground rules before the interview. Paul was up in Brainerd doing the drag racing scene, and the rules were that you could not ask him questions about acting or movies—only racing. I remember him sitting in his car and pulling his helmet up to show off those trademark blue eyes while I got to ask him a few questions about racing. He was very nice, and it was quite a thrill. I kept with the script, asking only racing questions. I had been warned that if I wanted a quick end to the interview, bring up a movie question.

On one Sunday night, I had Tim Irwin, the former mountainous offensive tackle for the Vikings, on my show. Tim is now a judge in Tennessee. "Big Ir" has an opinion about everything. He once told me after a loss that I had more concern about whether the Vikings won or lost than half the players on the team. He was just frustrated and venting.

So anyway, Tim is on my show live and we are watching some film of the game that day. The first play we show is Irwin missing a block, and his man creams the Vikings quarterback. It was one of those moments where he just got his butt kicked by a defensive end of the Washington Redskins. It was a big play in the game, and Tim says right on the air, "Why did you have to show that play?" I said, "Well, Tim, it was a big play. It happened in the game. I don't know what else to say."

At that moment on the set, you could cut the tension with a knife. There was a brief quietness that seemed to last a week, and then he settled down. But it was tense, and we were live on TV.

There was another night on my show that I will never forget. It kind of highlighted, at the time anyway, the "bad boys" of sports. I had on the show at the same time Warren Moon, who was coming off his domestic assault situation; J. R. Rider of the Wolves, who never showed up for anything; and "Black Jack" Morris of baseball fame. I have a picture of the three of them. I did three separate interviews, and it was really interesting. Actually, it went quite well.

I asked Warren some pretty tough questions about his case, and he was really outstanding. He wanted to talk about it and did a good job. J. R. Rider had trouble getting to practice, but there he was. He showed up for us and was always an interesting interview.

And Jack Morris . . . well, he was Jack Morris, a fine interview and much easier to talk with than back in his playing days. Back in the day, Jack was as surly as could be. Rod Carew was a lot like that when he played, and he always credited Harmon Killebrew with making him understand there was a right and wrong way to behave and treat people.

Actually, J. R. was more fun to talk with at any time than Christian Laettner of the Timberwolves. Laettner was so surly. I never wanted to be around him. The first time I met him, he came into the green room at WCCO for an interview before the draft. He had received all kinds of awards, and we did an interview with him.

I went out and introduced myself to Christian and was making some small talk with him. I recall mentioning to him that maybe he would end up with the Wolves here in Minnesota. His comment: "Yeah, whatever." It was like I was annoying him. And guess what? He ended up a Timberwolf.

Don Shelby was nearby and witnessed the whole thing. I remember Don and I later talking and saying, "You know what, this guy will probably end up playing here." And he did. He was just not a nice person. Actually, J. R. Rider was a nicer person, if you can believe that. I think he just kind of ran with the wrong crowd and got himself all messed up. But still, I would much rather talk with J. R. Rider than Laettner.

* * *

I have done interviews in which people have gotten mad at me. I recall Keith Millard of the Vikings flipping out on me, and I almost got into a pushing match with Mitch Berger of the Vikings over something. It's no big deal. It doesn't bother me.

Once during my show I had Ed McDaniel and Randall McDaniel of the Vikings on, and they gave me the silent treatment while we were live on the air. I asked a question and neither would answer. It was one of those moments. They had it all planned out and got me good. There was that few seconds of silence that seemed to last hours.

I remember thinking, "Okay, so this is the way we are going to do this tonight, is that right?" They had a good time with it and it was pretty funny—at least later on it was. They had a great time at my expense.

I had them both on the show quite often, and it was a great adventure because I was never sure what they were going to do. I really enjoyed working with them, as unpredictable as they were. That is the beauty of doing live television. You are never sure what might happen next, and whatever does can't be fixed with a tape delay.

Live is so much different than taped programs. Once you say something, it is out there. There is no seven-second delay to fix what might go wrong. Live television gives you an adrenaline rush. It gets the juices flowing. There is nothing quite like it.

* * *

Rosen's Sports Sunday now goes year-round, which we never did before, so we are constantly trying to find interesting things for our viewers. But I love the show and it is one of my favorite things to do.

Today, there are some really good players to interview on the local teams. With the Twins, Michael Cuddyer is a great interview. The Vikings have Visanthe Shiancoe and Steve Hutchinson. These are standup guys, athletes who understand their role in talking with the media, win or lose. They treat people with respect, and they realize that the media and others have a job to do and are willing to help out.

Nick Schultz with the Wild is someone I enjoy interviewing. He is a really nice person and always fun to be around. With the Wolves, Kevin Love is probably the number-one guy right now because he is basically the whole team and a good interview. In the future, I see Ricky Rubio's boyish charm making him a popular interview, and I see the possibility of him being a star player for many years.

Former Vikings coaches Brad Childress and Denny Green were tough interviews. I recall Green one time after a tough loss in Green Bay being asked something about the game, and he replied, "That's ancient history. Next question." I said, "Ancient history—it happened 15 minutes ago!"

I actually enjoyed talking to Brad Childress, especially about things other than football. Unfortunately, it took Brad a couple of years before we were able to see a warm side of him.

There were coaches and others who might say outrageous things, but you can have some fun with what they say and not make it personal. Mike Tice would say some incredible things, but he was extremely open with the media. Calvin Griffith was that way, too.

Things are always happening in sports that make for good coverage. We never have a lack of material, which makes it so interesting. Take the Minnesota Timberwolves. Glen Taylor, the owner, had to have been successful in many businesses to become a multi-multi-multi-millionaire, but his basketball team is run like a third-grade operation. In 2011, team president David Kahn and coach Kurt Rambis sat two feet from each other after the season and didn't speak because Rambis didn't know if he was going to be fired or not. He was eventually dismissed and the Wolves hired Rick Adelman as their new head basketball coach, but I felt the situation was handled poorly.

It was really just unbelievable! I was looking at some film depicting this situation and thought I must be having brain freeze to watch the comical atmosphere surrounding a big-league organization. At least the Wild had the decency to terminate Todd Richards after the season, but no, not our Timberwolves. It's a lot more fun for everyone to keep the coach hanging. It's sad and extremely insensitive and unprofessional. You don't treat people like that.

I don't do a lot of interviews with the Wolves because the fan interest level is at an all-time low. Maybe this will change with the arrival of Ricky Rubio and their recent number-one draft choice, Derrick Williams.

* * *

I love talking with new Gophers football coach Jerry Kill. He sugar-coats nothing. He tells the truth and gives no imaginary goals. I think he will do well. He is full of honesty and integrity. He fought the battle with cancer and hasn't got time in his life for a lot of B.S. He wants to win, and he knows it will take a lot of hard work to get there.

We need the truth as fans, and we need more of it. I think some of our professional teams in the area would do well by taking a course from Jerry Kill. We thrive on honesty. If we are not very good, tell us. Tell us what we have to do to be competitive. We just want to understand, and we can only get there from the truth.

Fans are more educated today with all of the Internet connections, Twitter, and blogs, and they know when they aren't getting the facts and the truth. It's tough to get things by them, so there is a reaction when there are attempts at denying the truth or when there is too much secrecy. They want accountability. There is a big investment in games—season tickets and so forth—and they want accountability.

* * *

I don't think I have ever had a doubt about truly loving my job. Every day I feel fortunate to have the opportunities that I have had. Interviewing some of the greatest names and people has made it so interesting. Everyone has been different.

In my career, I have had some classic interviews with some really big-named athletes. Reggie Jackson. O. J. Simpson. How about those two? I was doing a story on athletes and big-market advertising. We did some things with O. J. and the famous Hertz commercials. These guys understood who they were and how they could market themselves.

The story on athletes and advertising was extremely interesting. I mean, O. J. was interesting not only because of his football prowess but because of those Hertz commercials, which helped make him one of the most famous people in the world.

Look at the most famous sports commercial of all time: "Mean Joe" Greene of the Pittsburgh Steelers for Coca-Cola. His one line, "Hey kid," was maybe the best ever.

I'll finish with another favorite interview of mine. While attending the Harmon Killebrew funeral in Arizona last year, I met and interviewed a fan with a great story about Harmon. He talked about being a batboy for the Twins in 1962. After a game one night, Harmon invited several kids over to his house for a barbeque to thank them for their work during the season.

He told about getting home at about eight o'clock that evening with his mom at the door saying, "Where have you been?" The reply was, "Mom, I was at Harmon Killebrew's house." "Don't you lie to me, young man," his mom responded. "There is no way Harmon Killebrew invites you over to his house." It eventually got straightened out.

The man told me the story with the same passion and joy as he probably told his mom when she settled down. He told it to me almost 50 years later. He loved to tell it and I loved to listen to it. It was a great interview.

Four decades. Calvin and Sandy Koufax. J. R. Rider and Mickey. Dorothy Hamill, Reggie, and O. J. The list goes on forever. It has been such great fun. I'm a lucky man.

8

Bud

I was having lunch with a friend of mine, and the name Bud Grant casually came into the conversation. I jokingly added that the first thing that came to mind when I heard Bud's name was "fear."

Truthfully, though, the first thing that enters my mind when I think of Bud is loyalty. The word is a virtue of his and is something I have learned that he cherishes. It is a trait that he has with his family, his coaches, and certain players. Loyalty represents Bud Grant. He is true to himself and true to his principles.

Loyalty has a lot of meaning to me and is why Bud is so special to me. It is a word that reflects strength of character, a word that means that one accepts another despite all of their warts and flaws. Using war terminology, it means when you are in the trenches with them, they know that you have their back and they have your back.

I have certainly had a lot of those experiences with people I have worked with over the years. Bud had this with many of his players. His connection with players like Jim Marshall really stood out. Fran Tarkenton, obviously, was another, but Marshall in particular was one that he was probably the closest with through the years.

Bud had it with his coaching staff, his kids, his family, and his hunting buddies, who most people don't even know. He has always surrounded himself with people he can rely on.

When I was young in the business, I never recognized those kinds of qualities in people, especially Bud Grant. He was stoic and seemed so unapproachable. He had those steely eyes and a coldness that scared me during my initial contacts. But once I got to know him as a person, I saw things in him that were polar opposites.

While preparing *Best Seat in the House*, I was asked why I devoted an entire chapter to Bud Grant. I have known thousands of people in the media, in sports, through radio and television, and in my personal life—what makes Bud so special? I think it was this question that helped me to develop the most important part of the chapter.

Having the opportunity to do *The Bud Grant Show* with him for a couple of years was without a doubt one of the real highlights of my life and arguably one of the most significant of my career. He taught me more about life and common sense than anyone I have ever been around. He taught me things without even knowing he was doing it.

He taught me things like, "Don't worry about things you can't control." If it's out of your control, you can't fret about it. That was number one that I learned from Bud. He used to say that all the time, and I truly started believing it. I passed it on to my kids when they were worried about something. They would be upset about this or about that and I would say to them, "You know what, this is out of your control right now. You can control only what you can control, and there is no point in getting an ulcer over it."

Bud also had a tremendous skill of being consistent in everything he did. He was like a father figure to me even early on. He was such an icon to me and to most who knew him or looked up to him. But I must say, he was not easy to get to know.

He rarely ever called me by my first name, especially when I first got to know him. I remember the first time he called me "Mark"; I almost fell down. It was to me like getting the ultimate compliment. It was as if I had just received significant approval from my father. It was like doing something special and getting that pat on your back. It was that way for me with Bud.

I was a young guy when we first met, and from the beginning I literally idolized Bud. He would come into the studio and talk to Hal Scott, and he had this incredible presence about him—like nothing I had ever encountered before. I recall at practice he made Hal put his cigarettes out. Hal liked to smoke and they got along fine, but Hal would be told, "You're not smoking around here," and Hal did as he was told. He was telling Hal Scott this, and Hal could have told him to "go take a flying hike," but Hal put out the cigarette. He knew he was on Bud's playground, and Bud was the boss.

I will never forget the famous interview Bud had with Phyllis George of the historic and popular CBS Sunday football team, *The NFL Today*. They were out at Metropolitan Stadium with Brent Musburger, Jimmy the Greek, Irv Cross, and the whole CBS team, and Phyllis was interviewing Bud for a special. During the interview she said to Bud, "You're so stoic, Bud. Can I get you to smile for the camera, just a little smile, just once?" Bud looked at her and, in only Bud's way, calmly and stoically replied, "Say something funny, Phyllis."

Another thing about Bud Grant that few people realized was he was an incredible practical joker behind the scenes. He loved a good joke and was often the initiator with the best of them. He would hide animals of all types in the Vikings' complex at Winter Park on April Fools' Day, and he was first in line to enjoy a prank or practical joke on someone. He loved life and often exhibited it to those closest to him.

I learned so much from Bud. As I mentioned, there was the philosophy of control, his consistency, and I watched and learned from his great steadiness. He had so many ups and downs in his coaching life, and yet he handled them all so well. He had so much grace in the Super Bowl losses, yet he was so competitive.

No one was ever more competitive than Bud Grant. Although he rarely showed it, he wanted to win more than anyone I have ever known. There are stories of him on the racquetball court beating his opponents, and his competitiveness when he was playing sports was legendary.

Bud was a tremendous athlete and excelled at everything he played. Bud wanted to win, and yet when the game was over . . . well, "What are you going to do? It's over, forget about it. Give it your best effort and be done with it."

Bud taught me a lot about work ethic. "Give it all you have every day, and when you leave the practice field, the coaching office, or the game, be done with it and move on. When you get home, be home—not back at the office or on the field."

Eventually I did develop a positive relationship with Bud, but believe me, I had to earn it. It didn't just happen because I happened to have a job covering the team. I knew in order to have any credibility with Bud, I had to live up to certain standards. I had to be consistent in my reporting, my visibility, and my respect for him and the team. I learned how to approach him, what kind of questions to ask him. It took a long time.

In the early stages of my career, my hair was a little lengthy and Bud would sometimes come by and tug on the back of my hair and say something like, "Isn't it about time you get a haircut there?"

I really feel my acceptance came from Bud because I was consistent with my coverage and he respected that part of what I did. I had a good relationship with the players, and he recognized that as well. He looked for fair coverage and respect. I quietly and professionally went about my work.

I can recall times when we would be shooting coverage of their practice and Bud would come over and say, "Guys, turn the camera off right now, we are going to be running some plays that I would not like for you to film." And we would turn the camera off.

Now these were times when we had a lot more access to the team and what we would be covering. So Bud appreciated the respect we showed for his wishes and other kinds of things like that. Obviously, we never wanted to display any disregard for his wishes.

I think above all, doing the show with him was key to the development of our relationship. That was tough in the beginning. I was scared. *The Bud Grant Show* was the first of this nature in our new building.

In 1980, I was doing *The Ahmad Rashad Show* at WCCO, and Bud had his show on KSTP. Ahmad had to get permission to do the show from Bud, and this was really unusual at the time. Think about it. Bud had his show on the air, and Ahmad was doing his show at a competing station at the same time. Bud allowed it. He had great respect and loyalty for Rashad.

When I did the show with Bud, he protected me in some ways, too. For example, before the show he might say to me, "Be sure to ask me about this during the show." In other words, he meant, "Don't be afraid to ask me this point about the game." He helped me with some of the tougher questions. He wanted me to ask those because he knew the public expected him to answer them. Bud understood the importance of giving the fans what they wanted.

When we were doing the show, there were times he would come in and be on the telephone before we went on the air. Maybe the Vikings had just had a tough loss, and I would see him on the phone and just assume he was probably talking to offensive coordinator Jerry Burns or an assistant coach—something about the game and so forth—so I would stay away from him.

And even though I tried to give him his privacy, it was pretty hard because he was on the phone nearby. And then I would suddenly realize he wasn't talking to anyone about the game. That was past history for Bud. He was talking to one of his hunting buddies, making arrangements for their next hunting trip. He was setting up an appointment to be in the duck blind the next morning.

I think Bud was the first one who dismissed the notion that you had to be in the office 120 hours a week to be successful. He believed there were only a certain number of hours you needed to prepare a game plan and execute it successfully. He had his own way of doing business.

He was the most logical man I have ever known. During all the interviews and press conferences that I have attended with Bud Grant, I don't think he ever said anything that he regretted. He would always give that little clicking sound with his mouth and tongue if he had to think about something before he answered a question, and then he would answer the question with precise logic and thoughtfulness.

If he were coaching today, there would never be that ESPN moment when they would say, "Can you believe what Bud Grant of the Vikings said after the game or at his press conference?" Wouldn't happen. Now Bud might be inflammatory toward officials, but he would never give that ESPN moment. He knew exactly what he was doing at all times. If he ever said something out of character, you better believe he planned it out and knew exactly what he was doing.

Bud was a master at handling the media. He wasn't afraid to challenge reporters and, at times, make them uncomfortable. For example, someone might ask an irritating question and Bud might respond with, "You're not around here much, are you?" That's how he would put someone down. He could get personal, especially if you didn't have his respect.

Bud had a pecking order with the media. Everyone would be standing around with tape recorders, much different than the press conferences held today. But Bud would always talk to the print reporters first, so I would have my notebook ready and be nearby. I would make sure not to have my recorder out and on, because if you had it on when he was talking to the print guys, Bud might step over, put his hand on your recorder, and say, "I'll get to you later. I'll get to you in a minute." I never wanted that to happen. I had too much respect for him.

He would be very polite about it, but extremely firm. In other words, I don't want what I'm telling these guys to be recorded. That was just his way of doing business. Today, that wouldn't work because of the way the interviews are set up. Back then, we might have been in his office or out on the field. It was just a lot different, and Bud had his way.

During those times, there was no such thing as a media center. The formality of it all today is so different, and there is no opportunity for the luxury of control like Bud had. During most of the period when Bud coached, the media would walk into his office when the game ended and he would separate the print media from the electronic media. Anyone with a tape recorder or a TV camera would be considered electronic media. When the newspaper reporters were talking to Bud, we didn't have the cameras rolling. We would then get our chance after the print media was done. And he was consistent with that all the time. He had a way of doing business, and I picked up on that and it helped me establish credibility with Bud. He saw how I operated within his expectations, and he respected me for that.

Gaining my credibility with Bud took a long time. It didn't happen overnight. I was fearful of Bud in the beginning. Players were fearful of him. He just had that stoic, steely-eyed look about him that made it clear that "this is the way we do business."

I remember one time when I went to Chicago to do a story on the Bears. By then, Jim Finks, former Vikings general manager, had gone to Chicago, and we had a connection there. Ed Marinaro was there, and there were some others who had been in Minnesota at one time. I think Bud may have deep down felt a little betrayed by what I was doing and the story I brought home.

I went to Lake Forest, where the Bears trained. It was a phenomenal place; they had the best facilities. It was a very scenic and upscale environment, just a fantastic area to hold a team's training camp. So I came back with the story and told Bud that I had been there and what I had seen. No matter what I told him, he gave me a shot right back. He would say, "Well, is the food better? Do they have better practices than we do? Do they win more often than we do?"

I was giving him my impressions of what I had observed and in essence comparing it to the Vikings training camp at Mankato, and he absolutely wanted no part of it. He just shot me down, and I thought, "Oh, sorry I brought that up." That was his way of saying, "I don't care what they have there. Is that going to make them a better football team than us?" Changing the subject quickly when I got myself into those situations worked best. I learned quickly.

Bud was so different from other coaches. There would be times when I would be covering the team at training camp during practice and he would walk over as a monarch butterfly flew over my head and say—he would never say "Mark"—he would say, "Do you

Bud Grant and crew prepare for a preseason game. Bud was wearing his customary clip-on tie.

know where that butterfly is going?" And I would say, "I don't know, Bud, St. Peter maybe." Bud would say, "No, Mexico." "Yeah right, Bud," I would come back at him. And he would tell me for the next five minutes about the migration of the monarch butterfly to Mexico. All this while the Vikings practice was going on.

I thought at first he was pulling my leg, but he wasn't. He was giving me a lesson about the monarch butterfly and its migration habits. "Yes, this is what they do. They fly to Mexico during the summertime." This was Bud. This is what he did. It was never just all about football. He knew more about more things than anyone I have ever known.

R. J. Fritz would go fishing with him up in Canada and stop at the bait shop for minnows, and Bud would say to him, "What are you doing? We can catch our own minnows. We don't have to spend 99 cents a dozen on those." He had his way of doing things.

He would go hunting with players and drive forever and never say a word. I remember one of his former players telling me that they drove for hours, and the only time Bud said anything was when they made a stop at a filling station. Bud said, "Gas."

When I first came to WCCO in 1970, I was as green as it gets. Bud had been with the Vikings for three years already and had taken the team to its first Super Bowl. To say he was iconic in my mind would have been an understatement. He had built this powerhouse team full of incredible personalities, and he was the leader.

It wasn't too long before I started to get my feet wet covering the Vikings. I was sent to Dallas in 1973 to cover the NFC Championship Game against the Cowboys. It turned out to be one of the greatest games in franchise history. I was infatuated with the city and its history. I recall taking a cab out to the site of the Kennedy assassination.

The Vikings were an exceptional team at that time, and it happened to be Chuck Foreman's rookie season. To this day, I can't believe they sent me there for the game. I was a kid, 22 years old, and had only occasional contact with Bud. I never really formally met him, had only talked to him a few times, and was near him from time to time as I did my job.

I recall early on shaking his hand. It was special for me, but I saw him shake a guy's hand one time and later someone tried to reintroduce the person to Bud and I recall hearing him say, "I already shook his hand." In other words, he was saying, "I'm past the formalities here," so that kind of stuff leaves an impact on you. I thought I better know what I'm doing around here if I'm going to have any credibility and success covering the team and, most significantly, the coach.

I realized early on that brevity was important around Bud Grant. He wasn't a guy whom you wanted to buddy up to because he was different. I think his players had the same feelings, and they soon learned what the expectations were. He didn't have a lot of time for small talk unless perhaps it was about the monarch butterfly.

I was pretty close to Chuck Foreman. We were essentially rookies together the same year. And basically rookies were treated with disdain by Bud. They were to be seen and not heard. You can wait your turn. Earn your stripes. Get in line. Perhaps Chuck was one of the first to break through that barrier, likely because of his enormous talent. Early on, I was told that Bud told Chuck to "just follow Dave

Osborn around and do what he does." Bud liked "Ozzie's" work ethic.

I did a story about pain and injuries, actually a series, and I worked some with Tony Dungy on the subject. I wanted to shoot some stuff at Vikings practice with Jim Marshall and others on injuries and how they dealt with the pain associated with being a professional football player. I had to get permission from Bud to do it. It took awhile. He was very specific about what we could shoot during practice.

Eventually, he gave me some leeway to do my story. I think I had to some extent earned his respect. I was never sure exactly why, but I had gained some. I was young and eager, but I was present and I was there, around the team a lot. And Bud noticed and respected that. I learned to mind by his rules and be there.

When my connection with Bud first started, I only saw one side of him. I did my job. He was there and he was who he was. That was it. I never knew until much later on the other side of Bud Grant. I didn't know there was one. I didn't know the soft side that I later discovered. I just thought he was this really single-minded sort of disciplinarian who proclaimed, "This is the way we are doing business, this is the way we are going to win." And he had the people around him to get it done.

One of the first times I saw the other side of Bud was at Jim Marshall's retirement. There was no doubt that Bud loved Jim Marshall. They had a tremendous bond and still do to this day. Bud had great respect for Jim and how he showed up every day to play no matter how injured or hurt he was.

They used to have these weekly media lunches at a hotel out on Highway 100, and it was there I probably got to know Bud best. We would meet at noon and Bud usually brought a couple players with him, and there would be a lot of interaction with the media. Bud would make himself available, and I think because I always was at the luncheons, he became more comfortable in trusting me.

Bud kind of lost it a little when Jim retired after 19 years in the Viking trenches. It was shocking. I never had seen that side of him before. Here was this icon with the steely blue eyes showing emotion. I'll never forget it.

Bud was always in control. He was different in so many ways. When he was coaching, he never let the players hang around after the games and shake hands. He wanted them off the field and back in the locker room.

At the old Met Stadium, they shared the same sideline with the visiting team, so there was plenty of opportunity to visit with opposing players before or after the game. Bud would have none of it. He would look around. "Get off the field! You can fraternize all you want on the way to the bus or somewhere, but not on the field."

He wanted no part of seeing his players shake hands with their opponents. And it wasn't a matter of sportsmanship. It was far from that. He had principles and certain beliefs, and the players needed to follow them or they wouldn't be a Viking very long.

You see the games now and it's like old-home week—the hugging, laughing, and so on. And it was like, "No, not here, not with us. Get off the field." I don't think he even went to shake the opposing coach's hand. It wasn't done back then. The feeling was, "You're not our friends. We want to beat you. This is our livelihood."

It wasn't that he didn't have respect for the other team or the other coaches, such as Chuck Knox, Tom Landry, and many of the others. It didn't fit for Bud. He was perfect for that time period in professional football. He portrayed an image. The no heaters, no gloves, the short-sleeve shirts by several of the players, all the stories, it was Bud Grant. But behind all of it was a tremendous amount of pure common sense, and that really rubbed off on me.

He was so different from the rest. Here I would be doing my job interviewing Frank Quilici of the Twins, joking around with him and having a good time. He would be an easy interview, the life of the party so to speak. There was Cal Stoll over at the Gophers, the head football coach, such a nice guy, personable, cream of the crop kind of guy. And here's Bud, and I'm watching everything I do to be sure I earn and keep his respect. It was just that important to me.

Despite all of the things that made him who he was, once we got to know and respect each other, I found him very easy to work with, especially when we did the show together, which was actually toward the end of his coaching career.

The only time I ever saw fear in Bud Grant from my standpoint was one night when we were doing *The Bud Grant Show* and I had the flu bug. And I mean I was really sick. I should have stayed home, but I thought I would fight through it. Just before we went on the air live, I told Bud, "I don't know if I am going to make it tonight through the show, I am really sick."

Bud looked at me distressed and said, "Don't you do that to me. Don't leave me hanging here!" It was maybe the only time I ever saw him truly break character. To this day, I don't know how I ever got through that show, but I think Bud absolutely literally scared the hell out of me. He made it clear I was not going to get sick on his watch, and we made it through the program.

Anybody else, well, I don't know how I would have reacted. But Bud, he gave me a jolt and the show went on. It was like a coach's speech. "No, it's not going to be done that way. You are not allowed to get sick here on this show. Now let's go to work."

Bud Grant and former NFL commissioner Pete Rozelle before a Vikings game. *Diamond Images/Getty Images*

I was asked by a friend recently about Bud Grant. "What kind of a person is Grant?" my friend asked. I had to gather my thoughts some because if I had been asked the question early on in my career, it would have been a much different response than today.

If the question had been asked in the 1970s, the first word that would have come to mind is *detached*. He was detached from me and seemingly everyone else. I didn't really know him and I feared him. He was almost robotic in terms of how I saw him. But then I didn't know him at all back then.

* * *

Calculated. That's the word I come up with about Bud. Everything about him was calculated. There wasn't a misstep. There wasn't a moment where he was not supposed to be somewhere or act a certain way, talk a certain way. You never saw him step on himself. Calculated. Everything about him was calculated, planned, premeditated.

After years passed, everything culminated for me about Bud Grant when I was at the Pro Football Hall of Fame in 1994 when Bud got inducted. I had a chance to go there and see him break down with emotion. I saw him describe his players and talk about the moment, and I realized that this is one of the warmest human beings I have ever known. The man on that podium giving his induction speech was the polar opposite of the man whom I saw from a distance for many years.

The thought of this man with the coldness, the penetrating eyes, the icy stare, a man without a heart—nothing could be further from the truth. I know this because I have seen it. I have experienced it. From a reporter's standpoint, I'm not sure I ever truly realized it until I saw him on that special day in Canton, Ohio, when he got up to speak with the sunglasses on and broke down with passion and emotion.

He talked about growing up in Superior, Wisconsin, and how his dad took him to watch the great Don Hutson of the Green Bay Packers play. He spoke of trying to get his dad's approval, and to this day I get filled with emotion when I think of Bud's line at the end of his speech about his father. In referencing his dad, he made the comment as if he were talking directly to him: "The kid made it. The kid made it." And he sure did.

I think about his speech at Canton quite often, and in my most serene moments I hope Bud's comment about his dad thinking about Bud—"The kid made it"—perhaps also once in a while reflects Bud's thinking toward me, with me in the "kid" role. I feel that way about him and want to have "made it" in his eyes.

Over the years, we spent a lot of time together in a professional relationship. It wasn't that I wanted to feel that he liked me. It was more that I wanted him to respect me. I saw him regularly with other reporters, and I could easily see when that respect wasn't there. I did not want to be in that category. And I believe the reason behind that was that I had such an immense respect for him that I couldn't have imagined being in the class where he didn't respect me or that I didn't have credibility with him.

At Canton when Bud got emotional during his speech, while standing there with the dark glasses on, I think we were all just sitting there with our mouths agape. We realized the powerfulness of his speech, and coming from Bud—who was so filled with emotion and tears, which we had never seen before—it was really something, so powerful. I'll never forget it.

Through the years, our relationship got better and better. He impressed me so much and still does to this day. Bud has been retired from coaching for more than 25 years, and yet when I see him I tend to stand up a little straighter, talk a little more clearly, still seeking Bud's approval and respect.

He was like the teacher you always remembered. I wanted and want Bud to be proud of me. I wanted his approval. I wanted to be good in his eyes. I think I made it. I hope I did anyway. I believe I did. I can kind of tell the way he has talked to me over the years, the manner in which he has embraced our relationship.

I remember at Sid Hartman's 90th birthday party the way he treated my mom. He seems relaxed around me, a trust factor built up over many decades.

When the Vikings lost to the Saints in the NFC Championship Game at the end of the 2009 season, Bud was at the game in New Orleans as an honorary captain. After the game, I saw Bud near the locker room and thought, "Here we go again." And as painful as it was, there were two images at the time I will always remember about that day.

One was Adrian Peterson standing and looking out at the field, watching the Saints players and fans celebrate. He was motionless. And next to him about 10 feet away was Bud. He looked so sad, and it hit me. He was the honorary captain, and I just know he wanted to see the Vikings, his Vikings, win the game and get back to the Super Bowl. I talked to him briefly, and for a moment he put his coach's hat back on and somberly stated, "Turnovers, as I have always said, kill you." I felt sorry for him and wished at the moment I could have said something or done something to make him feel better. I felt bad enough, but to see Bud sad made me feel worse. He means too much to me. I wanted to fix it, but I couldn't.

Maybe I read into it too much, but I don't think so. It was hard for me to see him like that. There he was, Bud Grant, Hall of Fame coach, standing there alone. No one around him, just standing there. And the Vikings had lost again.

I believe that Bud rarely, if ever, revisits the past Super Bowl losses. There isn't much he can do about that now. He had his chances and they won't come again for him, but deep down I feel that he wants his team to finally win one, even if he is not on the sidelines.

Many thoughts raced through my mind when I saw Bud after the game. The reality is he has likely never lost a night's sleep over the past. But after the Saints' victory over the Vikings, it would have been pretty hard for him not to have relived those old losses. I just felt bad for him.

When I worked with Bud, I tried hard to be sure he knew that I recognized that my role in covering the Vikings was not about me. I was careful to be sure my reporting was on track and that I was just covering it and reporting on it, and that I was not the story. With some in the media the opposite is true, and Bud seemed to always be able to catch on to who was about that type of thing.

As time went on, Bud was great at assisting me with my stories and coverage of the Vikings. He returned my calls and was wonderful with the sound bites and giving me what I needed. He also listened to me and wanted to know what and why we were doing something. "Yeah, that makes a lot of sense," I recall him saying at times.

I mentioned how much I enjoyed doing the show with Bud. When Rashad left our station and Bud came over from KSTP to us, he had a contract to do a Sunday night coach's show after the game. The program was live and—win, lose, or draw—Bud was there ready to talk about the game.

Although Bud rarely showed much emotion on the sidelines during the games, I could usually tell by his demeanor whether the Vikings had won or lost the game. I would ask the questions and we would have an occasional interview, and the show lasted only 15 minutes back then.

I never spent a lot of time chitchatting before we went on the air. We just did our jobs. Bud would come in shortly before we went on the air, I asked the questions or opened up the discussion, and he left when we were done. As I think back on it now, it was different from today. I mean, how many coaches do live television interviews?

When Bud retired for the first time, I recall our show after Les Steckel was announced as the next coach of the Minnesota Vikings. We had on the show Tommy Kramer, Jim Marshall, Bill Brown, Bud, and Les Steckel, all sitting on the set. It was a half-hour special that night about the coaching transition, and there I was right in the middle of it. I had just flown back from Hawaii, where I had covered the story 24 hours earlier.

As I look back, it's almost as if I imagined the whole thing, except that I have a picture of all of us before the show. So, I guess I was there with the rest. It was quite a show that night.

For the most part, the coach's show was fairly easy to do. I would ask Bud a question and he would give a fair answer. For football fans, they knew that when Bud answered a question, they were going to learn something. He really knew the game and so much more than what had just occurred on the field.

Look at this cast on *Rosen's Sports Sunday*! From left to right: Les Steckel, Bud Grant, me, Jim Marshall, Bill Brown, and Tommy Kramer.

Bud means so much to me personally. I respected him so much as a football coach but so much more as a person. I learned so much from him and enjoyed being around him. I loved to watch how he operated. One of his colleagues once said that sitting down and having a conversation with Bud Grant was the equivalent to completing a five-credit course. How true that is.

Bud was attracted to and became close to players whom he respected, not only for their playing ability but for their loyalty and passion for the game. Jim Marshall epitomized those traits. Jim overcame so much to become the player he was. Jim was number one to Bud. He was the captain, and every Sunday he played his heart out. Bud had such high regard for him. The two shared a bond that was and remains astonishing. I saw it again during the 50 Greatest Vikings celebration. Their connection is amazing.

There were others, too, whom Bud really respected for their dedication to the team and the game. He was very close to Fran Tarkenton. Francis had such incredible ability and knew the game so well that Bud let him flourish at the quarterback position. I think Jim and Francis set the tone for what Bud expected, and they always delivered. Others like Dave Osborn, Mick Tingelhoff, and Bill Brown, with their uncanny durability and passion, brought great respect from Bud throughout the many years they played for him.

* * *

I always felt that there was some kind of informal connection Bud had to my family. My mom, who is in her mid-80s, has often spoken of remembering Bud's years playing basketball for the Minneapolis Lakers and his years as a great athlete at the University of Minnesota. The whole connection has come full circle, with me having my career linked with Bud Grant and having her and my dad share in all of it. Well, it has been pretty special for me and my family.

I have so much pride in my association with Bud. I recall taking my dad to the dedication for Winter Park. Bud was there, of course, and he made a joke to my dad, saying, "Maybe your son will teach me how to play tennis someday."

I was a decent tennis player and Bud knew it, so it made my dad feel great. My dad had taken me to all the games, and here he had a chance to meet Bud Grant. It was pretty special. After all, it was my dad who got me to all the sporting events and got me hooked on athletics, and here I am having the opportunity to introduce him to Bud. It was pretty cool. It's hard to imagine. And Bud was always so nice to my mom too, so each communication they had over the years gave me such pride. I used to think at the time, "Wow, this is really special."

I think because I did my job to Bud's way of thinking, we had a special kind of connection. No question, though, Sid Hartman was number one in his book. They have been friends for such a long time. And you talk about two totally different people, it's unbelievable. Sid doesn't hunt or fish, and they seem to be polar-opposite personalities. Yet, when Bud is inducted into the Pro Football Hall of Fame, who does he have introduce him? Sid Hartman. They have a connection lasting a lifetime. Loyalty. It's about loyalty, and Bud knows the meaning of the word—and practices it.

There are some other reporters who Bud respected, such as Ralph Reeve and Jim Klobuchar, reporters whom he got to know and respected because of their hard work and talent.

When the team would return home on the plane after games, the media often accompanied them. Bud had rules there, too, and we abided by them. Certain areas were off-limits to the press. He didn't want us talking to the players, and we had only certain areas we were allowed to be in. We knew there was a players' domain, and we knew not to enter it. There was an invisible line, and we knew not to cross it. Players' injuries and things like that, well, that was for another time, not on the plane ride home.

Bud sat near the middle of the plane, never in first class or anything like that, and kind of watched over everything. He used to go around to everyone after meals and collect meat bones and take them home for his dogs. He brought home "doggy bags." That was Bud.

Bud has told me to appreciate the good times you have with your friends and family. He truly understands the value and importance of these relationships.

I dedicated an entire chapter in *Best Seat in the House* to Bud Grant. I think that is a small indication of what I think of him and how he has contributed unknowingly to my life.

My book has given me somewhat of a platform to formally tell Bud what he has meant to me, so here it goes:

"Bud, I never played a down for you and I have never told you this, but I want to thank you for the tremendous influence you have had on my life. Reporters generally try to keep a reasonable distance from coaches, and I respect the premise. However, perhaps through some form of osmosis by merely being around you, I was greatly affected.

"I cannot tell you how many times over the years when facing a tough situation, I have asked myself privately, 'What would Bud say? How would Bud have handled this?' Your consistent, common-sense approach to everything you encounter has served you so well and has taught me more than you know.

"You have no idea what you meant to me as a young reporter coming up. You directed me and guided me in my career at a time when I was not getting it from anywhere else. I saw the way you treated people and handled people, and early on I knew it was the way I wanted to conduct myself.

"So Bud, my heartfelt thank you for everything you are and for the impact you had had on my career and personal life."

9

Harmon

My first thoughts about Harmon Killebrew? Paul Bunyan and Babe Ruth. Oh, how he must have struck fear in the minds and hearts of opposing pitchers who had to face him.

From a fan's perspective, it was always the anticipation. Let me put it this way, any time Harmon Killebrew was at the plate, whether at the old Met Stadium or if you were watching the game on television, you didn't go to the restroom, you didn't go to the concession stand, you put everything on hold. You hit the pause button on whatever you were planning to do. The fear was if you left the game for an instant, Killebrew might hit one of his monster home runs.

He is the only player I ever felt that way about when he came to bat. I just, putting it simply, didn't want to miss a single thing he did when he stepped into the batter's box. I always believed it was too risky to take the chance and miss one of his plate appearances.

The potential of seeing Harmon do something special was always there. You might miss one of his mammoth home runs or gigantic deep fly balls, and the thought was alarming. When I think about him, those are the things that come to mind.

Baseball has a slow rhythm to it. For long periods of time, there might be very little action on the field. The players are standing around

Look at those shoulders, arms, and legs . . . it has to be Harmon Killebrew! *James Drake/Sports Illustrated/Getty Images*

a lot, walking around some, and the pace is rather slow. It's that kind of a game. It is certainly very different from watching a football game or hockey or basketball. But with Harmon, when he came to bat, it was all different.

I recall that old financial commercial where everything stops because E. F. Hutton was going to say something. "When E .F. Hutton talks . . . " With Harmon, it was like that. When he stepped out of the on-deck circle and strode to the plate, everything stopped; fans pressed the pause button.

Every time I watched him play, I knew exactly when his next turn at bat was going to be. "Let's see now, he bats third next inning, or he will get up in the sixth inning if we get one man on base"—that sort of thing. It was always like that for me with Harmon Killebrew.

There was no other ballplayer who ever played for the Minnesota Twins where that feeling of expectation prevailed over you. As I mentioned, he was the only player in my lifetime with those kinds of credentials.

Maybe if Mickey Mantle of the New York Yankees had played here, I would have felt that way, but he didn't. I'm sure the New Yorkers probably were like that with Mickey in New York.

There was another player who had some of that type of feeling for me, but I never quite had the same reverence for him as I did for Killebrew. Frank Howard, when he was playing for Washington, had some of that plate anticipation, mostly because of his size. Howard was gigantic, 6 feet 8 inches tall, and menacing, but he never became the home run hitter that Killebrew or Mantle was.

There have been a lot of great home run hitters that I have loved to watch play: Frank Robinson, Rocky Colavito, Willie Mays, and, of course, Hank Aaron. But it wasn't quite the same as with Harmon.

I wanted to see the home run, and so did everyone else who came to the ballpark. You lived and died with the thought that maybe Harmon will hit one today. And maybe it will be one of his historic blasts. I felt it on the way to the park. I felt it before the game and every time it was his turn to bat. It was an adrenaline rush for me.

Harmon was so incredibly strong. He had massive shoulders and was very muscular and compact in his body makeup. He didn't have a polarizing, threatening air to him like Frank Howard did with his size, but he had this powerful, sturdy demeanor about him that once he dug in, he looked as though he was about to unleash something to be talked about for a long time.

Harmon was stocky and so well built at 5 feet 11 inches. He had huge shoulders, big arms, and God-given strength that was overwhelming. When he signed with the Twins at the age of 17, the Twins certainly knew it.

Harmon Killebrew was very important in my life, both personally and professionally. As a kid growing up in the Twin Cities, Harmon quickly turned into the guy we all pretended to be when we were playing baseball at the playground or in the backyard.

During the time period in my life when the Twins arrived in 1961, that was all we did as kids. We played baseball and dreamed that someday we could play in the major leagues. And while I played, I dreamed I was Harmon Killebrew. I had his No. 3 on my back. I knew his stance and his swing by heart. I hit those epic blasts just like "The Killer" right there in my backyard.

When the Twins came to town, as I mentioned in an earlier chapter, I was the first one on our block to own and wear a Minnesota Twins baseball cap. I wore it everywhere. They were our ballclub, and our hero, of course, was Harmon Killebrew.

The Twins were playing outdoors at Metropolitan Stadium in Bloomington back then, and as kids we were playing baseball outdoors in the summer and doing a lot of pretending. I lived in a sports-nuts neighborhood in St. Louis Park, and we played baseball with a great deal of passion and imagination. I don't know what all the other kids did, but when I came to bat, I would say to myself that I was Harmon Killebrew and it was the bottom of the ninth inning and "it's time to do something here."

Harmon gave us that. He was a folk hero for us. He was truly our Babe Ruth. He was our guy, a Minnesota Twin. And his name, I mean come on, are you kidding me?

His name wasn't Dick Jones or Bob Smith. It was Harmon Killebrew! I mean, you can't make it up. You always hear about great names: Dick Butkus of the Chicago Bears! Ray Nitschke of the Green Bay Packers! They had a ring to their name. Harmon Killebrew—it had the ring, the pizzazz. It was rhythmic. It always will be.

And remember the song. "There was Tony, the Killer, and Carew." Chills, chills, chills. "The Killer" as a nickname for the great slugger was so fitting, and ironically "The Killer" could not be further from the truth when describing Harmon's personality. He was the exact opposite. Harmon was as nice a person as he was a great ballplayer. They did not come any finer. He was a constant exhibition of class and kindness.

As kids growing up, watching the team develop and having that guy on our team hitting those magical, mammoth home runs was surreal. Here was this person bigger than life, and you hoped deep down inside that he would be that way in real life. You hoped that his personality and who he was as a person would be as iconic as he was on the field, on television, and in our living rooms. And he most certainly filled the bill.

All I knew back then was that I wanted to go to the ballpark so I could see Harmon Killebrew play. And maybe, just maybe if I were fortunate enough, it would be the day he hit a monster home run or maybe two.

And then I would come home and be him, act like him, and hit like him. If backyard imaginary worlds ever become a reality, I'll someday be with Harmon in Cooperstown. I would mimic his swing, walk like him, warm up like he did in the on-deck circle, and then, of course, hit one of his tape-measure home runs.

Unfortunately, I was never able to hit in real life the 500-foot home runs like Harmon was able to do. He had tremendous wrist strength and great bat speed, and he could really turn his powerful shoulders on the ball. And he had terrific timing.

I first got acquainted with Harmon Killebrew as a young reporter for WCCO television. I met him and spoke with him occasionally when assigned to do interviews for the sports news. Harmon was always very gracious. It was never about him but rather always about the team. He never focused anything on himself.

If you tried to talk to him about a personal accomplishment, he would acknowledge it but get right off the subject and back to the team. He would kind of brush it off and give the praise to someone else. "Well, you know, the other guys put me in a position to do it." Harmon was that way, deflecting things from himself and focusing on the Twins as a team.

He was always very humble about everything he did. He was incredibly modest and quiet. Yet, I was very nervous when I was around him. It wasn't that he did anything to make me feel that way. He was easy to talk with and easy to be around. It was just that he was Harmon Killebrew, and it seemed more appropriate for me to ask him for his autograph than to interview him.

The first time I met Harmon, I couldn't believe I was there with him. I was tongue-tied. And it wasn't just the first time; it was every time for a long, long while. I mean, this was Harmon Killebrew for crying out loud. It was my fault that I felt like that, not his. He always had a way about him that put you at ease. It was just who he was that made it difficult. I mean, this guy was an icon on the ball field and in life. He was extraordinarily special.

As I mentioned earlier, I was pretty much a rookie when I was assigned to cover Harmon as he approached his 500th home run. As Harmon got closer and closer to this monumental milestone, my assignment with a photographer was to be there when he hit it.

Remember now, this was long before baseball games were being regularly televised. The Twins in 1971 were coming off divisional championships in 1969 and 1970, but the 1971 team was not a great baseball team. For some of the games, the attendance was not very good.

On a warm summer night, they might draw only 12,000 or 13,000. It was not like today's media age in which there is often a heavy focus on the feat of a particular individual. Today, it doesn't seem to matter how well a team is doing. If an individual is hitting a particular mark in the record books, there is coverage by the media.

When a certain record is broken or a milestone is set, the event is celebrated and the player is put on a pedestal and there are press conferences and wide coverage. Back in Harmon's day, it was not the case. It was a totally different situation at that time.

I was out there night after night waiting for Harmon to hit his 500th home run. I had to be there. Every at-bat was an important one. We had to get every single at-bat on film. You only get one shot at something like this, and if you miss it, well, the result is obvious. There won't be a second chance.

We were using 16 millimeter film out there every day at the ballpark, and nothing happened. Nothing happened again the next day and the next. Finally in August 1971, he hit number 500 off Baltimore pitcher Mike Cuellar.

So now with the home run in the record books, it was my job to go and talk to Harmon after the game about the historic moment. The Twins lost the game and I went to the clubhouse for the interview. I had to send the film to the network the next day.

This was also going to be my big moment because they would be using my interview, my voice on this, which would allow me to join the union of which I am still a member to this day.

I walked into the clubhouse and saw Harmon sitting by his locker. You would not have known if he had just hit number eight of his career or number 500. The Twins lost the game and he was upset about that. He was more bothered by the fact that they lost than he was joyous over his 500th home run. I mean, he said a few things about it being great to have accomplished the feat, but again he was more concerned with the defeat.

"We lost the game," was probably the most significant thing he said. Can you imagine today's athlete being more concerned about the loss of the game than his own personal accomplishments?

This wasn't a game in which a player got four hits or hit a couple home runs. It wasn't a walk-off homer in the tenth inning. This was a game in which a man had just hit his 500th home run. Think about that. Five hundred home runs and exactly what that means. Harmon's humbleness was overwhelming.

With today's media frenzy and hype, first of all the game would likely have been televised on ESPN. The country and every baseball fan would have been waiting for the milestone to be reached. There would have been multiple news conferences, and the event would have been glamorized beyond belief.

I recall when Jim Thome hit his 600th home run in 2011. He was with the Twins at the time, and I lost count of the number of times his homer was shown on television—over and over again, during the game, after the game, on all the sports programs all over the country. There was a press conference for Jim after the game, and he was honored again when the Twins returned home from their road trip. He was given gifts and truly recognized for the magnificent feat that he had accomplished. Jim certainly deserved the coverage, but I always felt that Killebrew did as well.

For Harmon, there was no media attention to really speak of. There was no special media room set up. I think I may have been the only television reporter there covering the event. It wasn't anything like today. No one said, "Harmon, let's go through your career and talk about what it means to you to hit your 500th home run. Did you ever believe you would reach this pinnacle of success when you were growing up as a kid in Idaho?" There was none of that.

There was no massive celebration, and even Harmon, as I mentioned, was more upset over the loss that night. Later in the game, he hit home run number 501. I think back on the night and the home run and I feel bad. He was deserving of so much more attention for what he had accomplished in his career. It makes me sad to think back and to visualize him sitting by his locker as if nothing had happened.

At that time, I didn't know him. I was 19 years old, just a rookie in the business. He was always pleasant and nice to me, like he was with everyone else. He didn't know me, but he was cordial and respectful at all times. I was just a kid doing my job, and I continued to follow him and his career with the Minnesota Twins—only to have to watch his career come to an end in Kansas City, of all places. The greatest player in Twins history didn't even end his career here.

The Twins released Killebrew in 1975, and he signed with Kansas City only to be released again the following year. He hit .199 with 14 home runs, and then he decided to retire. In reality, he retired as a Minnesota Twin and was a part of the organization until his death in 2011.

Killebrew with the balls from his 500th and 501st home runs. *Bruce Bennett Studios/ Getty Images*

It was tough for Harmon to leave Minnesota, and I'm sure he would be able to tell story after story of Calvin Griffith's miserly ways in dealing with player contracts. There are thousands and thousands of stories about that part of Twins baseball.

In many ways, it is kind of an afterthought that Harmon ever played a year with the Kansas City Royals. For the fans, I don't think it was any big deal. He just happened to end his career there. But to us, even though he was in Kansas City for a short time, he was always a Minnesota Twin. It would have been nice for him to play his entire career in Minnesota, but it didn't work out that way.

* * *

Killebrew was a leader. He was a quiet leader who led by example and had great respect for the game. He expected the game to be played the right way. He was never judgmental and was always very accepting of others and their differences, whether it be their approach to the game or cultural differences.

He played with different personalities through the years, but Harmon was the marquee guy, and they all looked to him for leadership and as the person they could count on for the big play or the big home run. He earned respect by his consistency and the way he went about playing the game. At the same time, they knew he was their meal ticket, the guy who was going to get them to where they wanted to go.

Harmon would kid around once in a while, but he had his limits. After all, and he would have been the first to admit it, he was not the most exciting guy in the world. If asked, "What do you do for excitement?" he might come up with, "I like to wash dishes," or something like that.

It took awhile to get to know Harmon. Like Bud Grant in many respects, it was later in my adult life that I really got to know him. I was able to spend time with him and have conversations as almost a peer in some respects. Our relationship became closer in the later years as we got to know each other better. It took some time, though.

In the beginning, I was just a kid earning my stripes, hardly a time to become friends with an iconic figure.

I have devoted a chapter of this book to Harmon Killebrew because he was better than advertised. He was everything childhood dreams are made of. And he lived up to every ounce of expectations. He was a very important person in my life.

It doesn't matter what kind of business you are talking about—whether it be entertainment, politics, business, or sports—we as a society put people on pedestals. We like to build them up and tear them down. That's just how our culture works.

And Harmon, like everyone else, has had his issues, personal matters that have been a disruption in his life. But the fact is that when it is all said and done, he was truly far better than advertised. What I mean by that is he had a tremendous passion for others. The way he treated everyone was marvelous. He had a kind word for everyone. I saw that in him over all the years I knew him. He always found time to deliver a kind word for me whenever I was with him.

Harmon was for the most part a pretty private person—some say actually kind of boring. He got some criticism when he did the Twins telecasts years back for being too kind and not offering up negatives, even when deserved. He was low-key, quiet, and reserved.

For decades, I watched Harmon teach young ballplayers and touch their lives. I have watched him show young players how to sign an autograph. I saw him literally lecture young players on the importance of signing a baseball. "Sign the ball so that when they take it home they know who signed it, young man," I heard him say.

Now Harmon Killebrew is not necessarily an easy name to sign on a baseball or piece of memorabilia. It's not like, "I'd like to buy a vowel from Vanna White on the *Wheel of Fortune*."

It is a long name, but if you find something that he signed, the signature would be perfect, absolutely perfect. There is no doubt whose name is written. His writing is beautifully perfect. It flows like his career did. You look at some signatures that players put on a ball and there is no way you could ever tell who signed it. It is disrespectful to the fan and to the game. It is about respect for the game, and Harmon had it and he wanted to see it from others.

I understand the problems that go with it—long lines, long days—but to Harmon it was important, and he felt it was necessary to take the time and do it right. This small part of what he did was an extension of his love, passion, and respect for the game and the fans who adored him.

* * *

I'm somewhat of a romantic when it comes to a lot of these kinds of things. It goes back to my life as a kid, following sports, following baseball, going to games with my dad. I was asked once, I think it was by someone in the Twins organization, "What was the biggest moment that you had at the old Met Stadium watching the Twins play baseball?"

I didn't pause for one second or hesitate for an instant. I responded almost before the question was completed and said, "I was there the game before the All-Star Game in 1965 against the New York Yankees. The Twins were trailing 5–4 in the bottom half of the ninth inning and Harmon Killebrew hit a home run into the left field seats to win it. I will never forget it."

Just last year, I saw former Twin Rich Rollins at spring training and we talked about it. Rich had gotten a base hit to keep the inning alive, and then Harmon hit his game-clinching home run at the end. It kept the Twins in the pennant race, which they eventually won. They went on to face the Dodgers in the 1965 World Series. Later in the All-Star Game, Killebrew hit another, a three-run clout for the American League.

It was an easy answer to the question of my greatest memory at the old Met Stadium. I remembered it so well. I was with my dad, which made it more special, and I can picture the ball going into the left field stands like it was yesterday. It was an unbelievable moment. It was so sweet. I was dancing on air for an entire week after that.

I told that story recently to a friend about being asked for my most memorable moment at Met stadium, and before I could tell him what my answer was, he replied, "I was there. I saw it. Killebrew's home run in the bottom of the ninth to beat the Yankees the day before the All-Star break!"

I'm sure that anyone who was there that day recalls the memory as we do. I actually had a plaque made up with my quote about the home run, and I had Harmon on my Sunday night show, *Rosen's Sports Sunday*.

I shared the story with him. I told him about me being asked by the Twins the question about my favorite moment, and I told him my answer about his home run. He was so appreciative. He was like, "Wow, you remember that, Mark? After all these years, you remember that as your greatest moment at Met stadium?" I said, "*Remember it*? You made me the happiest kid in the world that day. It was one of the greatest moments in Twins history! How could I forget it?"

He truly appreciated it. He really did. It was like going up to an actor as my mom would do. "You know, I remember seeing you in such-and-such performance back in 1972," or whatever it was, and the actor replying with, "Wow, you remember that way back then? Thank you."

So, instead of Harmon going "Oh, yeah, thanks" and moving on, he made me feel really good that I chose that moment. He was truly appreciative. He was that way with people. It was never about him.

* * *

Our relationship got closer and closer as time went on. I have had the opportunity to play a round of golf with Harmon. I had had him on my show for many years. He was very involved in the "Miracle Field" organization, which has helped kids with disabilities to play baseball. He used to come into the Twin Cities every year and did a big event. As I mentioned, I also had a chance to play golf with him a couple years ago at Tom Lehman's fundraiser for cancer research. Wow, walking the golf course with Harmon Killebrew. It still feels like a dream.

I remember having a pretty big gallery following us, and it made me very nervous. Harmon told me, "Just hit one good on the first tee and on hole No. 10 because there won't be many with us after that." He was just giving me a little pep talk, and it worked some because on the tenth hole I hit a long 3 wood on the par-3 and put it right on the green. And Harmon gave me one of those "Nice going" compliments, and all I could think was, "Wow, Harmon Killebrew said 'Nice going' to me."

I recall that he was really hurting as we walked down the hill at the Minneapolis Golf Club to the tenth green. It was before he had his knee replacements, and he mentioned to me how he needed to get it done. So here I was, just casually talking to Harmon as we walked to the green. It was special—a memory never to be forgotten.

The other part about golfing with Harmon Killebrew was watching him drive the golf ball. It is sort of the same way when I used to put everything on pause when he came to bat. You never wanted to miss him use his driver off the tee. No, you do not want to miss that! Even the pro golfers would be envious.

It was always a great thrill to have Harmon Killebrew on my show. I was in awe every single time.

Seeing Harmon with a driver in his hand took me back to his days of holding a 36-ounce bat with pine tar on it about to launch the baseball some 525 feet into the stratosphere.

His home runs were unbelievable. When he connected, there was never a doubt. He hit it higher, further, and louder than the other hitters, like a missile being shot in the air.

I was at the stadium when he hit the gigantic blast into no-man's land, the upper deck at Metropolitan Stadium. No one ever had done that before or after. After Harmon hit the home run, the team replaced the seat with a giant target, to be remembered forever. I recall watching opposing players come in and stand at home plate and look to the location in absolute amazement. "You have got to be kidding me," was a common remark. "No one could possibly hit a baseball that high and far."

I can't imagine where that ball would have landed at Target Field, the Twins' new ballpark. Harmon was the measuring stick for long balls. He was one of just a few sluggers to clear the roof at the old Tiger Stadium in Detroit and he hit some incredible homers at Griffith Stadium in Washington when with the Senators and at Baltimore's Memorial Stadium. He could hit the ball as far as anyone.

Like most who were at the ballpark when Harmon reached the upper deck, I was in shock. It was truly an unbelievable sight to see the ball land where it did. There was a surreal moment that took over the ballpark. It was as if what we had just seen could not possibly have occurred. I'm convinced the opposing players would have liked to have come out of their dugout and given him a standing ovation. I don't know how you couldn't. I mean, no one could humanly hit a baseball that far. I was positively convinced of it, and I had just seen it happen!

And then what a lot of people don't remember, the next day Harmon hit another one that bounced off the facing of the upper deck. It was like he had a rocket launcher and was stationed at Cape Canaveral.

I know that Reggie Jackson hit some titanic blasts and Mickey Mantle had awakened the ghosts of the past with some of his home runs, but this? This was something!

I recall going with my dad to a game at Yankee Stadium and seeing Mantle hit a mammoth home run that is still talked about in New York. It was my first game there. We took the subway out, and Mantle hit one of the longest home runs in baseball history off the White Sox. He hit it left-handed, and it went over the fence near the outfield spot they called "Death Valley" because the field went so deep. So up until that point, it was the longest I had ever seen. And then Harmon hit his.

After, it wasn't like a pitcher would brush Harmon back or try to play some head game with him. No, no, that wasn't going to happen. They had too much respect for him to do something like that.

Harmon had some quirkiness to him also. Back in the day, when he started losing his hair a little, he always carried his cap in his back pocket while at the plate. This was so when he got on base and removed the batting helmet, he could in one sweeping motion take off the batting helmet with one hand and put the baseball cap on in an instant motion with the other hand. He was brilliant, like a magician at work.

I often wonder what he would be like playing today with all of his momentous strength. Remember, he played the game when the league was not watered down as it is today with so many teams. Those were the days when the players in the major leagues were all exceptional because of the few teams, unlike today.

I used to kid him about it. Once I said to him, "Harmon, how many home runs do you think you would hit in a season if you were playing today?" He said, "Maybe about 25." I said, "Harmon, only 25 home runs, come on, against this pitching?" I recall he looked at me with a little grin and said, "Keep in mind, Mark, I'm 68 years old."

As the years went by, I had him on my show so often that I got to feel as if I knew him pretty well. I felt somewhat close to him. I don't know if he felt the same about me. I hope he did. When I talked with him, I always felt that kid inside me. He never knew it, but I really did feel that way.

I mean, it's my show and I was going to be speaking with him as a peer, but yet inside me I was a kid all over again. Every single time.

I'm glad I felt that way. I mean, let's face reality here. I was talking to Harmon Killebrew. How could I have felt differently?

I know when I drive out to the Mall of America and see the street sign marked Killebrew Drive, I get goose bumps. It doesn't say Street or Lane; it says Killebrew Drive. So appropriate. Thousands of people pass it and drive on it every day and never give it a thought. There are likely many who don't even know who Harmon Killebrew is.

Every time I walk inside the Mall of America and see the place where home plate at the Met once was placed and see the spot where his mammoth home run shot landed, I close my eyes and try to recall every second of his at-bat. I think of the song "This Used to Be My Playground" by Madonna. I love the Twins and think about them often from the past, and a trip to the Mall of America brings me so many wonderful memories.

So much of my life was at the old stadium. I had so many great moments there with my father and so many of Harmon and what he represented to the Twins and to me. It has come full circle for me. I watched him as a youngster, interviewed him as a reporter, and called him my friend.

When it was announced that he was ill, I felt that he had just turned a corner in his life and had so much more to give. He left us too soon. He had so much more to give.

Because of this, I give the Twins franchise so much credit for the manner in which they treated Harmon and some of the other greats, such as Tony Oliva and Rod Carew, to keep them as a part of the organization. It is very special what they have done and what they continue to do for these players.

I love to watch parents take their kids to the statue of Harmon outside Target Field. And you just know what they are saying: "Now, that's Harmon Killebrew. He used to play for the Twins, and you should have seen him because he was really something! I know we have some great players like Mauer and Morneau, but you should have seen this guy hit a baseball."

For the kids, there is not much of an expression on their faces because, well, they are just looking at a statue. Maybe someday the kids will grow up and understand who this great player and gentle man truly was.

My real joy comes from looking at how excited fathers get. They want their kids to experience what they remember. I see it in their smiles. I see them pointing at the statue of Harmon, pointing to his mighty arms, his massive shoulders, and the great batting stance of his.

Harmon was so terrific with the fans. He was such a nice guy. The fans could relate to him because they got to learn and see what a nice person he was in addition to being a superstar athlete.

In many respects, he was mythical in terms of his personality as well. He could have had a bombastic personality, but he didn't. He wasn't a Mickey Mantle, a carouser, a nightlife person. It was like this guy was meant to be here in the Twin Cities.

If Mickey Mantle had spent his career in Minnesota, what would that have been like? If Harmon Killebrew had been a Yankee, what would that have been like? I guess we will never know the answer to that question.

Roger Maris was probably more like the personality of a Minnesota Twin, more quiet, more reserved. Roger didn't like the attention, all the celebrity status. He was a North Dakota kid. He didn't like being in the national media spotlight. He definitely would have fit in better here in the Twin Cities like Killebrew did.

* * *

I used to watch the old television show *Home Run Derby*. In fact, it was shown again not all that long ago. I watched one contest that pitted Harmon Killebrew vs. Mickey Mantle. It was something. They showed the part of the program in which the player not batting would do some of the commentary, and I remember Harmon saying, "Wow, Mickey really hit that one." It was just as pure as watching some kids at the playground pitching and hitting.

I think Harmon was deeply bothered by the cheating in the game, with the steroid usage and things like that. Some of the great records in all of baseball have been tarnished forever. Although Harmon had not been real outspoken on the subject, I do believe it is one of the reasons he had strongly supported the records being set by Jim Thome of the Twins.

Jim is like a left-handed version of Harmon, and I believe Harmon had such a great appreciation for what Jim did with his home run records that he just beamed when Thome hit one. Harmon could not have been more gracious when Thome passed his 573rd home run two seasons ago. Jim Thome has the same kind of reputation as Harmon with his engaging, respectful nature and obvious appreciation for the game of baseball.

It all seemed to work out for the Twins and for Harmon. Coming here from Washington as the hero with the new ballclub and a great personality, it was a great fit. The fans through the generations have looked at him as the face of the Minnesota Twins.

I give the Twins so much credit for recognizing the past. Harmon has his own section at Target Field, an area with tributes to his accomplishments. The pictures, memorabilia, and other things bring back the memories and remind us what this great slugger meant to the organization. One of the great quotes I recall was from former major league manager Paul Richards, who said, "Harmon could hit a baseball out of any park, including Yellowstone."

Upon viewing the area set aside as a remembrance to what he had accomplished, Harmon, in typical fashion, said, "Oh, this is too much. I don't deserve all this." It was easy for me to respond. "Yes, you do deserve all this. Look what you did!"

Besides the statue and his own section, Harmon has a gate named after him at the ballpark. All well deserved. He even has his own root beer named after him—another fitting tribute to a great slugger and wonderful man.

He hit more home runs than any player in the 1960s in a league with fewer teams and more quality ballplayers. He was one of the greatest home run hitters of all time. The game was different back then. To think of hitting 573 home runs, well, that's a pretty big number.

In baseball, numbers are more important than in any other sport. Stats are baseball. Killebrew was one of the greatest home run hitters of all time, and in the process he exuded class at the highest of levels. He was first-class all the way. He knew what his lot in life was. He knew who he was and what he had become. And through it all, it was his genuineness that always stood out. That's all we really want from anyone, for them to be genuine. He had the class and was purely genuine to a fault.

Harmon always had such an appreciation for his place in baseball history. He understood what he meant to the fans and, even more importantly, what they meant to him. His presence when he walked into a room was breathtaking. People looked up from what they were doing. They pointed toward him or mentioned, "There's Harmon Killebrew."

Even after all the years I knew him, I wasn't sure how to act around him. On the one hand, I enjoyed so much talking with him as a peer, and yet on the other hand—because I had admired him so much as a kid—I wanted to jump up and point to him and shout out, "You're Harmon 'Fricken' Killebrew!"

I can't begin to tell you how many times as a youngster that I went home after a game, went out in the backyard, threw a ball up in the air, and imagined I was Harmon Killebrew trying to hit the ball over my neighbor's roof. "Here we go, Harmon Killebrew's at the plate . . . " Over and over again.

I have my special recollections of his career. Obviously, his home run against the Yankees that I mentioned earlier before the All-Star break in 1965 was a great memory. Conversely, his shoulder injury in 1967 devastated me and, of course, the ballclub. As a fan, his injury truly crushed me. Those times really have stood out for me as both the positive and negative moments of his great career.

The games and the home runs are all memorable for all sorts of reasons. I remember how Harmon always tipped his hat to the fans. He was never one for curtain calls. They never did that much back in the day, but Harmon would always show his appreciation to the fans by tipping his hat as they cheered his home run. When he crossed home plate, he gave that little tip, telling all those watching, "Thanks, I hear ya."

I was so proud to have him as a friend. It made me feel so wonderful when he was nice to me, introduced me to his family, and all the other things he did for me and the community. He meant so much to me. It isn't just the memories; it's so much more than that. I thank him for being the personality I always wanted him to be. He taught me so much about humbleness, about how to treat people, and about how to be professional. He had class and presence, and it was everywhere around him. He was real with people.

I am 60 years old, for Pete's sake. I have been around broadcast journalism for more than four decades. I'm not wearing a baseball uniform in my backyard any longer, except perhaps on the days I get into deep thought about Harmon. Then even at my age, sometimes my mind takes me to my backyard and the uniform is back on again.

I am not naive. I know what it takes to be on top and stay on top. I think I have somewhat of an understanding of what he had to do just to be Harmon Killebrew and keep his magnificent reputation intact. I have such an appreciation for the road he must have traveled. The fact is, he was a baseball player, not a brain surgeon. He was just a baseball player, wasn't he?

Well, not in this community he wasn't. He was Harmon Killebrew. Because he showed how to combine talent with genuineness and appreciation like none other, he was a role model in every way.

When you watched Harmon Killebrew treat people the way he did through the years—the handshakes, looking people in the eye— it made him different and special.

* * *

I have had hundreds and hundreds of sports personalities on *Rosen's Sports Sunday*. When I sat there and said, "Good evening, everyone. Welcome to *Rosen's Sports Sunday*, live from our Channel 4 studios. And with me in our studio tonight . . . ." And I would just start smiling . . . I didn't even try to hide it . . . what else can I say? "Harmon Killebrew is here." And everyone who was at home and remembered was smiling right along with me.

"How are you doing, Harmon?" And his reply was always so sincere. "Great, Mark. It's great to be with you in the studio tonight. Thanks for having me on your show." And I'm just . . . "okay." He was so sincere. There I was, spending 25 minutes on the air with Harmon Killebrew.

It's not like his answers to my questions were that great. He was not going to set the world on fire with what he said. We have enough people around doing that. He just talked common sense about the way baseball should be played and the way many of us remember it being played.

I can't imagine how uncomfortable it would have been for him in New York, dealing with all the media and everything else. If he had been in pinstripes all those years, it might have been very difficult for him. But in Minneapolis and St. Paul, where he was so beloved, it became easy for him here. It was perfect for him in a state that recognizes Paul Bunyan—what a similarity.

Thanks, Harmon. You were always there for me. You turned my backyard hero into a real person of honor and respectability. You made a difference in my life and influenced me in such a positive way.

A few days before Harmon died, I sent him an email through Kevin Smith of the Minnesota Twins. I'm so glad I got it to him before he passed. The email read as follows:

Dear Harmon,

I'm having trouble finding the words to describe the level of impact you had on my life. You cast a huge shadow over my childhood here in Minneapolis as a kid growing up in the '60s. We all pretended to be Harmon Killebrew in our neighborhood baseball games. Your baseball card was the first one I grabbed with delight when I opened that package with the pink bubblegum.

My dad could afford to take me to about 15 games a year, and I mentioned to you that when asked after the demolition of Met Stadium what my biggest thrill was, without hesitation I said when Harmon hit that ninth-inning home run off the Yankees in the game before the All-Star break in 1965. I have a plaque proudly displaying my quote and a picture of the Old Met with you in it.

I want you to know that I am in the process of writing a book about my 40+ years of experience at WCCO TV, and I just recently completed my chapter about you and the impact you had on my life. I want as many people as possible to know that the Harmon Killebrews of the world are like that rare comet.

My first TV break was interviewing you after you hit your 500th home run in 1970. The Twins lost, so in typical Harmon fashion, you downplayed the importance of your individual achievement. In today's world, that player would have been all about getting on ESPN.

The amount of positive feedback I received every time you were on my *Rosen's Sports Sunday* show topped every other guest I've ever had on. I thank you from the bottom of my heart for teaching me the values that I try to live by every day. To understand our "celebrity" has meaning only when we give back to our community. On behalf of the countless people who have written or called me the past few days, we love you, Harmon. I love you, Harmon!

Mark Rosen
WCCO TV Sports Director

Harmon Killebrew's memorial at Target Field. A very sad day for me.

10

Radio and a Run for Governor

I really believe I had a chance to win. The chapter title is correct. I have been involved in radio broadcasting for many years and, yes, I really did run for governor for the State of Minnesota.

It wasn't one of those mornings when I woke up and decided this was a good day to announce my candidacy. It didn't happen quite that way, but close. The announcement came from KQRS radio in the Twin Cities that "Little Markie" Rosen was going to run for governor.

* * *

My son was born in December 1985, and I soon realized that my days of sleeping late in the morning were over. So when I got an opportunity to do some morning sports work for KQRS, I jumped at the offer.

Mark Steinmetz was the general manager at the station, and he called and said they would love to have me do some morning sports for them. No one was really doing this kind of thing back then, so I thought it would be something new and fun to do. At the time, Tom Barnard, a longtime radio personality, had not as yet started at KQ92.

I was told I didn't even have to go to the station to report the sports news. I could do it right from home. They set it all up for

My early days at KQRS in 1986, getting ready to broadcast from home with my young son, Nick.

me, and it worked great. The station ran a line to my home. I put on some headsets, and we were all set to do my three-minute piece in the mornings.

I did a typical short sports update for them after getting clearance from WCCO television to work at another station. I was already doing a little bit with WLTE radio with a call-in from time to time, but nothing really official. It turned out to be no problem for me to get up early in the morning and begin working in early 1986 for KQRS.

I had been doing the morning sports for a couple of months when I got a call in late March from the program director, who asked me, "Mark, have you ever heard of Tom Barnard?" I told him that I had heard the name but didn't know anything about him. I was told,

"Well, he is starting tomorrow morning on KQ. He is your new guy."
I thought, "Fine, okay."

For a short time, we went on the air together without meeting.
I was at home with the headsets and he was in the studio. One
morning, Barnard made some crack, kind of poking fun at me, and
we both started laughing. After that, we really hit it off. It was about
two to three weeks before we actually met each other, and it was then
we found out that we had a lot more in common than you could
ever imagine.

We were both born in North Minneapolis, although I was not
raised there like Tom was. We were born six days apart in the same
year. He is November 7 and I am November 13. We have always
remembered that. So we had a common thread that linked us, and we
hit it off very well on the air as well. We just seemed to connect and
really had a great time working together.

I was doing this little three-minute sports quip in the morning
with him, and this turned into a half hour and then even more. It
progressed to me doing my morning bit with Tom, taking my son to
daycare, and then driving over to the station for further air time in
the studio.

I would do two segments, with the second session lasting about
40 minutes. We would talk sports and everything else. We became
personality driven. We helped each other. I gave Tom the credibility
that he had been lacking, and he gave me the visibility and the
exposure I never had before.

The program just exploded in popularity. It went from about a five
share rating to a 15. It was Tom, his running mate Dan Culhane, and
me, and the show was a huge hit. As time went on, we really got into
the Twins and other subjects and started developing a tremendous
fan base. People really got into us. The station and our time together
became tremendously popular.

I was still very much involved in my primary job with WCCO
television, but in doing a three-minute bit on the air, I never really
had a chance to be myself. Radio work and Tom Barnard brought
that out in me.

I think I actually could have won the race for governor. Wouldn't that have been something?

At some point in 1986—I forget the exact date because of so much apathy in the governor's race—we spent a lot of time talking about it on the air. One day, Barnard came out and said that KQRS should endorse "Markie Rosen for governor." It started out as a joke, but it developed legs like you can't believe. The comment absolutely caught fire and spread everywhere. It was amazing how quickly it caught people's attention.

Now, of course, I could not officially declare my candidacy or I would have to be off the air, and as I say, it all started just as a joke. We thought it would be good to use as a fundraiser. But let me tell you, it was a grass fire in a dry field with lots of wind. In fact, later on, former Minnesota governor and past professional wrestler Jesse Ventura said to me, "It was you, Rosen, that inspired me to make the run for governor." So, I guess it is my fault that Jesse became the governor.

It just mushroomed. It did show that personalities, not only politicians, if you surround yourself with the right people, have a chance in even a high-profile race for governor. You can make it happen. Now, I had the benefit of being on the radio with this powerful station backing me up, and in addition they started a marketing plan. I was running for governor.

They sold buttons for 92 cents—get it, KQ92—with the proceeds going to the United Way. We sold tons and tons of buttons. The promotion also include a couple of songs sung on the air to the tunes of *The Dick Van Dyke Show* and *Rawhide*.

"Rosen, Rosen, Rosen, Little Markie Rosen, Channel 4 Markie Rosen, the sports guy . . ." It went on and on, and people loved it. There were lawn signs being put up all over, and the college campuses really went crazy with it.

In the beginning, WCCO television seemed somewhat amused by the whole thing. It was a lesson in marketing for them. They were locally owned at the time, and eventually the popularity of the show led to my demise at KQRS. KQ had marketed me, and nothing like this had ever been done before. WCCO certainly had not done it, and the whole experience was basically a new kind of programming concept.

Overall, it helped Channel 4 because I was getting all this attention. I had really responsible-looking people coming up to me on the street and saying, "Look, I am serious about this. I am going to vote for you for governor." I would reply, "Are you crazy?"

The governor's race that year, before I got all the attention, was between Cal Ludeman and Rudy Perpich. I don't think Rudy thought too much of what I was doing, but Ludeman actually attended one of our promotion fundraisers. I could not believe it, but there he was.

One of our events was a big fundraiser at the Met Center. The Lamont Cranston Band showed up, and it was quite a night. I was amazed at the people there. I had people from their teens, 20s, all the way to those in their 60s and 70s saying, "I'm going to vote for you."

Yes, it did start as a joke, but there became a point in the minds of many thousands where it was no longer a joke. "Little Markie" Rosen in their eyes was a legitimate candidate for governor of the State of Minnesota.

Cal Ludeman had a good sense of humor about the whole thing, and it was fantastic to see him at one of our events. Our goal with the whole thing from the beginning was to raise a lot of money, but it went farther than we ever anticipated.

We actually had an election headquarters. Do you believe that? Well, we did. It was at the Holiday Inn at the University of Minnesota. We had a ballroom much like any other candidate would have on election night.

The place was packed. I had a suite upstairs and would come down from time to time to address the crowd and make announcements. I would say something like, "I'm not conceding anything yet"—that sort of thing. I would make promises like "a CD player in every home if I am elected"—important things like that for the crowd to chew on.

The newspapers picked up on the whole thing and also ran with it. They had a lot of fun with it, and it gave my run for governor pretty good attention. I would guess we started the "run" in late spring, and by September it was humming—absolutely unbelievable!

In reality, it truly demonstrated how peeved much of the public was at the politicians for them to grab onto something like we were creating.

On October 18, we had a pre-game/election fundraiser with thousands of people in attendance. I recall getting up on stage and actually believing "I could win." I am convinced that if I had taken this whole thing seriously, put myself on the ballot, and surrounded myself with smart people, I could have won and been the governor. I am serious and sincerely believe it might have happened.

Please don't take this as an egotistical statement because I do not mean it that way at all. I am saying this because look what happened later on. Jesse Ventura, a professional wrestler, became the governor of the state. And if that can occur, well, then I know that I had a legitimate chance. I really believe that. Whoever thought Jesse could win?

I got 9,000 write-in votes. Nine thousand! Think about that. Nine thousand people got up on election day, drove to their voting place, went behind the curtain, and wrote my name on the ballot for the governor of Minnesota. Nine thousand people did that. I would have been hard-pressed in the beginning to think anyone would do it. But 9,000—are you kidding me? I felt bad for the people who had to count all the votes.

I had a lot of fun with it at the rallies and fundraisers, talking at the high schools, and the whole promotion aspect of it. But to this day, I still have people coming up to me and saying, "I voted for you for governor. You should have been our governor." I usually start

NINE THOUSAND VOTES!!!! Can you believe that?

laughing and reply, "Well, it's never too late." Now, I sometimes wish I would have won.

It shows you the power and influence that a person can have when you make a connection with people. It was a rally against the man, the establishment.

Cal Ludeman, at one point during a speech at our rally, referred to a T-shirt that said "Ludeman in 86 and Rosen in 94." I responded to the cheering crowd by saying, "With all due respect, Mr. Ludeman, I think it is the other way around." I appreciated the fact that he came out to our event, and although he didn't ultimately win the election, I have a lot of respect for him.

I also got to know Perpich a little bit, but as I said I don't think he was very amused by what I was doing. I think he felt I might take votes away from him, especially if it was a close race with Ludeman.

It was one of those moments in time where after it was over, you just kind of take a step back and say, "WOW, what in the world was that?"

Tom Barnard and I had great fun with it all, and we will never forget it. As for Tom, I always felt he took my election loss personally. He was quoted later as saying, "If I had done a better job as Mark's campaign manager, he could have been governor of the State of Minnesota!"

* * *

KQRS was a great place to work. I loved it. As we sat in that little smoke-filled trailer over on Lilac Way next to their building at KQ, and saw the comments coming in, we knew we had a program that had become something very special. The popularity of what we were doing was off the charts. Working with Tom and what we had done with sports had taken off.

The governor's race and that whole thing was big, but the show took off even more in 1987 when the Twins won their first World Series. KQRS was not the official radio rights holders for the team, but we were the station for the Minnesota Twins. The popularity of our commentary, especially on the team that year, was immense.

We had become the connection for the fans every morning. Every time the Twins were in first place, we would play what we called the "light and happy music." They didn't win all that many games that year, just 85, so they were in and out of first place quite often.

Fans would literally listen for the music. It really caught on with everyone. People would go nuts because if they heard the music they knew the Twins were in first place in the standings. It was almost like you could hear fans roaring through their radios. We were their connection.

The listeners were involved with us, and through us they became closer to their favorite baseball team. The Twins organization even picked up on it. They started playing the music at the Metrodome. That's how big this became. We had KQRS days at the Dome, and we set up in the second deck and people packed the place up there. So, we rode this mighty wave of our local heroes all the way through the season.

Many of the guys on the team fell into it with us and showed their support. They heard about it and realized what was going on. Players such as Gary Gaetti, Kent Hrbek, and others rode the wave with us and the fans. It was their generation, their time, and the connection was truly magical.

It became really clear the day the Twins opened the playoff series against the Detroit Tigers. Kirk Gibson was the left fielder for Detroit, and KQ brought in this guy to perform some type of voodoo, poke some pins in a Gibson doll, and other stuff to stymie Gibson. Everyone, and I mean absolutely everyone, in the left field stands knew about it.

When Kirk Gibson went out in the field in the first inning, he got this voodoo chant, which supposedly put a curse on him. I don't know if it worked, but he did nothing to hurt us. In fact, he sucked.

I just sat there with my mouth open. There were thousands of people who joined in, and it showed the power that the KQ morning show had with its listeners. First the governor's race and now this. I was having a really good time.

When the Twins went on to win the World Series, it heightened our popularity and ratings even more. I often felt more a part of it than just being behind a microphone on radio. I mean, fans called out my name on some occasions as much as the players' names. It was surreal. It was a ride on a magic carpet the entire season.

We always felt like we were the radio station that got them there. We inspired the fan base. We had a perfect storm of advertising, and with it we capitalized on a bunch of players who were still with the team that had in previous seasons lost a multitude of games.

They had so many players who had been on losing teams: Frank "Sweet Music" Viola, Puckett, Hrbek, Gaetti, and others. The fans got to know all these guys, and the station had a lot to do with that. I had a lot to do with that. We were very proud of the connection and the notoriety we gave to the ballclub.

Tom Barnard was a huge baseball fan, so we were able to break it down every day on the air and literally put a face to the team. This became the incredible connection with the fans. Tom did several bits that got a lot of attention. It was never mean-spirited, always in good fun. And the listeners loved it.

* * *

As I mentioned, our success at KQRS laid the groundwork for my eventual departure from the radio station. The television station had to be somewhat careful with how it played out because, while it certainly increased my profile on the air at WCCO television, it took time away from programming at WCCO radio. It turned into a very bitter departure for me.

My popularity at KQRS was the foundation for putting my primary job on the line at WCCO. It seemed as though every time we had something big occur with a rally or something, I got kind of a cold reception at the station. Deep down, I always felt they liked what was happening at KQ but they could never give me a real thumb's up because what was going on hurt WCCO radio.

It wasn't that easy to fix, either. They couldn't just tell me to stop at KQ and put me on WCCO radio. I had a contract, and in the past they had approved my work there and had not been interested in me working at WCCO radio.

I was okay with that and I was happy to start radio work at KQRS. By 1988, my contract was up there and I was told by WCCO management that maybe it was time for me to take a look at WCCO radio. And I thought, "Here we go. This is not going to be good." It became a real battleground—and a public one at that.

KQRS weighed in on it. Ron Simon was my agent, and he did the negotiating for me. Ron Handberg said something to me at the time, and I know he didn't mean it, but he said, "I think every KQ listener that you brought to Channel 4 is now here to stay, so it's time for you to move to WCCO radio." I thought, "He really didn't say that, did he?" In this business, you never stop marketing something like what we had at KQ. It was exactly the demographic we wanted for WCCO television.

Jim Rupp was the CEO at the station, and I knew he had a job to do. I knew it was his job to get me to WCCO radio. I had two terrific bosses at WCCO when I joined the radio station.

Steve Goldstein was the general manager and John Quick was the program director, and they were very sharp people. They had a vision for what the radio station would be like.

They had the superstars there. They had Boone and Erickson. They had Steve Cannon. Sid Hartman was there, and they had them all and they wanted me to be a part of it. But I didn't want to go. I was happy with what I was doing. I was very happy at KQ and I wanted to stay.

We had discussions. It got very public, and fans chimed in with "Saving Rosey" bits. There were roses sent to the station—that kind of thing. It was a very difficult time. It was a very tough position to be in. I was really caught between a rock and a hard place.

While all this was transpiring, no one ever came directly to me and said, "Look, you are either going to sign with WCCO radio or you are out on the street." That didn't happen, but it was certainly implied. I didn't want to lose my television job. It was my "A" job, and I was certainly tuned in to that aspect. I understood what was happening.

All of this had nothing to do with how WCCO radio was handling the negotiations. They were extremely fair to me in every respect. KQRS kind of felt that there was not much they could do, and their offer to keep me was not anything to write home about. I was hoping they would make the negotiations tougher by trying harder to keep me, but it didn't happen. They actually sort of threw in the towel, thinking they were in a losing battle. Apparently, they were not in a position to compete with WCCO.

KQRS was not happy at all about the situation. They felt like they had helped develop the popularity I had achieved and did not want me to leave. Deep down, though, they understood the dynamics that were going on.

To me, it was heartbreaking. I had to make the call. Steve Goldstein knew how hard this was for me, and had it not been for him, it would have been a lot more painful.

My last day at KQRS was very difficult for me. It was a very sad day. I gave a little talk on the air, thanking everyone, and afterward I really broke down in tears. I hated the thought of leaving something I had enjoyed so much. I loved the people there and loved working with Tom Barnard, who became as close to me as a brother could be. It was very hard to say goodbye.

I felt it was unfair what happened, and I still do to this day. It was the first time I really understood the politics of this business. A lot of my coworkers even thought the whole mess was craziness. They felt WCCO television should want you at KQ because of the popularity and demographics. But it didn't work that way. In fact, the CEO of both WCCO television and radio, Jim Rupp, made a television statement that it was time for "Little Markie" Rosen to grow up and become "Big Mark" Rosen. That hurt.

Jim Rupp was a stuffy guy, a stuffed-shirt type. And he gave marching orders to his subordinates at the television and radio stations. It wasn't pretty as they filtered down to me and basically said, "You can't do this anymore."

I got it. I understood it, and I suppose if I were in their shoes, I might have felt the same way. Still, it didn't make it any easier for me. So I moved on, believing maybe it was meant to be. Maybe it was the best it was going to be.

I did it all. I had the great relationship with Tom Barnard. We did the governor "run," had the Twins connection, and had a tremendous impact on the radio market. Maybe it was time. I told myself that anyway, and it helped some. Those three years at KQRS were magical, make-believe years, and I walked away with my head held high and a deep fondness for the people there.

Tom and I have a bond like brothers. For a while, we didn't talk or see each other. Tom is a very emotional guy, and the whole thing was very troubling to him. He was not upset with me, but he took the whole situation very hard. It did affect our relationship because I was not with him every day like I had been in the past, and that hurt both of us.

We got along so well. I was the one guy who really challenged Tom on that show, and he loved it. We knew each other inside and really connected on the air. We had a chemistry and rhythm that you could not make up.

I was replaced at KQRS by the sportscaster at Channel 5, Mark Curtis. He replaced me right away, and it was a disaster of epic proportions. Tom was mad that I was gone, and Curtis walked into

That's Tom Barnard, over my left shoulder. We became great friends and have remained so to this day.

the wrong place and got blistered. No one wanted to listen to him. The chemistry was off. I listened to the show in the morning and it was painful. Mark ended up leaving, and I think he is still on the air in the Phoenix market in news. It was just the wrong timing for him. He was a good guy, but it didn't work. It was a really bad gig for him.

* * *

So it was over at KQ, and I started with WCCO radio in 1989. They really laid out a welcome mat for me with a big Sunday morning breakfast at the Bierman Building on the University of Minnesota campus. They had a huge number of sports personalities attend. Players such as Kirby Puckett and Kent Hrbek, coaches, athletic directors, and many others all showed up, and it was a pretty special event for me. I was very honored by their kindness.

My dad came with me, and the station even invited the public to be there. I was very appreciative of the event, which was sort of their way of welcoming me to their family.

I was on the radio twice in the morning doing sportscasts with the anchors, and then I was on with Sid at 7:40 a.m. That was always interesting. And in the afternoon, I would be on with Steve Cannon and all the little Cannons. I got to officially meet his cast of voiced characters: Morgan Mundane, Ma Linger, and Backlash LaRue. It was quite a group.

It doesn't get any bigger than that. Boone and Erickson were still on, Sid, Cannon—I mean, wow, I was with some big-time talent. I did my sports bits with Charlie Boone and Roger Erickson, and then I would come on with Sid and we would banter back and forth, argue—you know how Sid is. I was doing all this strictly from my house in the morning. With Cannon in the afternoon, I did go to the station once in a while, but not very often.

Working with Steve Cannon was really tough at first. I ended up loving Steve, but in the beginning not so much. He really tested me. Here was a guy who rarely ever used call-ins. He called the process of the call-in a "crutch," and he did not like it. He had his cast of characters and thrived on them during his show.

Cannon was a radio dinosaur and a brilliant personality. He was an iconic figure in these parts of the Midwest and a local favorite among listeners. But as I said, he tested me. He would say in his deep, profound voice, "All right, Mark Rosen, who did you talk with at the Twins today? Who did you talk with at the Vikings offices?"

I recall one day when I was extremely busy with some other project, or whatever it was, and told Steve that I was tied up with something and didn't get a chance to speak with anyone from the teams. And Cannon said back to me right on the air, "Well, then, what good are you then?"

I was shocked. I couldn't believe he would say something like that live on the radio. I went, "Whoa!" I remember calling him at home that night and saying, "Steve, what was that about? It was just one of those days. I wasn't able to make my usual rounds like I normally do." He said, "Well, I just wanted to test you." And I told him, "Well, that was really unfair. Don't do that again." And he never did.

We ended up being very good friends. I used to pick him up and we would play golf together and he would give me his philosophy on life. I thoroughly enjoyed the time I spent with Steve. He was extremely opinionated about things and a very reclusive individual in a lot of ways. But when Steve Cannon was your friend, believe me, he was your friend.

He used to bring his bag lunch to work every day and would poke fun at himself for doing it. I would sit down with him at Twins games, and I often gave him a ride to his car when I was going back to the television station. So, I spent a lot of time with Stevo. We would talk religion, philosophy, sports, and whatever else was on his mind. We would gripe about things and talk about business, the weather, the economy—just about everything.

Steve was a mentor to me, too. This was Steve Cannon, for crying out loud. He passed away a few years ago, and I was really sad about his death. He was such a tremendous talent.

The one thing I will always recall about Steve was how much he hated doing the Minnesota State Fair from the WCCO radio booth. I think mostly it was because he couldn't have his group of characters with him. I guess Morgan, Ma, and Backlash were uncomfortable with large crowds.

They were all missing from the fair, and it took something away from the program because his fans loved his alter egos. He was so incredibly talented in that respect, and his audiences were mesmerized by his voices to the point of many not understanding the cast's true background.

Many never heard the actual story of Steve and Morgan's first encounter. It seemed that Cannon was attending the famous New York Giants and Baltimore Colts NFL Championship Game at Yankee Stadium in 1958, and the seat next to him at the game was empty until a "down on his luck" Morgan Mundane sat down. They struck up a conversation, and the rest is history. I'm not sure how Ma Linger and Backlash came to join Cannon.

I am so proud to say that I worked with Steve. There was never a point when I was at WCCO radio or KQRS that I didn't have great people working with me. I was blessed to be around people like Dave Moore, all the great reporters and photographers, Tom Barnard, Steve Cannon, Boone and Erickson, Sid, and the list goes on and on.

It was unfortunate for me that eventually Steve Goldstein left the radio station. It is a fact of the business. The really good people often move on, so it's important to not hitch your wagon to a star because it might not last. John Quick also left, so the people responsible for getting me to WCCO radio were now gone. They had inspired me to go to WCCO, even though I didn't want to go, but I really liked those guys and knew how professional and talented they were.

When Steve left, management brought in Rand Gottlieb. He was the general manager with the bright idea of putting Steve Cannon and Ruth Koscielak together. If you wanted to watch disaster in the making, that was it. Steve Cannon didn't like to take calls from the outside, let alone have a co-host. That was a radio minefield, to put it mildly.

When I first heard of the decision to put the two together, I thought, "Hmm, now that decision is a real head-scratcher." Well, it was more than that. It was a time bomb! It was a horrible match. Listeners reported tension in their cars while they listened. You could be 50 miles away from the studio and feel uncomfortable driving along and listening.

Steve was an extremely strong personality, and he could be a real SOB—and he didn't care. They never, ever got along. I don't think Steve ever disliked Ruth. I don't think it was that. It was more, "Hey, you are in my living room and you weren't invited. Now get out!"

Rand was fine as a boss. I got along with him, and for the most part I was happy at WCCO radio, but it was not ever going to be the same as it had been for me at KQRS. If everything had stayed the same over there and here, I might still be there. I mean, Tom Barnard is still there. Maybe I would be, too—who knows for sure?

The ironic thing, and I'll throw this out there to chew on, was that in 1988 I was down at spring training with the Twins. Tom Barnard was there, too, and he told me he had a handshake agreement to leave KQRS and go to WCCO radio. He had an agreement to go before I was going there. I was dumbstruck. I said, "You're what? Are you kidding me?"

He had a basic agreement with Jim Rupp and was supposedly set to eventually replace Steve Cannon. To me, this was staggering news. I kept the words "Are you kidding me, are you kidding me?" from coming out of my mouth about every two seconds.

Tom can tell the story better. I don't want to speak for Tom, but as I recall, Tom was upset that he never met face to face with the brass to iron out the deal. They were only negotiating with his agent. I remember him telling me, "Look, if they don't want to meet face to face with me, then I'm not going to work for them." So, it broke off before anything became finalized. But I remember his words like it was yesterday that he was going to WCCO radio. It was one of the most stunning days of my career.

At one point, the general managers at WCCO radio changed. They brought in a new guy, and he was difficult to work with. I never felt this general manager really understood the station's vision. He was quick to point out to me with a couple warnings that things were happening from a financial standpoint and I needed to be prepared for some cuts.

Eventually, there was a parting of the ways. It wasn't like I was fired or anything; I just left by mutual agreement. It was okay. I wasn't upset about leaving WCCO radio. I guess it was more like it was the right time for it to occur.

I had been there for about five or six years, and then I stayed out of radio for a few years. Then one day I got a call from Doug Westerman at KFAN, and he wanted me to do some radio work for the station. At the time, I was ready to jump back in, and again I had to get permission from WCCO to make the move.

It was pretty easy to get the okay because it was obvious that WCCO radio was not going to use me. I started working with Bob Yates in the morning. Paul Allen was not there yet, and then a little later I worked some with Dan Cole, "The Common Man," and Chad Hartman and Dan Barreiro in the afternoon. Eventually Hartman and Barreiro split, and I went with Hartman in the afternoons and stuck with "Common" as well.

It has worked out great. I am doing what I liked to do on the radio. In reality, I have grown over the past decade with the station. They have become the sports station of the area now, having the Vikings and the Gophers in football and basically sports, sports, sports all day. I enjoy everything I do at KFAN. Working with the morning crew is great, and "Common" reminds me of my days at KQRS.

* * *

I think radio is really important for me to do because I believe it keeps your mind sharp. You have to be able to think on your feet, be ready in an instant to respond and question. All of this keeps your juices flowing, thus making you better prepared and confident in all of your work tasks. It keeps me thinking young all the time. I recognize our audience and it keeps me invigorated, and that's important to me.

I think I am the same on the radio as I am on television, but on radio you have a better and longer opportunity to make a point on something significant. For example, last year I had the time on the radio to rip into our local politicians for taking the entire legislative session to *not* balance the budget. It was outrageous behavior, and I let the listeners know how I felt. "They had five months to balance the state's budget and they couldn't do it, and now we are going to continue to pay them for their incompetence while they work during a special session to try to do what they should have done during the regular session. If any of us performed our work like they do, we would be fired!" On television, it might not fit really well with the sports, and there would not be the time to do it.

Now, I have a forum on the 5:00 p.m. sports on WCCO television in which I can do this type of thing from time to time. When the Twins were going so badly last year, I did a rant one night and it was timely. I went to the news director before I went on and told him what I had planned. It was more a radio piece, but because of the way it is set up at five o'clock, it fit well.

I told our news director, "I've had it with this team and the way they are playing. I'm going after them today!" And I did. Don't get me wrong, it is not as if this is only what *I* have to say. I have enough people coming up to me during the day expressing their displeasure. So, hopefully in some respects, I represent the voice of the fans.

It's not personal! I didn't go after Danny Valencia, the Twins third baseman, and say, "He's a really bad person. He doesn't help grandmothers cross the street and he ignores kids seeking autographs." I don't say or mean anything like that. I said, "Maybe the pitchers in the league have caught up with you. I don't understand why general manger Bill Smith can put Alexi Casilla at shortstop as an everyday player. And this decision is based on what?"

I did let them have it and there was the television forum to do it. But most of the time, ranting works better on radio.

On television, it is harder to sometimes be yourself because of the bright lights and all that goes with television. If you were sitting with a friend having lunch and a camera and microphone with bright lights and sound equipment were in your face, I think you might be a little more conscious about what you are saying. But for the most part, from experience, I am pretty relaxed, and I think radio has helped me with this.

I try to be careful with what I say on both radio and television. You have to know your audience, and I try to keep updated on who our listeners and viewers are. We have had some really good training with consultants through the years, and that has been very helpful also.

* * *

I have been blessed to have had a wonderful career at WCCO television. I mentioned that it is my "A" job and always will be. I have loved my radio work also, and I truly think that each has helped me to be better at what I am doing. I hope so anyway.

I have been on the air for too many years to be worried about job security. But I do concern myself with the insecurities of always wanting to be better. I may think to myself after being on the air, "Did I say that the right way? Could I have been better?" But I guess that is healthy, to be concerned about how you do your job and always wanting to find a way to be better.

I live in a vacuum. I am never sure whether people like what I am saying. I love it when I get an email, a phone call, a comment, a letter that says I did a good job. It means a lot to me. We all need it from our bosses, our peers, our audience.

When Dennis Swanson, my boss from CBS, came up to me and told me, "Do you know how unique you are? People just don't do what you do anymore. You have such a great ability to adjust to things." This was such a huge compliment coming from him, and I will never forget it. We all need those kinds of things in our life—recognition, appreciation, and support. It doesn't often go with the territory.

I love to connect with people, whether it's on the street, at a game, at a movie theater, or via email. I care deeply how people react to what I say and do. So, when someone takes the time to tell me something positive, it rips into those insecurities and I am greatly appreciative.

As I sum it up, radio has been wonderful to me and for me. I have loved it all, and the "run for governor" . . . well, that was just a bonus.

11

The Heart and Soul of Broadcast Journalism

I have learned a lot over the past 40-plus years in broadcast journalism. I want to transgress for a second back to the first chapter in *Best Seat in the House*, in which I talk about my first days at WCCO television.

When I was 17 years old, still in high school, and walked into that television newsroom as an observer—my Field of Dreams, by the way—I never gave a thought to anything but pure fascination of what was happening before my eyes. I never gave any attention to the fact that I knew absolutely nothing about the business that had immediately grabbed onto my heart and soul. I truly didn't know what I didn't know.

In front of me was a top-notch, grizzled crew, and I didn't know anything about anything. I often think about the lessons I learned and about what it takes to be successful in this business. I learned it is an arduous, long process. It is something that to this day, after all these years, I have not fully figured out.

It's kind of like going 3-for-5 or 4-for-5 at bat in baseball, or 4-for-4 with no home runs. It sort of feels like there is more work to

A pre-game broadcast from Soldier Field in Chicago.

be done. There is work still left out on the field. I'm doing okay, but there is so much more.

I wrote this down once, a message that I have tried to pound into my kids' minds: "If you want to avoid disappointing others, don't disappoint yourself." This is the key thing I have always tried to remember. Don't slack off. Don't take shortcuts. Don't look for the easy way. Ask a lot of questions and do the best you possibly can.

In order to believe in this kind of statement and to follow through on this belief, you have to have a high level of integrity and curiosity. You have to know who you are. I get asked all the time by high school kids, college kids, "I want to do your job. What can I do so I can get a job like you have? What advice do you have for me?" I say, "Well, there is no easy path." This is not like becoming a lawyer, a doctor, or a teacher, where you go to school and become one of the people who work in those professions. Maybe you go to graduate school, go to medical school, finish, and get a certificate on the wall and hope to then become successful in your chosen field.

This is very different. You will likely have to work in a small town, possibly in some remote place where the favorite eating establishment is the local Dairy Queen at the end of town. Maybe there is a hardware store in the middle and the television station signal crackles in the evening before it goes off the air at seven o'clock.

Your salary, well, maybe it's just enough for a cheese sandwich at lunch and probably dinner, too. You have to love your job to put up with this in the beginning. But it all too often works this way.

My situation was a little different, and I will mention that fact in a second. But money? In the beginning for me, there was none. In the beginning, I worked for free. Oh, my gosh, when I was first officially hired, I believe my first paycheck was for $22.00. For me, this was pure gold because I finally got paid. I used to have to ask Hal Scott, "Do you think I might be able to get paid one of these days?"

As far as the different situation, I started my career at WCCO television, which was similar to how my friend Dave Winfield began his career. Dave never spent one day in the minors; his professional baseball career began in the major leagues. I never had to spend a day in the minors either. That's the difference, and I get it.

I have told people a hundred times over that what happened to me could never happen again. No boss at a major television station would ever allow some 17-year-old high school kid who knew nothing about the business to come in and just hang around.

It was unheard of then and even more so today. It would never happen. No one would allow someone as young and green as I was to stay through those early-learning time periods. I would have been banished to the minors to learn the ropes.

"Come back and see us when you know something, kid," I can hear the response to my thought process of wanting to come in, observe, and just hang around. I was extremely fortunate.

This is a business in which you have to love what you are doing. You have to sacrifice your personal and social life. You have to sacrifice maybe getting a better-paying job. I knew all that and I made plenty of sacrifices, but I also knew always in the back of my mind that this could come to an abrupt end on any given day, any day that I was there.

I was never comfortable enough to think that because I was on the major league roster I would never get the call someday to "come and see the boss and bring your playbook with you." Believe me, I understand it all. It is what makes my story so incredibly unique.

In this business, I think the best advice I can give young prospective journalists is "you need to be you." I have had many young women come up to me over the years and say, "I want to be an anchor. I want to be like Pat Miles. I want to be like Amelia Santaniello." I say to them, "That's great, but I would first be concerned with working on your reporting skills."

You see, I know young people look at the national anchors and the local anchors and deep down feel, "I could do that. I want to do that. I'm attractive looking. I can read. That can't be so hard to do. I want to do that." And again, my advice goes to the heart of the business. You have to work on many things, especially the reporting skills. There is much to do and to learn before you walk into a major newsroom and announce that you want to become an anchor. You have to work on your writing skills, your communication skills, your listening skills—all things that take many years of practice and repetition.

I will say this, and I sincerely mean it from the bottom of my heart. Nothing gives me more pride than to see one of my former interns make it in the industry. I feel like a proud papa. I can usually tell within a very few days whether someone has the ability to make it in the business. It is usually quite easy to identify if they "have the right stuff."

I can easily see if they have the drive, the passion, the curiosity. I look for their attention to detail—the "What else can I do?" as opposed to the "What time can I get out of here today?" approach.

We have had interns who have gone to the other markets and moved up the ranks and become successful. But I have to say, I am also brutally honest with them, and in the process I've hopefully given them the right kind of guidance.

Again, I started at the major league level as a kid. But at the time, there were only four local stations. There was WCCO Channel 4, KSTP Channel 5, KMSP Channel 9, and WTCN Channel 11. There was not ESPN or Fox Sports North. We had no such things as the Internet, blogs, Facebook, Twitter, or any of the other mass media communications. Now it has exploded, and with it come many thousands of young people who want to get into the business.

I cannot recall many, if any, of my friends saying, "I want to be involved in television sports when I grow up." Television sports when I started, in all honesty, was not that big of a deal. Local television was not that big of a deal. I just happened to find my calling. But today, wow, for every job that is out there, there are 5,000 people who want it—if not more.

So, you have to distinguish yourself in some way. And the route isn't mapped out for you. There is not one road or another that is better to take. You have to find your path, road, method, and hopefully it works out for you. That's what I tell young people today who have the journalism desire.

I tell them to try to get connected any way they can. If you cannot find a way in as a sportscaster, grab something else—anything to find a way in. Prove yourself, and then you will find a way to move around. I had the passion, desire, and interest, but so what? I had to prove myself by doing any and every single thing they had for me. Remember what I said earlier: "Empty wastebaskets, pick up the cigarette butts, that's okay. Do you want me to wash the floors before I go home?" Find a way.

Maybe there is a job as a technician, a photographer, a custodian, whatever it is—take it. Obtain as much knowledge about the business as possible. Knowledge is power. The more you can do to get your foot in the door, the better off you are. Whatever skills you can gather will serve you well in the future.

In the process, you may find that the wait is too long or the right opportunity just never seems to come your way, and you give up. Some do. They don't have the patience, and the fact is there are no guarantees.

It is easy for people like Oprah Winfrey and others to say, "Pursue your dreams. Find your passion." This is good advice. Yes, of course, you want to do that, but you also have to pay your bills. You have to be realistic about it. I never want to see someone with passion and dreams to stop and give up. I hate it when it happens, but I don't believe it necessarily represents a sign of weakness. Sometimes reality just strikes and someone realizes, "Look, I have taken this route as long as I can." There is nothing wrong with that, either.

It is okay to say, "I'm going to be a Don Shelby or a Mark Rosen," but you also have to have a plan B if it doesn't work out—because it may not. It is hard to find careers these days, especially in this business. It is rare to find someone with a 40-year career any longer.

When I get the opportunity to speak to high school or college classes, I get energized. I really do. I thoroughly enjoy it. They are wide-eyed, and they want to know about the business. I try to give them the best possible advice because I have been in their shoes. I sat there in those same kinds of classroom desks wondering how it was all going to work out.

It is very important in this business to learn from the beginning. In other words, pay your dues. With some young entry-level workers or interns, I see a feeling of entitlement. They feel they should be assigned more to do. Sometimes we see those who are with us as interns only because they thought it would be really cool to work at a television station. I haven't seen as much of that lately, but once in a while we will get a student who really has no interest in a career in television.

At WCCO, we are pretty selective. We take time to carefully go through résumés and screen applicants very closely. I see a tremendous increase in the number of young women who are interested in this kind of work, and this is particularly gratifying to me.

I often get asked about the importance of the pretty face in television. I don't want to say that looking nice doesn't have value, but I think your face can do other things for you other than just look good. Facial expressions are important, and the way someone makes a presentation is important.

I think we see this being the case on the network right now. ESPN has a woman whom I greatly admire named Doris Burke, who interviews NBA players and coaches. She is a sideline reporter for the most part, but she does other assignments as well. Her questions, mannerisms, and character make her outstanding at what she does. She is attractive, but no beauty queen, and it doesn't matter one bit because she is so competent at what she does. She is accepted entirely for her skills. I think there are times when the beauty queen or the male model image can work against someone. There has to be some real substance to the person. Michele Tafoya is a good example. She is a natural—a good, solid reporter.

One of the things I have really tried to do as I have approached 60 years of age is to keep myself vital. I take care of my skin. I've lost some

Smiling and feeling good after a regular workout with Ron Henderson, the Fitness King.

weight and do what I can to look and feel healthy. I work out with the Fitness King, and I feel good about that. That doesn't take away from the fact that people know what I look like. I'm not trying to be Brad Pitt or Robert Redford here. I know what I am and that's fine.

I'm not sure if 60 is the new 40, but I think I look and feel better than I did when I was 40. It sounds kind of weird to say that, but I really do. It is important that I feel good about myself. I also know I do a better job on television than I did when I was 20 years younger. I believe I am better at my job right now than I ever have been. Granted, men have an advantage in this business, as very few women have the opportunity to work well into their 60s.

With all of the experience I have had, I know I am so much more relaxed on the air at this time in my life. I am much more myself now than ever before. The hardest thing you have to do on television is be yourself.

I always tell young people to write some copy about a Twins or Vikings game. And in most cases, when I read it over I will say back to them, "If you were telling a friend about the game, is this the way you would talk to them? It doesn't sound like it to me. You would never use those words. So why use them when you are trying to write a script?"

I fell into that trap early on, but I learned from it. I can write sports copy in my sleep at night, but the trick is to write the copy in *my* words, exactly how I would say it to someone over lunch. It is the most fun and challenging part of my job, and I love doing it.

It is unlike what the news anchors are involved in because I write my own material. I don't need an editor's approval—I don't even have an editor. I am able to do my thing, and when the day is over, it is all mine. I rise or fall on my own, and I really like the independence.

I have learned through the years to be careful not to overwrite. Let the picture do the talking. There were so many people who gave me the guidance I needed and really taught me the ropes. Hal Scott was the one early on. Doug Nemanic, my photographer, stressed the importance of describing my reporting to my audience. Remember back a few chapters when Doug told me, "There is nothing in that script you just wrote that tells me you were there and witnessed what you are reporting on." What great advice he had for me.

Whatever the conditions are for the event, you must take the listener or viewer with you. Have them believe they were beside you and saw what you saw. Take them into the clubhouse. Take them to the sideline of the field.

After the Vikings lost the game to New Orleans in 2009, keeping them from the Super Bowl, I saw Vikings running back Adrian Peterson standing outside the locker room in full uniform staring toward the field. He was watching the Saints celebrate. His hands were on his hips, and a forlorn look was on his face. I will never forget that image.

Seeing Bud Grant standing by himself over in the corner . . . the loneliness of that moment. The starkness of what could have been and what should have been. The feeling of Adrian Peterson standing there. He was the only Vikings player out there. That's what separates being a good journalist from one who doesn't pay attention to the details of what is going on around them.

Now I didn't have pictures of what I just described, but in my mind's eye I saw what was occurring after the game. I saw Adrian Peterson watching the celebration, wishing he could turn that clock back 10 minutes.

When the Vikings lost to Atlanta in the devastating 1998 NFC Championship Game at the Metrodome, I was walking off the field and saw Vikings wide receiver Cris Carter bawling his eyes out, tears running down his cheeks. Now that is something you don't forget.

When I'm writing a sportscast for television, I try to bring myself and my emotions to it to make it real. I try to give the viewers my feelings and observations of what I'm reporting to them. You have to be able to talk through the camera lens. You have to visualize the people—the viewer, the listener—and talk to them.

If you are giving a speech before a large audience, you have the opportunity to move your eyes from side to side and see how the audience is reacting to what you are saying. Television journalism is basically done in a vacuum. We hope there are people out there who are reacting to what we are saying, but it's hard because we don't see them.

When the night is over and the broadcasts are finished, we go out to the parking lot, get in our car, and go home like everyone else does when the workday is over. I only hope I have communicated what I wanted to say for the listener in a manner that brought them beside me.

It takes a long time to be a good communicator. It takes a lot of experience. It is a skill that just doesn't happen overnight. It is being you. As I have communicated over and over, it is the hardest thing to do.

I see these young reporters come in and they are talking to me like a normal person, and all of a sudden they have to do their audition tape with a coat and tie on. The light comes on and the director says, "Okay, here we go." And all of a sudden they become someone else. They are not the same person. Watch the great ones on television because they make it look so easy. They have perfected their craft and it is a constant process.

The advantage I had of being so young in the environment with such a tremendous talent base was that I learned so much every day. I would have been cheating myself if I didn't take advantage of every single second.

Ron Handberg, our news director back when I started, was also a writer and a very good one. Today, news directors don't write; they are copied. Ron Handberg was an accomplished writer and author himself. He was a magnificent news writer. He was so succinct in his work. He spared so little in words. He got right to the point.

Al Austin was another. Bob McNamara of our station used to say that Al was the best writer he had ever seen. His investigative work was meticulous. He was such an incredible talent and did such a fantastic job with editorials as well.

McNamara was adept at writing to pictures. If you read his script with no pictures in front of you, it would make no sense. You can be the best writer in the world, but if you can't write to the pictures and work with the photographer, there is no story. McNamara was the best at it.

I tell the interns and young people in the business, "You have to be a part of a team. This is a team. You can't come up with a story idea and simply write a bunch of words to it. This is teamwork. You have to work together, work with your photographer. 'Oh, by the way, did you get that picture? You mean you didn't get that shot of the kid crying over there in the corner?' You have to work as a team, or else what you do will have no value. Helping each other out is what makes it all work."

R. J. Fritz was a really good writer, too. I was blessed with being around all these people in the newsroom who understood what it took to make a good newsworthy story. They had the talent to make it happen proficiently and brilliantly, and I was blessed to be around them. Caroline Lowe was another—a terrific crime reporter.

* * *

I think I have been successful and lasted this long in the business because I pay attention to details. The little things make the difference. Sure, you have to perform. That's a big part of it, but in doing so you have to pay attention to the little things. You have to work to make it right and then be yourself. Be the same Mark Rosen on the air as at the movies.

I absolutely love it when someone says to me, "Hey, Mark, you are the same guy I see on television." Well, I am the same guy. That's who I am. I am not acting.

Success in television comes with teamwork and the ability for people who work together to get along. Consultants are brought in from all over the country to emphasize this, but it is not a matter of just throwing bodies together with a little training. It is putting people together who have the right chemistry. You can't just come out and say, "Okay, now let's be a team." That doesn't work any more than it would to throw a sports team together and say, "Okay, guys, we're a team now." You don't have to have everyone always like each other, but there is a need for respect and sincerity with each other.

Working together as a team comes from an ability to understand the importance of the final product and how the various components have to come together if there is to be any chance of success. Each person's role has to be understood and respected by the other members of the team, with the same ultimate goal in mind. In sports, we call it winning. In the business world, we call it orchestrating success. In life, we call it making a difference.

I am always amazed by the people I come across in my career who are driven to succeed. There are plenty of people who work hard and enjoy success as a result. That's great, but I'm talking about the type of person who is so incredibly driven to succeed that they seemingly never rest until they have risen to the top and conquered the mountain, walking the dangerous terrain and winning the battle in the process.

I remember back in the mid-1980s when Lou Holtz came here to resurrect the downtrodden Minnesota Gophers football program. The Gophers had been virtually obliterated by all competition the previous season. It was head coach Joe Salem's last year, which had included a savage 84–13 drubbing at the hands of the Nebraska Cornhuskers.

It didn't take long for Holtz to begin the program's turnaround. In the second and final year of his short stay in the Twin Cities, he had his Golden Gophers throwing the ball into the end zone on the final play and nearly upsetting the highly ranked Oklahoma Sooners.

How does that happen? How does a football team with virtually the same players lose 84–13 one season, and then, in just a very brief period of time, come to the point of almost engineering one of the greatest upsets in college football history? It happened because a football coach came to town with an unstoppable, burning desire to win. He brought with him a staff that knew how to coach, work together, and mesh all the pieces.

I can recall near the end of one of the non-conference games in either Holtz's first or second season, the Gophers had a substantial lead late in the game. The opponents threw a long desperation pass down the sidelines which was caught for a garbage-time touchdown. It didn't change a thing. The Gophers had won the game in a lopsided victory, and all the touchdown did was add seven points to the opponent's score. Holtz went nuts. I watched him running up and down the sidelines, ranting and raving like a wounded bull. I have no clue what was coming out of his mouth, but I'm glad I wasn't the one bearing the brunt of his tongue lashing.

The long pass play had nothing to do with the outcome of the game, but it mattered to Holtz. It was a breakdown of what had been taught, prepared for, and planned. It demonstrated that all the hard work in preparation for that type of play had been for naught, and Holtz was not going to stand for it. It was not a part of his game plan for perfection. It was a chink in the armor, and it was not acceptable.

Now that particular example makes a point on a large scale, but it is the reality of what I do when I appear on WCCO television three times a day at 5:20 p.m., 6:20 p.m., and 10:20 p.m.—and on a much larger stage when we do *Rosen's Sports Sunday* programs. If I go on the air and do my piece and I don't give it my very best, then I know I have failed. And giving my very best, as I have said before, does not mean showing up a few minutes before the lights and cameras go on, reading a piece on the air, and going home.

It means working closely with my producer, our camera folks, and the newscasters to ensure that the product we present will be delivered smoothly, as if my audience is in the same room with me and we are just conversing.

I have tremendous regard for all of the people I work with and know that any success that I have had in this business comes from the assistance I have received from others along the way. Teamwork, teamwork, teamwork—I cannot emphasize it enough. When I am working with an intern or new staff member, it is a message I have to make sure they understand and truly grasp, because there is no chance for success without it.

When Lou Holtz went ballistic on the sidelines of a football game, he was communicating in his own way that failure had occurred. Teamwork failed at that moment, and that was not to be condoned.

Even in the short two- or three-minute segments that we do on the news three times a day, I cannot accept failure and must operate under the foundational premise that we will give it our very best, but we can always make it even better. That's why I often take the time to go back and look at the tape of the broadcasts. What did I do wrong here? How can I make it better at 10:20 tonight? Did I make my point, or how can I say it differently next time?

There is an old film clip of a former Washington Redskins football player talking about what it was like when Vince Lombardi arrived in Washington D.C. to coach the Redskins, after he left the Green Bay Packers. I recall the film narrator had preceded the player's commentary on Lombardi by saying something to the effect that Washington was "first in politics and war, but last in the National Football League." The fact is, the Washington Redskins were an absolutely horrific football team at the time.

The player said that the team had lost so often that a win was something to really celebrate. The Redskins had finally won a game, their first under Lombardi in the preseason, and the team came to a meeting the following day feeling pretty good about the unusual occurrence of winning a football game. They were amazed to learn that the coach didn't share their sentiment. "He was screaming and yelling," recalled the player. "We wondered what was the matter with the man. But we learned that winning wasn't enough for him. It had to be done the right way."

Again, I'm not Lou Holtz or Vince Lombardi—and I'm not by any stretch of the imagination saying that I should be raking the sidelines or the film room during or after a game. The point I'm trying to make is that it's all about doing the right thing and doing it the right way—doing your very best all the time. It is essential to deliver the best possible product to your audience. This is what broadcast journalism is all about: communication with one another as the product is being put together, and then delivering the news to your viewers in a positive, succinct, and balanced format.

It is all about commitment. "A Commitment to Excellence" is one of my favorite slogans. Al Davis, principal owner of the Oakland Raiders until his death in 2011, also loved the statement and had it posted so everyone in the organization could see it.

Another of my favorite quotations was said by philanthropist T. F. Buxton: "With ordinary talent and extraordinary perseverance, all things are attainable." I know a chief executive officer who had these words put on a large sign and mounted in a company lunchroom for all to see. These are powerful words. "A Commitment to Excellence." "With ordinary talent and extraordinary perseverance, all things are attainable." I love it. I believe it.

We can always do it better. I have a fantastic crew that I work with everyday. And I have been truly blessed with being around great people in the past, whom I mention throughout this book. But I know we can all do better. It is the striving for excellence that keeps me going, keeps the juices flowing, and fires me up every single day before the lights and cameras go on.

I know I am repeating myself again when I say that I have learned so much from others. But I truly believe that it needs to be repeated. I know that there are so many wonderfully talented people who can teach all of us ways to do things better. I believe there are informal mentors out there who we can watch, learn from, and observe. And it never has to get to the formal level of teaching or coaching.

I learned from watching Dave Moore, Bud Grant, and Harmon Killebrew. I learned from Dave Winfield, Kirby Puckett, and Jim Marshall. We didn't sit down in a classroom where they taught by writing on a blackboard or lecturing. I watched them live, and I learned.

I would never expect myself or anyone else to be someone's clone. But I do think many of the great ones have character traits we can learn from. We can find ways to utilize these traits within the constraints of our own personalities, mannerisms, and methods. Dave Moore had an uncanny ability to relate to people with a style of trust and confidence. People trusted Dave Moore. They had confidence in him. Why? Because he could communicate—and he did it in such a friendly yet purposeful style. He gave us the news, and we respected the way he did it.

Bud and Harmon were very different yet had their ways about them that were revered by others. Bud had a tremendous gift for managing people. He knew everything that was going on around him. And Harmon? So gracious, so nice, so incredibly humble.

Winfield, Puckett, and Jim Marshall were all so different, but they taught me so much: Dave with his exuberance and commitment to the game, Kirby with all his emotion and passion for life and everything around him, and Jim Marshall—there will never be another like him. Jim will run out of time long before his curiosity and emotion for living leave him. I have learned from them all and have such a profound appreciation for each of them.

Every one of us has people around us, those who we interact and communicate with and who can teach us. Teach us to be better. Teach us to try harder and to instill in us the old Army slogan: "Be all that you can be." We only have to observe. Why wouldn't we?

One of the major aspects of my work is giving the scores and the inside workings of all the Twin Cities sports organizations, whether the information is positive or negative. That's my job, and I love doing it— but also remember, I am a huge fan. These are my teams, and like many other fans, I live and die with their success and failure.

I grew up loving the Vikings and the Twins and struggled mightily when the North Stars left. Despite their past problems, I'll always be a fan of the Timberwolves, and I love the Wild even though they are relatively new to Minnesota. And with it all, I have to provide the information to my listeners. It's what I do, and I have to do it professionally and balanced. My mentors have taught me not to settle for less.

I am impressed by the success of the Wilf family who own the Minnesota Vikings. Zygi Wilf is a solid businessman—but he is also a football fan! He is passionate about winning and probably would trade a number of lucrative real estate deals to bring a Lombardi Trophy home to the great fans of the Minnesota Vikings. He has spent the money—no question about that—and has tried to put the pieces in place to build a sound, winning foundation. He has surrounded himself in the business world with successful people who work together toward a common goal. He has made a strong effort to do the same in football but will have to continue to tinker and modify to find the right combinations—both on and off the field—in order for the team to get back on the winning track again.

Jim Pohlad, owner of the Twins, has seen this type of success with a management team in the front office and on the field that has managed to remain relatively intact for decades. When Jim and team president Dave St. Peter made the decision to bring former general manager Terry Ryan back to the position to replace Bill Smith, it was the first major change in the organization for many years.

We're all excited about the bigtime changes general manager Chuck Fletcher has made with the Minnesota Wild. Fletcher has made some significant moves to strengthen that organization, as has the Timberwolves' owner, Glen Taylor. With a roster of exciting young players and a seasoned veteran in coach Rick Adelman, the 2011 season has given Wolves fans hope for the first time in several years.

However, these leaders are not doing it alone. They are relying on their people to advise, assist, and recommend. The professional sports teams who have reached the pinnacle of success have done it by great organizational management. It is the same for us in the newsroom. We are each striving every single day for success, and the process never slows down or takes a vacation. Each day a new challenge is before us.

To assist us in our goal to be successful and improve our product every day, we have amazing technological tools at our fingertips. I couldn't do anything live from the 1980 Olympics—I had to do it all by telephone. Can you imagine what it would have been like to do the sports segment of the news live outside the arena at 6:20 p.m., minutes after the U.S. team beat the Russians? Now we can do it anywhere in the world, but we have to work together to make it happen. Thankfully, we have engineers like Art Phillips, who I have seen lie under a truck on a bone-chilling night to fix the generator so we could get that once in a lifetime live shot on the air. It's people like Art and others who make it happen.

We are colleagues that work together in the world of broadcast journalism. In the end, we formulate a trust and a bond that never wavers.

* * *

A few years ago, I had the opportunity to work with two experienced managers. Ed Piette became our general manager, and Jeff Kiernan was the news director. He became one of my favorites of all time. He is working in Chicago now and is just a great guy. He is a tremendous person. And Ed, who I knew from his days at KSTP, was great to work with also. He had a great sense of humor, and the two of them made a great combination. He was a winner, wanted things to be done right, and knew how to push the right buttons with people. He was a great leader.

I have had the honor to work with the best and most talented people in broadcast journalism for the past 40 years. I have learned so much from them. One of the things I was taught early on was to be able to control my emotions and do my job. I work hard at this, and most of the time I'm pretty successful.

Pay attention to yourself and do what you need to do today. I learned that and try to live by it. I feel so strongly about the whole respect thing and how you treat people.

This is a tough business. I love to work with young people, including our interns as they learn the business. To succeed in this business, you don't have to be a superstar. I try to tell them you don't have to be the one at the head of the class. You don't have to be the one who was captain of four teams and a well-known individual coming into this field of work. Sometimes the person on the end of the bench, who shows up every day for practice, can be as good or better than someone else.

I was sort of that guy at the end of the bench. So, I have a soft spot in my heart for people who show up and cheer their teammates on and want to be there and be a part of the team. I think that translates well between sports and business. If you give it your best shot with your best possible effort, your chances to succeed are immensely increased.

If you are passed over for that promotion or the corner office, don't burn bridges. It's something that sports and business can teach. They go together. Work hard, keep your head high, and things will go well in the long run.

I think oftentimes that people who have come along the hard way and have to work for what they have make some of the best employees.

They get it and demonstrate it by their honesty, integrity, credibility, and work ethic.

Take a look at some of the very best local athletes, such as John Randle and Mick Tingelhoff of Minnesota Vikings fame. Neither John nor Mick were drafted by NFL teams. Each was signed as a free agent. No team thought that either was good enough to be one of their college draft choices. And what did they do? John is a Pro Football Hall of Famer. Mick started at center for the Vikings for 17 seasons, and he should be in the Hall of Fame as well.

The 2011 Minnesota Lynx are another example. Coming off six consecutive losing seasons, this team came together and won it all. Although the fan base will likely never equal that of the baseball Twins, football Vikings, hockey Wild or basketball Timberwolves, the Lynx brought the Twin Cities to life in 2011, winning more than just a title in the process. These great athletes look at themselves beyond winning, more as seasoned role models and as trailblazers for generations to come.

When I walked the celebratory parade route on Nicollet Mall, I saw the faces of the youngsters in the crowd. They were the same faces of joy, admiration, and passion present with the young boys and girls as they watched Kirby Puckett and Jack Morris after the 1991 World Series. The Lynx players had captured their souls and imaginations in a similar fashion.

This organization set a goal and they achieved it while coming together as a team. Lindsay Whalen was always thought to be our own, right here from our Golden Gophers, but she and her teammates accomplished so much more. This is an abundantly talented team that has richly identified with the fans and community. They have created a strong base for years to come. In addition to being great athletes, they are even better personalities who have openly expressed such appreciation for the support they have received. We waited a long time for a professional sports team to win a championship in the Twin Cities. We haven't had a title to celebrate in 20 years—not since the Twins won the World Series in 1991. But the Minnesota Lynx won more than a championship. They won our hearts.

* * *

For more than 40 years, I have truly put my heart and soul into my career. The journalist has to be able to put personal stories and all aspects of reporting to the public into a message that the viewers can understand and find interesting. It must be done in an honest, personal, and straightforward way. Work within yourself to set a tone of honesty, integrity, credibility, loyalty, passion, and hard work.

Be yourself. Don't talk down to people. Don't talk to them like they just got off the Greyhound bus. Respect everyone's intellect out there while communicating effectively.

I want to pass along a great quote, my all-time favorite, that conveys a wonderful message. The author is unknown, but I read it in one of Tim Russert's books some time ago. It simply read, "The only place where success comes before work is in the dictionary." That says it all.

The story can be as simplistic as a high school baseball game or as monumental as winning a gold medal at Lake Placid. It is all-encompassing, but the key is the story behind the scenes, not just the box score. It is the person behind the box score who counts and represents the heart and soul of broadcast journalism.

12

Greatest Loves and Passions

I have been very fortunate to have a family and a career that have energized my love and passion for life. For more than 40 years, I have had the privilege of looking forward to going to work every day. Few people are able to say that about their careers.

I mentioned earlier that one of the hardest things to do in television is to be yourself. It can be an extremely intimidating environment. It is not a normal setting. People with a camera, lights, and a microphone are following you around all day, and unless you are the Kardashians, performing in front of all this broadcast equipment is not an easy task.

Being yourself and acting as planned isn't always easy. It is certainly easy to say to someone when the camera, lights, and microphones go on, "Okay, now be yourself." Well, as you can imagine, it's just not that simple.

A lot of it is attitude—being secure in my own convictions, my beliefs, and my style—but it is also about developing an understanding of just being myself. It has enabled me to relate to people at all levels, whether they are a chief executive officer of a major corporation, an elite high-profile athlete, or the person working at a fast food restaurant. I enjoy interacting with people, being engaged.

I try to be the same when the lights go on as I am during my free time. I never want to fall into behavior like "leave me alone, get out of my face, I'm off duty, get away from me." If I had that kind of personality or attitude, I doubt I would have much respect for myself.

Sometimes with the workload and the timing of the sports news, it can get hectic, but yes, I do have a life outside of television and radio. My work takes me away from home a lot, but I've worked hard to balance my priorities. I think I do a pretty good job.

* * *

I met my wife early in my career. Denise was working at the station as a nighttime artist. It was her first big job after graduating from the Minneapolis College of Art and Design. She had grown up in Gary, Indiana, not exactly the garden spot of America. She lived near the Michael Jackson family, and, in fact, "little" Michael performed at their homecoming dance. Think about that for a minute: Michael Jackson at your homecoming.

Eventually Denise ended up in Minneapolis, and I met her while we both were working at WCCO television. She was working the same night shift with me during the Watergate scandal. She used to come down to our basement newsroom and work on what we called "flops," which were flat pieces of art material on which she could trace pictures of Richard Nixon, John Dean, and others.

As for me, well, I was 22 years old, had no social life whatsoever, and spent most of my time working. One day she struck up a conversation with me. I think we talked some about the White Sox because she was a fan, but the fact that she appeared interested in just talking to me was almost overwhelming.

We started dating, and now, after almost 35 years, we are still together. She has put up with me for a long time. I'm not going to sugarcoat it and say it's been an easy ride; most marriages aren't. When you sign on to my kind of lifestyle as a broadcaster, it is a challenging existence. I never knew for sure whether I would be spending my career here in the Twin Cities or in numerous other locations around the country.

Spending more than four decades at a television station is very unusual—hard for most in the industry to fathom. I could have ended up in any number of markets, from Green Bay to Buffalo, like many of my colleagues have.

In the early 1980s, we actually commuted between Minneapolis and Chicago (before kids) when Denise took a job as a creative director of a department store. It was at that time when I imagined moving to Chicago. I've always loved the city. They have a great sports market, and I've always fed off its energy.

I kind of idolized the broadcasters at the CBS station, WBBM TV, in the early 1980s. Johnny Morris, the former Chicago Bear, was their sportscaster, but they also had news anchors Bill Kurtis and Walter Jacobson, who believe it or not are back anchoring the 6:00 p.m. news again at WBBM for my former news director, Jeff Kiernan.

The thought of going to Chicago passed quickly because I was promoted to the weekend sports job at WCCO. Again it sounded good, but I was working nights and weekends and Denise was working Monday through Friday during normal hours, so the word *normalcy* really didn't exist.

I did not get a chance to go home very often during the dinner break when my kids were growing up. I'm not looking for sympathy because it was my choice for this kind of career, but it was and still is the reality of the work. And of course, I wish I had been around more and hadn't been gone so much.

For the most part, Denise had to be a single mom. I was not there at those crucial times—after school, at dinner, after dinner, getting the homework done, "clean your room" time, "too much video game time" . . . all the important early years of a youngster's life.

When I was off, nothing was more important to me than being with my kids. I put aside my hobbies to create my own special relationships with my son and daughter as individuals and as a family.

I wasn't the family disciplinarian, mostly because I wasn't around during those crucial times. I wasn't there to see what was happening on a daily basis, so it would have been unfair to jump in with my opinion. It wasn't like in the old days when many of us were growing up and our mothers would exclaim, "Wait until your father gets home from work!"

The other issue is the simple truth that because I was on TV every day, it was tough on my kids, especially my daughter. Some people think if you are a television celebrity, you must have immense wealth, which is ridiculous. In addition, our privacy in public is often tough to come by. Also, people, especially kids, think because I work in sports I know all the superstars and can get them to do anything for me.

I just happen to do sports on television and radio. I am not better or more successful and important than anyone else's dad who might be a teacher, pharmacist, mechanic, or any other profession. This is my job, and to me, it is what it always has been. I understand there is a celebrity aspect that goes with the position. The media to a great extent and the athletes in this town are the ones who get noticed and appear in gossip columns the most.

My daughter's friends on occasion have said, "Your dad's Mark Rosen; can't you get Randy Moss to come to our school? Can you get this player's autograph for me? Can you get this, can you get that?" It hasn't always been easy. I know that my son, Nick, felt many times like "I just want my dad to be my dad; I don't care about this other stuff."

Nick really liked sports and played high school soccer and got quite active in skiing. My daughter, Chloe, was on the swim team in high school. It wasn't easy catching many of their games or meets. It seems like I was always checking my watch to see when I had to leave. I often would have to rely on a late-night phone call to get filled in on the details.

Even when we have our time together, I often have people approaching me at dinner, events, or wherever we might be and want to talk baseball, the Vikings, or whatever the hot topic in sports might be. Yet, I find that it is hardly a sacrifice to be nice to people. I feel if they are appreciative enough of my work to come up to me, then I can surely return the kindness.

Ninety-eight percent of the time, people are understanding and just great about it. Many times I end up asking them more questions about their life than they do about mine.

No question I do stand out in a crowd. I'm about 6 feet 6 and, yes, the initial interaction from people usually goes like, "You don't look that tall on TV."

* * *

Sports is a great common denominator. The news anchors get a much different response from people. It's a much easier icebreaker to ask me about the Twins or the Vikings than someone asking Frank or Amelia about the state budget crisis or their property taxes. They normally get the "How are the kids?" line.

Our meteorologist, Chris Shaffer, is on the same playing field as me, except he gets blamed a lot more for an actual forecast than I do for my prediction on a football game. It seems people are always upset about the weather.

The reality of all this is people invite us into their homes every day. It's a very special thing. I have spent my entire life in this community. This is my home, and it pleases me to no end that they feel I am, in a sense, part of their families.

The irony to all of this is that becoming a part of others' families has taken time away from my own, and I do get melancholy about it.

My kids are grown now. My son is working in Los Angeles and my daughter is going to college in Chicago, and I look back and think, "Where did the time go?" Today I see my friends who have young kids and I tell them, "Enjoy this time—never take it for granted. I missed too much."

My kids are now young adults. They are pursuing their own dreams, but as my mother has told me many times, you never stop being a parent.

Nothing gives me more satisfaction than getting that message or text from my daughter simply saying, "Gee I miss you daddy, I need a hug."

With my son, Nick, at Chicago's Soldier Field before a Bears–Vikings game in 2005.

Our son Nick is our birth son. Chloe was adopted from Korea at five months of age. Becoming involved in Children's Home Society and bringing a baby into our home who has grown into this extraordinary young adult is my single greatest accomplishment. I am so proud of my kids and who they have become. We did a lot of traveling when they were young, and I know it helped them to develop a strong sense of independence. But it's the simple pleasures that resonate the most.

My dad worked for Paramount Pictures for 40-plus years as a sales rep. He was gone a lot when I was growing up. Because of my family history with movies, my kids stepped into the mold and have a deep appreciation for film.

Chloe, like myself, has become a huge Alfred Hitchcock fan, and she is constantly challenging me on which are his best films of all time. She has also become an accomplished master scuba diver. It used to drive me crazy when she would tell me she was going wreck diving at 110 feet with sharks nearby.

Chloe's adoption was surreal. I think back to that phone call we got from the Children's Home Society in September of 1990. After two and a half years of waiting, our daughter was on her way from South Korea.

Our Channel 4 sports photographer, Dave Halpern, came out to the airport with us, and one of the great joys of our lives was watching her come off that plane with her escort. I remember Nick, who was five at the time, saying on the tape, "Is that Chloe, is that Chloe?" And I remember like it was yesterday, putting that little baby in my arms and knowing my life had just changed forever. I just melted. I kept thinking, "This is my daughter." It was a phenomenal moment.

From where she came, Chloe had little chance for success in her world. Over and over I tell her, "Pursue your dreams. You have so much to learn and so much to give."

Because of our experiences with our adoption, it has opened my eyes to help out all the more with charities that reach beyond our borders. I get asked to get involved in a number of wonderful charities.

Children's HeartLink has been one of my favorites. It has been an honor to serve on their board of directors and host their annual fall gala, raising money for such a wonderful cause.

Infants as young as Chloe was when she arrived here are operated on for congenital heart disease. The conversations with doctors who tell me their experiences and what they have been able to accomplish are absolutely jaw-dropping. And they come up and thank me!

The doctors and all their supporting staff are the real heroes for what they do. The kids whose lives have been saved have traveled from all over the world to take part in the annual gala and make every second of my participation worth it.

Don Shelby taught me a lot about the importance of mentoring others. There are so many young people in our community who just need a pat on the back, an encouraging word, the attention and love to get them back on track.

Both of my kids went to Minneapolis city schools, but more and more, including our suburban areas, the number of kids who have one parent, or who are being raised by grandparents, is staggering. The

With my daughter, Chloe, in Hawaii, 2008.

ACES Foundation (Athletes Committed to Educating Students) is another pet project of mine. They specifically target inner-city schools at those vulnerable junior high ages, when one bad decision can lead to a lifetime of misery.

I cannot imagine a greater satisfaction than getting involved in charitable work. The fact is, it is not about reporting on the Twins or the Vikings; it is about what you have done to give back to others.

I take my name and my credibility very seriously. I was lucky. I had people like Phil Jones, Bob McNamara, Hal Scott, and Jerry Bowen to mentor me. Without them, I wouldn't be where I am today. So if one of these kids has a question about broadcasting or any subject, I hope I can make a difference.

Look at the Hall of Fame career of Randall McDaniel, one of the greatest offensive lineman in NFL history. As a teacher today, he is simply known by his students as Mr. McDaniel. Now that's a Hall of Fame life!

My passion in life is trying to make a difference. I appreciate my job today more than at any other time. I feel I am better at my job now and, in many ways, I feel like I am just starting out.

When I was at Harmon Killebrew's funeral last year, I realized the importance of what his life meant to so many others and to me. He represented to me my passion.

Hey, life is difficult. We have to work hard to succeed, and many times that's not even enough. I know I have paid my dues. When I see people who are trying to take shortcuts in life, I know they are missing out on what it takes to be successful.

There are simply no shortcuts. There are no overnight successes, no matter what field you get into. Hard work is the key.

Through my work at KFAN radio, I got the chance to meet John Kriesel, who had served our country in Iraq and lost both of his legs when his Humvee was hit by an IED. He was given a second chance in life. Look at him now. He's State Representative John Kriesel, who spoke his mind as a strong individual, not along party lines, during our state shutdown last summer. I have the ultimate respect for John and others like him.

My dad was a World War II veteran who landed at Utah Beach. He was part of our greatest generation who rarely spoke of their time at war. I've always had a built-in respect for veterans. When they talk, I listen. Life is about respect for others.

I get up in the morning with the same level of excitement I had when I first walked in the doors at WCCO TV in 1969. I'm so fortunate to feel that way after all these years. I'm excited to get to work. What will this day bring?

The thanks I have for people who appreciate the fact that I am just me, Mark Rosen, means the world to me. The fan in me is still there. The kid in me is still there. If I ever lose that little kid and fan inside me, I'll know it's time to move on.

My life has been a wonderful and magnificent journey. Thanks for taking the time to sit next to me. I sincerely hope you have enjoyed having the best seat in the house!

Afterword

When I first met with Jim Bruton about working together on *Best Seat in the House*, it was at Joe Senser's restaurant and sports bar in Bloomington. How appropriate. Joe remains not only one of my favorite Vikings of all time, but one of my favorite people. Back in his playing days, we would occasionally have dinner at the very spot that now has his name on it. It was called Mother Tucker's restaurant back then. It didn't take long for Joe and I to become friends after he was a sixth-round pick of the Minnesota Vikings in the 1979 NFL Draft. A lot has happened in the three decades that followed.

It is so different today with the salaries of players in major league sports. It is so much more of a business. There is so much more of an attitude of "How can I market myself? How can I take advantage of a short career?"

I recall former Vikings running back Dave Osborn saying, "We would have played for room and board." Not in today's world; there is no such attitude.

Recognizing that we are in a different time and that prices have skyrocketed in every facet of our economy, it still is refreshing to remember the old days in sports and how different things were. In 1956, Mickey Mantle hit 52 home runs, drove in 130 runs, and batted .353 while winning baseball's Triple Crown. He made $32,000 that season. Taking nothing away from the outstanding abilities of

Twins catcher Joe Mauer, but it was equivalent to half of Joe's salary for one game.

Former Minnesota Vikings quarterback Fran Tarkenton retired in 1978 as the highest-paid player in professional football at $175,000. Can you imagine what Fran would be paid in today's extravagant market?

The reality is that players for the most part don't need us in the media anymore to get their agenda out. There are vast available resources that never existed in the past.

I often miss those days. It also seems as if our personal relationships meant more back then. We actually had to pick up a landline phone and call someone to make plans. There was no email, Internet, Facebook, Twitter, blogs, or cell phones. It was different.

Things have definitely changed in sports journalism. We have less access to teams. Security is tighter. In the past, it was more of a fraternity atmosphere. We had more freedom. There was an inherent trust. I can recall walking through the hallways at Winter Park unescorted. I would stop in and talk to Bud, talk to the coaches and front office folks. It was the same with the Twins and the Gophers. It's just different. I miss it. Don't get me wrong. I still enjoy good relationships with many of the players, coaches, and others whom I cover; it's just not the same.

Today, our sports information comes from all directions. It is mind-boggling, to say the least. Sports is 24/7. It comes from everywhere: ESPN, all the talk radio and numerous stations, networks, and social media. Sports news comes at us like an out-of-control freight train. Yet, what is important is the perspective we present and represent to the public. It is not just about what happened on the day of the game or who did what, when, and where. It is much deeper than that, and my job is to put a real perspective on what is happening. An opinion? An analysis? Yes. That's what I mean, as long as it is supported by the happenings on the field of who did what, when, and where. This is an integral part of my job, and I don't see any change in that aspect over the years.

Since my first day on the job, I have always found it essential to give a personal perspective on sports. Report the weather, the kind of day it is, and what elements the runners have to overcome at the state high school cross country meet—and most importantly, take my audience with me. I learned that right from the beginning, and the thought process remains with me today in everything I cover.

Is it easier with today's technology? Of course it is. But there was something special to me about the old 16 mm film and how it was processed and all that went with it. It would take forever to list all the technological differences, but maybe a good comparison puts it all in perspective. We would take our 16 mm film and have it processed similar to taking your camera film to the drug store. There was no videotaping, and I certainly never had the luxury or the availability of a laptop, which I have used to do editing in the back seat of a rental car on the way to the airport.

There is no more grainy film. We have high-definition, which is incredible. We don't write up a script on a typewriter and then race up five flights of stairs to get it to an anchor like I often did at the old WCCO studio. Today, producers can change or add words right on the teleprompter as the program airs. It is quite a difference.

Anytime I'm in New York, I love to visit the Museum of Television and Radio. You can spend hours watching your favorite episode of *The Fugitive* or the day we witnessed the first live murder on television, when Jack Ruby shot Lee Harvey Oswald in the basement of the Dallas police station.

I talked earlier in the book about breaking news. Ruby's action was real, live breaking news. That type of journalism hasn't changed a lick. It still comes down to how it is reported, the opinion, the analysis.

When it comes to technology, the genie has left the bottle for good. Virtually everyone with a cell phone has the chance to record news as it happens. Granted, it may be Lindsay Lohan entering a store in Beverly Hills; sadly enough, someone will surely find a way to make something of that video. Or perhaps it is someone in the World Trade Center towers taping the destruction with their cell phone. Everything is live today. When it is all said and done, however, the fundamentals of news gathering and reporting remain. And that won't change despite the avalanche of Twitter and Facebook connections.

As I glance toward the future in sports, my two chief concerns are the growing number of serious injuries, specifically concussions among boys and girls participating in sports, and the overriding pressure from parents for their kids to excel. I have a great deal of respect for the volunteer coaches and referees who understand the nature of playing amateur sports for the right reasons. Too many parents are finding it more difficult to find a "healthy balance" of involvement in their child's sports experience.

When I see six-year-olds already "specializing" in one sport or attending endless so-called "elite" camps, I want to send Hall of Famer Paul Molitor over to their homes to give a lecture on why so many kids drop out of organized team sports by the time they are 12. Why? Because they are no longer having fun.

And for sure, it is not just the overactive parents who cause me concern, but the violence we see from fans today at sporting events. We can look at what has happened on the West Coast during football and baseball games and the acceleration of this type of dangerous behavior. Around here, of course, we can recall with shame the infamous 1975 bottle-throwing incident, when the field judge at the Vikings playoff game against the Dallas Cowboys was struck in the head.

It bothers me that fans bring their dangerous behavior to the stadiums and ballparks. Who brings a gun to a game? Some people do, and that really is scary. But in society today, we don't see violence just at the professional level in San Francisco or Vancouver. It was right here in Dinkytown after the University of Minnesota hockey team won the NCAA title—twice! It is a concern today—and one not given that much attention in the past.

Of course, there are problems and there are concerns. I certainly am aware of all that. But as far as the job goes, I still love every aspect of it. Fun is what I continue to have at my job. The challenge to bring more positive stories about people participating in sports is what drives me. It doesn't matter if the story centers around the backup offensive guard of the Vikings or Jenny, who overcame personal obstacles to earn a spot on the St. Louis Park girls basketball team.

It's what I love to follow, learn from, and report. Even after all these years, the fire inside me still burns. I love what I do.

The job has changed a lot, but I am convinced that I'm better at it. I am more confident every day. I have learned a great deal through the years, as it takes a really long time to be yourself on television. Getting comfortable in your own skin is not easy in front of the cameras and lights. Every day is a new learning experience. Every day brings new challenges. My mentors at WCCO television would never settle for less.

A friend asked me at lunch recently if I still was enjoying my job after more than four decades in sports broadcasting. He said, "Mark, you have been doing this a long time. Is it still fun for you? Do you still enjoy going to work every day? Do the bubblegum cards still come alive?"

They were easy questions, each deserving of a one-word response: "ALWAYS!"

A Tribute to
WCCO Television

You let me "hang out" in the newsroom when I was 17 years old, and later hired me to work in the sports department. You have stayed with me and supported me for over four decades while showering me with standards and professionalism worthy of the highest esteem. You have set the bar above the top of the ladder and filled my days with excellence, passion, and multitalented colleagues. Honesty, integrity, credibility, and loyalty have been your trademarks. You have provided me the opportunity to get up every day and look forward to going to work. It is an honor to be on your team and I have loved every minute. To you, WCCO television, my heartfelt thanks!

—Mark Rosen

Index